D1535098

VOLTAIRE

Selections

THE GREAT PHILOSOPHERS

Paul Edwards, General Editor

VOLTAIRE
Selections

Edited,
with Introduction, Notes, and
Bibliography, by
PAUL EDWARDS
Brooklyn College and New School for Social Research

A Scribner/Macmillan Book

Macmillan Publishing Company
NEW YORK

Collier Macmillan Publishers
LONDON

Copyright © 1989 by Macmillan Publishing Company,
a division of Macmillan, Inc.

Printed in the United States of America

Macmillan Publishing Company
866 Third Avenue, New York, New York 10022

Collier Macmillan Canada, Inc.

Library of Congress Cataloging-in-Publication Data

Voltaire, 1694–1778.
    [Selections. English. 1989]
    Voltaire: selections / edited, with introduction, notes, and
bibliography by Paul Edwards.
        p.   cm. — (The Great philosophers)
    "A Scribner/Macmillan book."
    Bibliography: p.
    ISBN 0-02-331610-1
    1. Philosophy. I. Edwards, Paul, 1923–   . II. Title.
III. Series.
B2172.E5 1989   88-11085
194—dc19   CIP

Printing: 1 2 3 4 5 6 7   Year: 9 0 1 2 3 4 5

I don't have a scepter, but I do have a pen.

VOLTAIRE

I cannot find words in which to express my delight in Voltaire's sharp, swift wit which penetrates in a moment to the inner core of humbug beneath pretentious trappings. I wish the world contained more of his deft light-heartedness. We have all grown serious and forgotten how to laugh.

BERTRAND RUSSELL

Preface

In France in the eighteenth century *philosopher* or *philosophe* referred primarily to a group of writers who attacked traditional religion and political absolutism in order to bring about a more rational and humane society. Voltaire's role as a *philosophe* is well known. It is generally agreed that few men in any age did so much for the cause of religious toleration, and his struggles against judicial barbarism have also frequently been celebrated. It is much less well known that Voltaire wrote extensively on topics of concern to philosophers in the more academic sense of the word. In French there are some excellent anthologies of Voltaire's philosophical writings in this sense, but no such book exists in English.

The aim of the present volume is to fill this gap. I have brought together Voltaire's most interesting discussions of the existence of God, the problem of evil, the mind – body problem, free will, the reality of matter, miracles, and the foundations of morality as well as of specific ethical and political topics such as suicide and toleration. Most of the selections are from works that were already translated into English in the eighteenth century, some even during Voltaire's lifetime. One major item, however, is made available here in English for the first time. This is the *Treatise on Metaphysics*, perhaps the most systematic of his purely philosophical writings and a work thought too dangerous to be published during his lifetime. I have also included Rousseau's letter to Voltaire on Providence of August 18, 1756. This letter, provoked by Voltaire's *Poem on the Lisbon Earthquake*, was one of the defenses of optimism that prompted Voltaire to write Candide. It is one of the most famous documents of the intellectual history of the eighteenth century, but it has never before been available in English.

My introduction gives a fairly detailed account of the highlights of Voltaire's extremely eventful life, and it offers a critical introduction to several of his philosophical theories. A major portion is devoted to an examination of Voltaire's numerous versions of the design argument for the existence of God. This argument continues to have great appeal to ordinary believers and one version of it, which is stated by Voltaire with his usual clarity and vividness, has the support of some very able and sophisticated contemporary philosophers like Richard Swinburne. It has also been defended, implicitly if not always explicitly, by a number of influential scientists who champion it as "the anthropic principle." A detailed critical discussion of this version of the argument is therefore of some interest, and I have tried to show why it fails and indeed why it must fail.

What makes Voltaire so enjoyable is not simply his mastery of language, but also the seemingly endless stream of illustrations that enlivens his discussions of even the most abstract questions. His reading was enormous and enormously varied and his memory prodigious, even in old age. Sometimes when he realizes that his readers are unfamiliar with the facts he spells everything out. Frequently, however, he refers to persons and events that were familiar in his day, but about which modern readers are liable to know little or nothing. Wherever I was able to obtain it, I have supplied the relevant information in footnotes, some of which are quite elaborate. These footnotes have become an essential part of the book. Many of them deal with incidents of persecution of the most horrible kinds, which were the result of religious and political intolerance. Voltaire could easily have written a fascinating and gruesome book bearing some such title as "History of Suffering Due to Fanaticism and Intolerance." The stories related in the longer footnotes might well constitute the core of such a history.

Numerous friends and colleagues have been kind enough to offer their help at various stages of the preparation of this book. My friends Maurice Cranston and Richard Popkin, both of whom possess vast knowledge of the intellectual history of the seventeenth and eighteenth centuries, answered innumerable tricky questions. I have also been fortunate to obtain the advice of three leading specialists in the French Enlightenment — Professor W. H. Barber, the General Editor of the new and definitive edition of the *Complete Works of Voltaire*, Professor Haydn Mason, general editor of *Studies on Voltaire and the Eighteenth Century*, and Professor Aram Vartanian who is noted for his outstanding contributions to the history of materialism in the seventeenth and eighteenth centuries. Mde. Larissa Albina kindly checked out Voltaire's marginal notes on the copy of Hume's *Inquiry Concerning Human Understanding* in Voltaire's library which has been kept in Leningrad ever since Mde. Denis sold it to Catherine the Great after Voltaire's death. Professor Robert Brown of the Australian National University at Canberra helped to clear up problems relating to Voltaire's discussions of Hobbes and Locke, and Professor Norris Clarke, S.J., of Fordham University advised me on the content of certain Catholic teachings criticized by Voltaire. Professor Anthony Manser of the University of Southampton helped to translate some obscure passages in Rousseau's letter on Providence. Professor Haskell Block tracked down the source of Voltaire's quotation from Corneille in *The Ignorant Philosopher* and offered much other helpful advice. My introduction was read by Professor Mason as well as by Professors Donald Levy, Terence Penelhum and Michael Wreen all of whom made valuable suggestions. My friends Mary Ward and Ronald Warsager helped in countless ways and especially in connection with the new translations and the extensive revisions of the older ones. Professor Howard Dunkle was kind enough to supply translations of the numerous Latin passages quoted by Voltaire. Mr. David

Bostock, Father Frederick Copleston, S.J., Mr. Joseph Dempsey, Professor John Pappas and Mr. Nicholas Walter kindly answered various questions relating to the material in the explanatory footnotes. I am profoundly grateful to all these individuals who have given so freely of their time.

It has occasionally been observed that Voltaire was not a profound thinker. This charge may well be true, but he possessed many other qualities that compensated for lack of profundity. These include a tremendous vitality, an almost unique gift for exposing pretentious humbug, and a glorious sense of humor. Perhaps nobody before or since has been so successful at demolishing opposing positions by laughing them out of existence. I hope that the present book will show the reader that philosophy and serious thought can also be fun.

New York City, April 1988   Paul Edwards

Contents

Introduction

François-Marie Arouet, known to the world as Voltaire, was born in Paris in 1694 into a prosperous middle-class family. His father, a notary with distinctly conservative views, sent the boy to the Jesuit school of Louis le Grand, where he received an excellent classical education. He was extremely precocious. At the age of twelve he wrote polished verses that delighted his teachers. To the chagrin of his family, he abandoned the study of law for literary pursuits, in which he was spectacularly successful almost from the start.

In 1718 his first tragedy, *Oedipe*, was performed with great success, and his plays dominated the French stage for the rest of the eighteenth century. His epic poem, *La Henriade*, which appeared in 1723, celebrated Henri IV, the last liberal French king. Although the poem was banned because of its undisguised hostility to Christianity, *La Henriade* had a vast circulation and was hailed by critics as the greatest epic in the French language. Voltaire's unorthodox opinions did not prevent his being a favorite at the court. The queen was said to have wept over his plays, and she gave him an allowance of 1,500 livres from her purse. This relatively serene period came to an end in January 1726 when a young nobleman, the Chevalier de Rohan, stung by some of Voltaire's derisive remarks, had him beaten up. Voltaire not only failed to obtain justice but, because of the influence of the well-connected Rohan family, it was he who ended up in the Bastille. The episode left an indelible impression on his mind and made him an unrelenting enemy of judicial arbitrariness and cruelty.

THE ENGLISH INFLUENCE

Voltaire was released from the Bastille on condition that he live at least "fifty leagues" away from Paris. For a variety of reasons he chose to go to England. He had been on friendly terms with several of the British ambassadors to Paris. Probably at the suggestion of one of them, Lord Starr, Voltaire had sent a copy of *Oedipe* with a special dedication to George I, who responded in cordial terms, sending Voltaire a fine gold watch and a gold medal with an engraving of his likeness. In 1722 Voltaire had met Lord Bolingbroke, a highly cultivated Tory exile who introduced him to Locke and other leading British thinkers. Voltaire could not read English at that time, but he was greatly attracted by what Bolingbroke told him and he had decided to visit England several months before the Rohan episode.

When Voltaire arrived in London in May of 1726, he was supplied with numerous letters of introduction from highly placed Englishmen living in France, including Horace Walpole, then the British ambassador to Paris. Voltaire spent two and a half years in England. He mastered the language and diligently studied the works of the English philosophers, scientists, and social reformers. His reputation as a brilliant poet and playwright and the generosity of Bolingbroke, who had been restored to favor, enabled Voltaire to gain entrance into the flourishing literary and theatrical world of London. Bolingbroke introduced Voltaire to Alexander Pope and his circle, and through Pope he met such outstanding writers as James Thompson, Edward Young, John Gay, and Jonathan Swift, for whom he felt a special affection.

Voltaire was also admitted to the circle of Caroline, the Princess of Wales, who had a deep interest in science and philosophy. Caroline, a German, had been on friendly terms with Leibniz before marrying the Prince of Wales. At one time she had tried to mediate the dispute between Leibniz and "Chevalier" Newton, and subsequently she acted as intermediary in the celebrated Leibniz-Clarke correspondence. It was to her that Leibniz repeatedly expressed his despair over what he believed to be the evasive and incoherent answers of Clarke, especially on the subject of universal causation. Newton had been a frequent visitor at the meetings of Caroline's circle, but by 1726 he was too ill to attend. However, Voltaire did meet George Berkeley (who was not yet a bishop) and Samuel Clarke. Voltaire did not take Berkeley very seriously as is evident from the article "Body" in the *Philosophical Dictionary*. Clarke, on the other hand, became a major influence in the formation of his views. For several years Voltaire was a believer in free will, and his arguments on this topic are taken straight from Clarke. He also endorsed the cosmological argument for the existence of God in the version that appeared in Clarke's first set of Boyle lectures entitled *A Demonstration of the Being and Attributes of God*. Most important, it was Clarke who made him see the full significance of Newton's achievement. For Voltaire, Newton was not only the most stupendous thinker in the history of science. In demonstrating that the universe has an orderly plan, he also provided decisive evidence for the existence of God. In a letter to the Abbé d'Olivet in 1736, Voltaire describes Newton as the greatest man who ever lived compared with whom the giants of antiquity are like children at play. About Clarke as a human being, however, Voltaire's feelings were mixed. He described him as "a man of rigid virtue and gentle disposition, more fond of his ideas than desirous of propagating them," but he added that Clarke was "wholly taken up with calculations and demonstrations," and in fact a "veritable reasoning-machine."

Unencumbered by any sense of false modesty, Voltaire was a master in the art of self-promotion. During his stay in England he arranged for a second and substantially revised edition of *La Henriade*. His plan for such an edition had already been announced in a letter to George I in October 1725. Horace Walpole had become one of his propagandists, writing to an influential friend that Voltaire was going to England "to print by subscription an excellent poem, called *Henry IV,* which on account of some bold strokes in it against persecution and the priests, cannot be printed here." The new edition was dedicated to Princess Caroline and she, along with George I, headed the subscription list, which included numerous members of the nobility and the government, distinguished writers and scientists, wealthy merchants, and even several well-known Protestant clergymen. The embassies of Denmark, Brunswick, Sweden, and Holland also appeared on this list, but not those of France or any other Catholic country. Several Voltaire scholars have noted that the publication thus became, in the words of Haydn Mason, "a manifesto of Protestant liberal Europe under English leadership, arrayed against Catholic absolutist Europe." On top of everything, Voltaire reaped a huge profit estimated by Mason at 30,000 francs.

On returning to France he wrote the *Lettres philosophiques,* which appeared first in London in 1733 in English translation as *Letters Concerning the English Nation,* and a year later in Paris. Over 250 years after its publication, this slim volume is still delightfully readable. Gustave Lanson, perhaps the greatest of Voltaire's numerous biographers, called it a "revelation of Voltarian prose — limpid, alert, sharp-edged, an incomparable filter of ideas bubbling over with delightful wit." The intent is serious but the manner gay and irreverent. The gravest discussions are enlivened by hilarious anecdotes. Even at this stage nothing that was in any way ludicrous on the human scene escaped Voltaire's watchful eye. In later years the wit often turned malicious, but here the humor is gentle and the overall effect exhilarating.

The *Lettres* was aptly described by Lanson as the first bomb hurled against the *ancien régime* and became the inspiration of liberal reformers throughout the European continent for the rest of the century. During Voltaire's stay in England, an exceptionally liberal government was in power, and he therefore tended to exaggerate the prevailing degree of freedom and toleration. In the *Lettres* he praised English institutions and, by implication, condemned conditions in France — the wealth, intolerance, and immense power of the church, the despotism of the king, and the privileges of the aristocracy. He recommended equal status for merchants and nobles, a fair distribution of taxes, and toleration for all religions. England, he wrote, is a land of sects and "an Englishman, like a free man, goes to heaven by whatever route he chooses." The *Lettres* also contain an exposition and defense of the empricisim of Locke and the methods and achievements of Newton, accompanied by satires of the theories of Aristotle and Descartes. The French edition contained an additional "letter" on Pascal, whose gloomy fideism is vigorously opposed. Pascal's notorious "wager," as well as his appeal to the heart, were anathema to Voltaire, who thought that our opinions in all fields should be based on evidence. "The interest I have in believing a thing," Voltaire wrote, "is not a proof of the existence of that thing." As if to confirm his strictures, the authorities at once moved to suppress the *Lettres*. The publisher was sent to the Bastille, Voltaire had to flee from Paris, and the courts condemned the book to be "torn and burned in the Palace courtyard . . . by the common executioner, as being scandalous, contrary to religion, good morals, and the respect due to the ruling powers."

With the publication of the *Lettres*, Voltaire became the first of the "*philosophes*," the free-thinking critics of established institutions, passionately devoted to their reform and if necessary their destruction. The entrenched powers of church and state were not slow to perceive the threat. "Just what is a *philosophe*?" asked the Abbé Molinier. The answer was as simple as it was frightening. A *philosophe* is "a kind of monster in society who feels under no obligation towards its manner and morals, its proprieties, its policies, or its religion. One may expect anything from men of their ilk."

CIREY

Most of the fifteen years following the publication of the *Lettres* were spent by Voltaire in the company of his learned mistress, Madame du Châtelet, at Cirey in Lorraine. This was one of the most peaceful periods of his life. Between 1734 and 1737, he composed the *Traité de métaphysique*, which is the most systematic and closely argued of his philosophical works. It was "written for" and dedicated to Mme. du Châtelet, but it was also undoubtedly written for the world at large. She thought it a particularly dangerous work, and Voltaire made no effort to publish it during his lifetime, but he did not forget about it in later years. When he wrote *The Ignorant Philosopher* in 1766, he called it his "second *Traité*." What presumably made it so dangerous was Voltaire's determined and extremely skillful attack on the Cartesian soul and his wholly negative discussion of belief in life after death. He concludes that "all probabilities" are against survival, something he never repeated in any of his published works. He also insists here, in contradiction to later published pronouncements, that no undesirable consequences are likely to result from a rejection of belief in rewards and punishments in the next world. Unfortunately, we do not possess the *Traité* in its final form. There is evidence that he revised it in 1737, but the only copy found after his death, which was obtained by Beaumarchais for the Kehl edition of the *Oeuvres Complètes* (1784–1789), is dated 1736. This may account for the truncated and shapeless form of several of its discussions.

In 1738 Voltaire published *Éléments de la philosophie de Newton*, to be followed in 1740 by *La métaphysique de Newton*. The former is a very lucid exposition of the main scientific ideas of Newton accompanied by a demonstration of the superiority of Newton's mechanics and cosmology to those of Descartes, whose views were still widely preferred by French scientists. Historians of science think so well of this book that its original English translation of 1738 was reprinted in 1967 in the Cass Library of Science Classics. The *Métaphysique de Newton* covers some of the same ground as the *Traité*, but there are some significant changes in Voltaire's views. The design argument is now enthusiastically endorsed with hardly any mention of the cosmological argument. Perhaps more important, Voltaire no longer shows much affection for libertarianism, which had been vigorously defended in the *Traité*. The "freedom of indifference" is not denied, but it is said to be manifested only in exceedingly trivial contexts. Clarke is criticized for saying on this subject exactly what Voltaire himself had said in the *Traité*, and Anthony Collins, whom Clarke had criticized, is warmly praised. Collins, a leading English deist, had published his *Philosophical Inquiry Concerning Human Liberty* in 1715 in which he offered a tightly knit defense of the doctrine of necessity, or what we now call determinism. Voltaire eventually accepted the views of Collins on the subject in their entirety, and in all his later works refers to Collins with the greatest respect. The *Métaphysique de Newton* was incorporated as the opening part of a new edition of the *Elements* in 1741, and it was this composite work that was brought out in English translation in Tobias Smollett's edition of Voltaire's works in the 1760s.

The fact that Voltaire wrote a "Treatise of *Metaphysics*" and that one of his two books on Newton has the word *metaphysics* in its title may give the false impression that Voltaire was a friend of metaphysics in the sense in which this word has commonly been used in recent times. It is true that he believed in God and this belief would usually be classified as "metaphysical," but Voltaire would have insisted that it was an empirical hypothesis that was the most plausible explanation of certain facts. He was also intensely interested in the problem of free will and the relation between the body and the mind; and these are often called "metaphysical" questions. However, for speculative metaphysics he had nothing but contempt. In 1744 in his *Courte réponse aux longs discours d'un docteur allemand* ("Brief Response to the Lengthy Discourse of a German Doctor"), Voltaire relates a conversation he had in England with a "very enlightened person." He recalls remarking that Clarke was a much greater metaphysician than Newton, to which the enlightened gentleman replied, "that may be, but you might as well say that one is better at playing with balloons than the other." Since then, Voltaire adds, he had dared to puncture some of these metaphysical balloons and discovered that what comes out of them is nothing but hot air. "Metaphysical phantoms," he had written earlier in the same discourse, "pass away as things seen in a state of delirium." Almost thirty years later, in the article "Xenophanes," in the *Questions Concerning the Encyclopedia* (1772), he praises Bayle, as he had done on several previous occasions, for ridiculing the "chimerical reveries" of Plato, Pythagoras, and the pre-Socratics. "My sage," he concludes the article, "is the investigator of natural history. We learn more from the experiments of the Abbé Nollet [a French eighteenth-century physicist] than from all the books of antiquity." It is not difficult to surmise what Voltaire would have said about the metaphysical balloons launched since his day.

In the eighteenth and first half of the nineteenth centuries, Voltaire was regarded not only in France but also in other countries, especially Germany, as a major dramatist of a stature comparable with that of Corneille, Racine, Goethe, and Schiller. This view has long been abandoned and a good deal, although by no means all, of his poetry rings dull to modern ears. Voltaire's place as a major historian, on the other hand, is more secure than ever. In 1731, shortly after his return from England, he published the first of his great histories, the *History of Charles XII*. This book was a moving account of the Swedish king who had died in 1713 and whose inordinate passion for glory and conquest had brought ruin to himself and his country.

It was in Cirey that Voltaire did much of the research for his other historical works which were to appear in the 1750s. Because of his reputation for flippancy, it is worth emphasizing that, barring occasional lapses, the histories are based on solid and extensive research. The *Century of Louis XIV*, which became one of his most famous and controversial books, was not published until 1751 during his stay at Potsdam, and the multivolume *Essay on the Manners and Spirit of Nations* appeared in Geneva in 1756. This is a universal history written by a historian with a truly cosmopolitan outlook. History is not to be reduced to an account of Western civilization and its origins in the Greek and Jewish traditions. Voltaire set out to "render justice to all nations" and he did it to the extent to which information then available allowed this. Arab, Chinese, Japanese, and Indian civilizations are discussed at some length. Non-Christian civilizations are portrayed in more flattering terms than the Christian civilization of the West, but Voltaire does not deny that at certain times the papacy and Christian teachings played a useful role in presenting checks to violence and military barbarism. The picture of the Middle Ages is nevertheless jaundiced and has been justly criticized by later historians. The overall verdict on human history is a mixture of gloom and hope. In all places humanity has gradually formed laws and customs to make life bearable. Much of history is indeed a record of atrocities and the teaching of absurdities, but experience has shown that certain conditions make for happiness and certain others for misery. War and fanaticism are the most obvious causes of unhappiness and the cure, insofar as there is one, is the cultivation of reason and the critical spirit so that the human race will no longer submit so easily to lies and tyranny. The *Essay* was a tremendous success. It was almost immediately translated into English, and between the time of its publication and its appearance in the Kehl edition of 1784, it was reprinted sixteen times.

Because of their glittering style and streams of amusing anecdotes, Voltaire's histories can still be read with pleasure, but their significance greatly transcends their literary merits. Explanations in terms of divine providence that fill the volumes of earlier historians, including Voltaire's illustrious predecessor, Jacques Bossuet, are not allowed, and, particularly in the *Essay*, history is treated as the story of peoples rather than of rulers and military leaders, with special emphasis on progress in the arts and sciences and their impact on society.

Voltaire's view of "great men" had been stated several years earlier in a little poem with which he began one of his letters to Frederick the Great (May 26, 1742). "I do not like heroes," he wrote, "they make too much noise in the world. I hate those conquerors . . . who have placed supreme happiness in the horrors of combat, seeking death everywhere and causing a hundred thousand men of their own kind to suffer it. The more radiant their glory, the more odious they are."

VOLTAIRE AND FREDERICK THE GREAT

Mme. de Châtelet died in 1749, and the following year Voltaire accepted an invitation from Frederick the Great to become "philosopher-poet" in residence at Potsdam where he stayed for two and a half years. There had been extensive correspondence between the two men going back as far as September 1736 when Frederick was Crown Prince, and they had met in 1740 and 1743 after Frederick became king. In 1740 Voltaire had published in the Hague, with his editorial changes, the *Anti-Machiavel*, Frederick's youthful critique of Machiavelli's political philosophy. Frederick liked to call himself "the *philosophe* of Sans Souci" and on certain important issues he was a true disciple of Voltaire and the French Enlightenment. He rejected and disliked Christianity and all revealed religion, predicting that Christianity would not last more than another two hundred years. He genuinely believed in religious toleration and popular education, instituting some admirable reforms to put these ideas into practice. He was something of a dilettante in the arts, writing bad French poetry and mediocre music, chiefly for the flute, which he is said to have played exceedingly well. He wrote excellent prose and he had a good understanding of philosophical questions. Such questions played a major role in the first years of his correspondence with Voltaire, and Frederick easily held his own. In a letter dated April 19, 1738, he pointed out the flaws in Voltaire's defense of free will, and these criticisms contributed to the change in the Voltaire's views on the subject. In 1770 Frederick wrote an able critique of certain of the arguments in Holbach's *System of Nature*. Father Copleston devotes the opening pages of the chapter on the German Enlightenment in Volume 6 of his magnificent *History of Philosophy* to Frederick. His bibliography lists almost a page of works about him, some of them by distinguished philosophers like Dilthey and Spranger. Frederick greatly preferred the use of French both in writing and in conversation, having nothing but contempt for German letters. He read the Greek and Roman classics, admired Locke and the English deists, and venerated Bayle to whom he referred as the greatest "dialectician" who ever lived, but it is probable that Frederick never heard of Kant and he showed no interest whatsoever in the works of Lessing and Mendelssohn, the leaders of a flourishing enlightenment centered in Berlin, just a few miles from his palace at Sans Souci.

One might have thought that Voltaire would accept Frederick's invitation without a moment's hesitation. Even after becoming Royal Historiographer in 1745, he was not at all appreciated at the French court and his writings continued to be suppressed. At Potsdam he was going to be feted as the superstar of a colorful and distinguished group of scholars with whom Frederick had surrounded himself. He would be paid an excellent salary and, perhaps most important, for once he was going to be able to publish his books under his own name without fear of the censors or the police. Nevertheless, Voltaire hesitated as he had never before and as he never did again in making a major decision. He may well have had forebodings that sooner or later he and Frederick would quarrel and that his stay at the Prussian court would come to a bad end. It was no secret that Frederick had a cruel streak and in spite of his declarations of eternal love and friendship, Voltaire may have felt that he would become one of the targets of the king's cruelty. Frederick himself had been the victim of tortures and humiliations at the hands of his coarse and brutal father, Frederick William I. At the age of eighteen, Frederick decided to escape to England, but the plan was foiled. He was arrested and imprisoned and his friend and accomplice, Lieutenant Katte, was sentenced to death. Frederick was forced to witness the beheading. Voltaire was aware of all of this and he also knew all too well that in spite of his many liberal ideas, Frederick was very far from approximating to Voltaire's idea of a philosopher-king. Although Voltaire was too polite to say so to his face, he disapproved of Frederick's propensity for aggressive warfare and the Machiavellian ways in which he conducted his relations with other nations. The bloody battles described in *Candide* are modeled on Frederick's wars with Austria and the later even bloodier Seven Years War (1756–1763), which was still raging when the book was published. In his *Mémoires*, written in 1769, Voltaire wisely observed that "if Machiavelli had had a prince for a disciple, the first thing he would have advised him to do would have been to write against Machiavelli."

However, Voltaire did go to Potsdam, and at first everything went smoothly. He enjoyed his new surroundings and had a great deal of spare time. His only official duty was to correct Frederick's French writings, which took up one hour a day. Frederick, like Voltaire, was a great conversationalist and so were a number of the other distinguished guests. Many years later Voltaire still remembered the lavish midnight suppers as "feasts of reason, wit and science." However, before long there was trouble. Voltaire simply could not resist the temptation of ridiculing Frederick's French poetry. He is supposed to have complained that the king sent him his dirty linen to launder. Voltaire strenuously denied having made that remark, but one of his enemies reported it to Frederick anyway, and Voltaire did not deny saying, when his role was compared to Plato's at the court of the tyrant Dionysios, "but Plato did not waste his time correcting bad verse." Frederick on his part made many wounding comments, which were carried back to Voltaire. The atmosphere was gradually poisoned.

To make matters worse, Voltaire became embroiled in a financial scandal. His wealth was not due to royalties from his books and plays but to skillful and audacious investments and speculations, some of which bordered on criminality. The details of the so-called Hirschel affair have never been fully cleared up. Some writers say it was all Hirschel's fault, some say it was Voltaire's, but Frederick was probably correct in describing the affair as a case of a "scamp who wanted to cheat a crook," leaving us free to decide who was the scamp and who the crook. Even Besterman, whose biography of Voltaire comes close to being a hagiography, admits that Voltaire should not have engaged in such a transaction, adding that "though venial by conventional standards," it was "positively virtuous by comparison with the corruption in business manners of much of the French nobility." To recover a large sum Voltaire was compelled to bring suit in a Berlin court. He won the case, but to the delight of all his many enemies and to the great embarrassment of Frederick, all kinds of unsavory details about Voltaire's machinations were revealed. During the case Voltaire was lodged in the king's Berlin palace. In a polite but firm letter, dated February 24, 1751, Frederick set out his guest's misdeeds. "I kept the peace in my house until your arrival," he wrote, "and I warn you that if you have the passion of intrigue and cabal you have come to the wrong place."

Frederick should have done one of two things. He should either have sent Voltaire packing or he should have taken him back without rancor, giving his unruly guest an opportunity to behave with greater circumspection. He did neither. He took Voltaire back but started tormenting him. The midnight suppers became a nightmare for Voltaire. Frederick acted as if Voltaire did not exist. His jokes were ignored, but Frederick heartily laughed at the jokes of his other guests, singling out Maupertuis for special attention. Voltaire's letters to Paris betrayed such misery that the Count d'Argental, his most loyal friend, implored him to come home. Voltaire stayed, but an explosion was not far off.

For several years prior to 1750, the above-mentioned Pierre-Louis Maupertuis, a physicist and mathematician of considerable attainments, had been president of the Prussian Academy of Science. Maupertuis was a pompous and jealous man and from the beginning there was feuding between him and Voltaire. Voltaire resented Maupertuis' treatment of a German scientist by the name of Koenig, and when Maupertuis published a volume containing some foolish speculations, Voltaire wrote a savage parody called *Diatribe du Docteur Akakia*. He read his satire to Frederick, who enjoyed every word but at the same time forbade its publication. Voltaire ignored the order and went ahead with publication of the *Diatribe*. This was, in effect, the end of the Potsdam episode. Frederick's rage knew no bounds, and Voltaire fled from Sans Souci to rented rooms in Berlin. On Christmas Eve of 1752, the public executioner burned the pamphlet in the street under Voltaire's window. Biographers of Voltaire have tended to put most of the blame on Frederick, but a kinder and less imperious man would sooner or later have lost his patience and invited such a trying guest to depart.

Some years later, all was forgiven, and the two resumed their amicable correspondence. In one of his letters, Frederick wrote with much justice: "Would that Heaven, which gave you so much wit, had given you judgment proportionately!" In spite of all of the backbiting and unkind remarks on both sides, there was a great deal of affection between the two men. In 1760 it was reported to Voltaire that Frederick was contemplating suicide because of serious reverses in his military fortunes. Voltaire wrote him a moving letter telling him why he must go on living. When a statue of Voltaire was commissioned by some of his Parisian friends in 1770, Frederick wrote to D'Alembert that Voltaire's works "will last longer than the basilica of Saint Peter, the Louvre, and all those buildings which human vanity consecrates to eternity." After Voltaire's death in 1778 when memorial services were prohibited both in Paris and in Geneva, Frederick arranged for one in Potsdam, and himself wrote the eulogy.

THE END OF OPTIMISM

After the break with Frederick, Voltaire was without a home for a year and a half. Much of this time was spent in Colmar in almost complete isolation. At one period he did not leave his quarters for eight months, dividing his time, as he put it in a letter, between illness and work. He was not particularly dejected and he wrote to his niece that his real vocation was that of a monk. Early in 1754 it was made clear to him that Louis XV would not welcome his return to Paris. Voltaire then began to look for a new home in the area of Lausanne and Geneva. His financial speculations had made him enormously rich, and in January 1755 he bought a chateau in Geneva, which he named "Les Delices." The outstanding literary event of these years was the publication in 1759 of *Candide*, the celebrated satire of metaphysical optimism.

It is of some interest to note that for many years Voltaire himself had been in the camp of the optimists and that his progress toward the position reached in *Candide* was very gradual. In the *Philosophical Letters*, in response to Pascal's gloom, Voltaire declared that animals were generally very contented and that many human beings led reasonably happy lives. Rather smugly, he observed that when he looked at Paris or London he saw nothing remotely like the "desert island" to which Pascal had compared our "mute universe." What he saw were "opulent" and "civilized" places where men were "as happy as nature allows." To Frederick he had written in a similar vein in 1738 that "when everything is counted and weighed up . . . there are infinitely more enjoyments than bitternesses in this life." Professor Barber has pointed out that during the Cirey period, Voltaire's personal contentment and philosophical optimism were reflected even in his dramatic works and in the earlier of the philosophical tales. In his first play, *Oedipe*, the dominating theme was the horror of fate, but in the only dramatic work of the 1730s, the opera libretto *Pandore*, in which such a theme occurs at all, "Destiny" appears as a beneficent and rational power who succeeds without difficulty in preventing the tyrannical Jupiter from destroying the world. In *Plato's Dream* the conclusion is that, although not perfect in every detail, the universe as a whole is as perfect as its inevitable limitations permit. This is less extreme but not so very different from the optimism of Alexander Pope's *Essay on Man* in which it had been maintained that really "there are no evils," but if there were any "particular evils, they compose the general good."

There is a marked change of emphasis in some of the philosophical tales of the late 1740s, especially *Zadig* (1747) and *Memnon ou la sagesse humaine* (1749). The main theme of both is the totally undeserved suffering of just and even noble men. Memnon is trying to lead the life of a perfect philosopher. His generosity leads to a series of disasters, leaving him destitute, humiliated, ill, and blind in one eye. In a dream a "good genius" from a distant star appears who assures him that his fate will soon change. "Are those poets and philosophers wrong," asks Memnon, "who tells us that everything is for the best?" "No," replies the good genius, "they are right," but we have to view events "in relation to the gradation of the whole universe." Memnon is not convinced, and the story ends on a skeptical note.

Zadig, an even nobler protagonist, concludes after a series of misfortunes that the world is "governed by a cruel destiny which oppresses the good." At this stage he meets a mysterious and venerable hermit who performs a number of exceedingly strange acts. The last of these in particular seems an outrageous display of ingratitude. Zadig and the hermit are given shelter by a virtuous and charitable widow. After they leave the hermit drowns the widow's nephew. In response to Zadig's expression of horror, he explains that the widow's nephew was destined to murder his aunt in a year's time and Zadig himself in two years. It is perhaps reassuring to know that such defenses are not admissible in courts of law anywhere in the civilized world, but the hermit reveals himself as the angel Jesrad sent from heaven to enlighten Zadig — to make him see that in the long run the wicked are always unhappy and that evil always leads to good. The story has a happy ending, but Zadig's critical faculty is intact and he is not convinced by Jesrad. His question of why evil should exist in the first place is never answered. In these stories Voltaire has not yet abandoned optimism, but he recognizes that there is a great deal to be said against it and that there are many questions to which the optimist has no answer.

The total abandonment of optimism seems to have occurred during Voltaire's last year in Potsdam. For several years, beginning in 1752, there is much gloom in his correspondence. The mood of these years was no doubt strongly influenced by the tribulations at the Prussian court and his unsettled life prior to the purchase of Les Delices. Voltaire's views were also in all probability shaped by his extensive reading of history in preparation of the *Essai sur les moeurs*. As noted earlier, Voltaire came to regard history as predominantly a record of atrocities. Such a conclusion is hardly compatible with the view that whatever is is right or that ours is the best of all possible worlds.

Not long after Voltaire took up residence in Geneva, on November 1, 1755, Lisbon was shattered by one of the worst earthquakes ever recorded, with 10,000 people killed and another 10,000 seriously injured. This event provoked Voltaire's *Poème sur le désastre de Lisbonne*, a powerful pessimistic tract whose upshot is that we cannot reasonably believe in a God who cares for our welfare. The poem gave rise to numerous heated replies, the most famous being a long letter from Rousseau to Voltaire, which was published in Berlin without the authorization of either man. (It is reprinted as an Appendix to the present volume). Rousseau argued that the earthquake was a just punishment of men who had abandoned a natural country life for the artificial pleasures of big cities. If they had lived in villages, the number of victims would have been much smaller. What is more — and here Rousseau refers not unfairly to Voltaire's *Zadig* — "an accelerated death is not always evil." There is no certainty that a single person who perished in the Lisbon earthquake suffered more than he would have done in the ordinary course of events when he would have died anyway, and very possibly a death involving more drawn-out suffering than the quick end resulting from the earthquake. As the only alternative to a suicidal pessimism, we must continue to have faith in the goodness of God — we must believe that in the long run things turn out well and that from a sufficiently broad perspective everything will be seen to make sense. The answer to the defenders of God's goodness and justice in the face of such disasters as the

Lisbon earthquake was *Candide*, and metaphysical optimism has never recovered from this blow. When metaphysical optimists appear on the scene, as they still occasionally do, it is usually sufficient to remind the world of Dr. Pangloss, perhaps the most delightfully absurd character in all literature. "What is optimism?" asks a character by the name of Cacambo. "Alas," replies Candide, "it is the mania for pretending that all is well when all is ill."

It needs to be emphasized that the specific target of Voltaire's ridicule is not only Leibniz but the whole school of Leibnizian philosophers with their metaphysical jargon, their pontifications, and their preference for abstract speculation over concrete experience. It has often been claimed that Voltaire misunderstood Leibniz's dictum that ours is the best of all possible worlds. This may be so, but it is hardly relevant. For the position attacked by Voltaire has had a great many defenders, whether Leibniz himself endorsed it or not, and it was high time to demonstrate its absurdity. Moreover, if Leibniz did indeed mean something other than what "best of all possible worlds" naturally suggests, he was surely guilty of an outrageously misleading use of language.

Voltaire's name did not appear on the title page of *Candide*. Instead the reader is told that the book has been "translated from the German of Dr. Ralph." This information was supplied in the first edition that came out early in 1759. In the edition of 1761, the reader is told that the book has been "translated from the German of Dr. Ralph, with additional notes found in the doctor's pocket after his death in year of grace 1759." Voltaire vigorously denied authorship of *Candide*, but he was not displeased by the book's enormous popularity.

THE WAR AGAINST CHRISTIANITY

The Calvinists of Geneva were by no means pleased with Voltaire's presence in their city. They objected to the theatrical performances at his chateau and they were particularly displeased by certain statements in the article "Genève," written for Diderot's *Encyclopédie* by D'Alembert at Voltaire's suggestion. In 1759 Voltaire purchased a magnificent estate at Ferney, a few miles over the French border, where he lived unmolested by French, German, or Swiss authorities until shortly before his death.

When Voltaire settled in Ferney, he was sixty-six, immensely famous, and immensely rich. He was to live another eighteen years, and this final period became the most rewarding and productive of his life. He waged two campaigns that shook Europe like nothing since Luther's break with the Church of Rome. The two campaigns were intertwined, but only the first was the result of deliberate planning.

It is not clear when Voltaire lost what little belief in Christianity he may ever have entertained. What is certain is that he opposed Christianity throughout his adult life and came to regard it as a major aberration of the human mind, as well as a terrible disaster for the human race. He believed Christianity had to be destroyed before one could achieve a rational and humane society. Christianity, he wrote to Frederick the Great, "is the most ridiculous, the most absurd, and bloody religion that has even infected the world." However, Voltaire did not openly write against Christianity until the 1760s. From then until his death he waged an unrelenting campaign against "the infamous thing," as he called it. During the Ferney years, letters to his friends always concluded with the slogan "Ecrasez l'infâme." There has been some debate as to exactly whom Voltaire had in mind when he spoke of "l'infâme." Sometimes he probably meant persecuting intolerance in general, but is seems clear that on most occasions he referred to the "most absurd" and the "most bloody" of all religions. Many years earlier he had remarked that it took twelve men to establish Christianity but that it might take only one to cause its downfall.

The first of his major anti-Christian publications, *The Sermon of the Fifty*, was published in 1762, but it had been written several years earlier, possibly during his last years at Cirey. This pamphlet reads like a declaration of war on Christianity, and it is written in a deliberately inflammatory style. It attacks Christian mysteries like Transubstantiation as absurd; Christian miracles as incredible; the Bible as full of contradictions; the Jews, whose religion had led to Christianity, as an ignorant and mendacious people; and the God of Christianity as a cruel and hateful tyrant. The true God, the sermon concluded, "surely cannot have been born of a girl, nor died on the gibbet, nor be eaten in a piece of dough." Nor could he have inspired "books, filled with contradictions, madness, and horror." May the true God "have pity on the sect of Christians that blasphemes him!"

As another installment in the war against Christianity, Voltaire published in Holland, also in 1762, extracts from the *Testament of the Abbé Meslier*. Meslier (1664–1729) was a country priest who, while living an outward life of conformity, had been a complete unbeliever with an intense hatred for the Christian religion. In the 1720s he decided to write down his ideas but to keep them secret during his lifetime. In addition to an uncompromising attack on Christianity, the *Testament* contains defenses of atheism, materialism, and political revolution. In a passage that has often been quoted, he expressed his wish to abolish injustice by "hanging and strangling with the bowels of the priests all the nobles and rulers of the world." Voltaire had heard about Meslier's *Testament* from his friend Thieriot as early as 1735 and he apparently made substantial extracts from it in 1742. The extracts that he published in 1762 deal primarily with miracles and the evils of the Christian religion. Voltaire did not publish the sections in which Meslier advanced atheism and revolution. In his unsigned introduction Voltaire professed to deplore the "melancholy spectacle" of a priest, with a fine sense of justice and a highly developed intellect, condemning Christianity in such harsh tones. During the remainder of his life Voltaire frequently referred to the case of Meslier with mischievous delight, speaking again and again of "the sad and dangerous moment" when the dying priest accused himself for having professed and taught the Christian religion.

Unquestionably, the most powerful and also the most delightful of Voltaire's missiles against Christianity was the *Philosophical Dictionary*, which is widely regarded as his true masterpiece. This melange of witty reflections on a great variety of topics attempts to demolish the enemy by laughing him out of existence. Voltaire wrote the first articles in Potsdam as early as 1752. He kept jotting down ideas for a number of years, but he did not begin serious work on the *Philosophical Dictionary* until late in 1762. The first edition, then one small volume, appeared in Geneva in June 1764 with a false London imprint and without Voltaire's name on the cover. As usual, Voltaire strenuously denied his authorship, but nobody took the denial seriously. The first edition sold out immediately. The Genevan government condemned the book to be burned in September 1764; liberal Holland followed suit in December, and in Paris it was publicly burned in March 1765. In July of that year, it was put on the index by the Holy Office.

In spite of these condemnations, new and enlarged editions appeared year after year. In the final form given to it by Voltaire, the work was published in 1769 in two large volumes. It was reprinted in this form several times during the remaining years of Voltaire's life. In 1770 he began to publish another even larger work arranged in dictionary form under the title of *Questions sur l'encyclopédie*. *Questions* eventually became a huge compendium running to nine volumes. It contained a great deal of new material, but it also reprinted several of the articles from the original *Dictionary* with additional sections. It goes without saying that the *Philosophical Dictionary* outraged Voltaire's clerical enemies. Some started compiling "antiphilosophical" dictionaries that, as Voltaire would have put it, "regrettably" did not remotely rival the original work in popularity. From this time on, Voltaire came to be regarded by Catholic apologists as the Antichrist. Almost half a century later, Joseph de Maistre still proclaimed that hell had put "its entire power into the hands of Voltaire." Voltaire did not at all mind being called the Antichrist. In fact, he often referred to himself as "Beelzebub's theologian" and he knew that the hatred he provoked proved the enormous effectiveness of his campaign.

L'HOMME AUX CALAS

Voltaire's second campaign, against judicial barbarism, did a great deal to prepare France for revolutionary change. It was precipitated by the judicial murder of Jean Calas, a Huguenot trader in cotton goods, who, on the basis of malicious rumors, had been arrested for murdering his son. The rumors had it that the son, Marc-Antoine, was planning a conversion to Catholicism and that, to prevent this, his father and the other members of the family had strangled him. Marc-Antoine had not the slightest interest in a conversion and committed suicide in a fit of depression. The accusation leveled at the Calas family was unsupported by anything that would pass as evidence in a civilized court, and it was clearly inconsistent with common sense and all the known facts. The family was nevertheless tried and found guilty by the judges of Toulouse. The family property was confiscated, and Jean Calas was condemned to be broken at the wheel and then burned at the stake. The other members of the family were banished from France.

The sentence against Jean Calas was carried out with unspeakable brutality on March 10, 1762. When Voltaire heard about the execution, he resolved to rehabilitate the wronged family. He mobilized all his influential acquaintances at Versailles, including Mme. de Pompadour and the Duke of Richelieu, and his powerful friends elsewhere, especially Frederick the Great and the Empress of Russia. He published pamphlet after pamphlet, in several languages, exposing the judges of Toulouse. The Toulouse authorities would not make the court documents available, and at first the king and the government refused to overrule them. Eventually the public clamor became so great that a new trial was ordered. On March 9, 1765, forty Paris judges declared Jean Calas to have been innocent in a unanimous decision. The Calas property was restored and the king granted 36,000 livres as compensation to the widow. There were festivities in Paris. Crowds gathered to applaud the widow and the judges. Voltaire, who always referred to this case as "mon meilleur ouvrage" (my best work), was from then on known as "the savior of the Calas."

Another case from the same part of France in which Voltaire intervened concerned Pierre Paul Sirven, a well-to-do Protestant, and his wife who had been sentenced to be hanged for the murder of their daughter. Here, too, it was charged that the daughter had been planning to become a Catholic, and the evidence again was incredibly flimsy. Fortunately, the Sirvens fled to Switzerland before their trial. It took Voltaire nearly nine years to establish their innocence and to have their fortune restored. The Sirven case, Voltaire wryly remarked in a letter, lacked "the éclat of the Calas case" because "nobody was broken on the wheel."

The same could not unfortunately be said about the beheading of the nineteen-year-old Chevalier de la Barre for blasphemy. La Barre and his young companion Gaillard d'Etallonde were accused of mutilating a wooden crucifix, making blasphemous remarks about the Virgin, and singing blasphemous songs. D'Etallonde escaped before the trial, and la Barre, pleading guilty to the other charges, steadfastly denied mutilating the crucifix. He was tried and found guilty of all charges by a court in Abbeville, near Amiens, on February 28, 1766. He was condemned to have his tongue cut out, his right hand cut off, and to be burned at the stake. The verdict was appealed to the *parlement* of Paris. Voltaire and most observers expected that the sentence of the Abbeville court would not be upheld and that la Barre would get off with a prison sentence. However, chiefly because of the ravings of the Paris clergy about the dangerous spread of infidelity, the *parlement* ratified the original conviction. It spared la Barre from having his tongue and right hand cut off, but the death sentence was confirmed, substituting decapitation for burning at the stake. To extract a further confession, la Barre was to be tortured before his execution. This incredible sentence was carried out on July 1, 1766. After his beheading, the corpse was burned along with a copy of the *Philosophical Dictionary*.

Voltaire was powerless to save la Barre, but be obtained a position for d'Etallonde in the Prussian army and tirelessly worked for his rehabilitation, which was not granted until 1788, ten years after Voltaire's death. No case infuriated Voltaire more, and none contributed more to his determination to change the French legal code and its administration. "The atrocity of this act," he wrote to d'Alembert, "seizes me with horror and anger.'" "What an abominable jurisprudence," he wrote to Beccaria two years later, "which sustains religion only by means of the public executioner. This is what is called a religion of love and charity." Eight years after la Barre's beheading, Voltaire remarked to Condorcet that rage came into his heart and tears into his eyes every time he thought about this horror, which he described as "a hundred times more hellish than the assassination of Calas."

Voltaire was involved in many other cases. He succeeded in freeing Claude Chaumont, who was on the galley bench because he had attended a Protestant service. He also was able to free Jean Pierre Espinas, who had spent twenty-three years in the galleys because he had given lodging to a Protestant clergyman for one night. Not all cases involved religious bigotry. A particularly monstrous case, quite as horrible as that of Calas, concerned a farmer from the village of Bleuville, identified by Voltaire simply as "Martin." The farmer's shoeprint or a print resembling that of his shoes was found on a highway on which a man had been murdered. The only witness who had seen the murderer as he was fleeing testified that he could not recognize Martin as that man. Martin exclaimed, "Thank God!" which the judge interpreted to mean, "Thank God. I committed the murder but I have not been identified." He thereupon condemned Martin to the wheel, and this insane sentence was carried out at some time in 1767. "When he was stretched out on St. Andrew's cross," Voltaire wrote to d'Alembert, Martin asked permission from the executioner "to raise his arms to call heaven to witness his innocence. . . . He was allowed that favor after which, his arms, thighs, and legs were broken, and he was left to die on the wheel." The "little property" of the family was confiscated and the family itself fled to Austria. Voltaire did not hear about this case until July 1769 when another man confessed to the crime. Voltaire tried to obtain the rehabilitation of the wronged family, but without success. All he could do was make the facts public.

Another terrible case concerned François Montbailli and his wife, an entirely respectable couple who had never been in trouble with the law. In 1770 Montbailli's mother, who was an alcoholic, was killed in Arras. The "proofs" against the couple, according to Voltaire's account, would have appeared ridiculous even to the judges who condemned the family of Calas. Montbailli was tortured and, in spite of his protests of innocence, both he and his wife were sentenced to death. Montbailli was broken on the wheel, but the sentence of his wife was postponed because she was pregnant. Voltaire succeeded in obtaining a new trial in which she and her husband were declared innocent. It was, Voltaire remarks, "a miserable restoration, unattended with either satisfaction or recompense."

One of the most celebrated cases concerned General Lally, the French royal commissioner in India, who had been defeated by the English and was executed on unproven charges of disloyalty. Voltaire pursued his efforts to vindicate the general's name for ten years and received the news of his rehabilitation as he lay dying in Paris in May 1778. It roused him to write the last letter of his life. "The dying man revives upon hearing this great news," he wrote to the general's son, "... he will die content."

VOLTAIRE AND BECCARIA

As part of his campaign for judicial reform, Voltaire published two of his most constructive and universally admired books, *Commentary on Beccaria's "Of Crimes and Punishments"* (1766) and *Prix de la Justice et de l'humanité* (1777). Beccaria's book, which was a devastating attack on the legal and judicial systems then in operation in almost every country in the world, had been published in Italy, at first anonymously, in 1764. Beccaria's *Treatise*, as it is usually referred to, expressed sentiments shared by humanitarian reformers in many countries, and it became one of the most influential publications of the century. It was placed on the index, but this did not prevent Catholic rulers from openly endorsing the reforms it advocated. Maria Theresa of Austria and Archduke Leopold of Tuscany were among those who announced their intentions to reform the laws of their countries in accordance with Beccaria's recommendations. Leopold did abolish both torture and the death penalty shortly after his accession in 1765, and in 1786 he promulgated a new legal code that was closely modeled on Beccaria's recommendations. Catherine the Great of Russia declared herself a disciple of Beccaria, just as she had previously declared herself a disciple of Voltaire and Diderot, but in her case it was mostly talk, and the

Russian criminal code was not significantly improved. Thomas Jefferson and John Adams in America and Jeremy Bentham in England expressed enthusiasm for Beccaria's ideas, and even the reactionary Hegel, who continued to regard suicide as a crime and taught that capital punishment constituted an "annulment of murder," mentioned Beccaria with respect in his *Philosophy of Right*. Article VIII of the Declaration of the Rights of Man adopted by the revolutionary National Assembly of France in 1789 reads like a quotation from Beccaria's *Treatise*: "In order for punishment not to be, in every instance, an act of violence of one or of many against a private citizen, it must be essentially public, prompt, necessary, the least possible in the given circumstances, proportionate to the crimes, dictated by the laws."

Perhaps nothing pleased Beccaria more than the endorsement of Voltaire, who had been his idol for many years. A copy of the original Italian edition of Beccaria's *Treatise* was given to Voltaire in October 1765 by James MacDonald, a young Scottish visitor. Voltaire, who could read Italian, was enthusiastic and called Beccaria his "brother." In June 1766 the Abbé Morellet, who had brought out a French translation of Beccaria's book a few months earlier, visited Voltaire at Ferney. The two men had extended discussions of the topics covered in Beccaria's book. Until then Voltaire had believed that to avoid such outrages as the judicial murder of Calas and la Barre, it was sufficient to break the power of the intolerant Church and to rectify certain abuses in the administration of the law. Now for the first time he realized that nothing less than a total reorganization and reform of the French judicial system was required. He decided to write a book of his own to complement Beccaria's work. The *Commentary* was written in July and August and appeared in September of 1766. The title is misleading since what Voltaire produced was really an independent work. In many of the subsequent editions of Beccaria's book, for example, in eleven out of twelve English editions before 1800, Voltaire's *Commentary* was printed along with Beccaria's text. Beccaria's book would undoubtedly have been a huge success even without Voltaire's endorsement, but especially in England and America, its impact was in large measure secured by the publication of Voltaire's *Commentary* within the same covers.

"The misfortunes of the wretched in the face of the severity of the law," Voltaire observes early in the *Commentary*, "have induced me to look at the criminal code of nations." Most of his scorn and outrage are directed at the French legal system. The punishments inflicted on defendants judged guilty were usually quite out of proportion to the severity of the offense. Most of the judges were venal and incompetent and immediately treated the accused as an enemy. If a person had the misfortune of being accused of a crime, his chances for acquittal were exceedingly dim regardless of how flimsy the evidence. In some of the most moving pages he ever wrote, Voltaire describes the plight of the criminal defendant in eighteenth-century France. He is at once locked up in a dungeon, he is not allowed to communicate with anybody, and he is loaded down with irons as if he had already been condemned. In criminal cases the defendant is not allowed a lawyer. The witnesses against him are heard in secret by a judge who can usually make them say anything he likes. Cross-examination is hardly ever permitted. If a witness, realizing that he has made a false or misleading statement, wishes to retract, he is liable to be tried for perjury. In these circumstances it is often the wisest thing for the defendant to flee, but the law specifies that flight is to be regarded as tantamount to guilt. Who would not be terrified by such a proceeding and who can be certain of not being crushed by it? "Oh judges," Voltaire exclaims, "if you want accused innocent men not to flee, give them the means of defending themselves."

On some issues, notably the death penalty, Voltaire was less radical than Beccaria. Voltaire was certainly no friend of capital punishment, but he could not see his way clear to supporting the total abolition recommended by Beccaria. Surprisingly, Beccaria did not use what is unquestionably the most powerful argument in favor of abolition, that, because of its finality, judicial errors cannot be rectified. Morellet did make such an observation in the notes he added to the French translation of Beccaria's *Treatise*, and Voltaire could see its force. His discussions of miracles show how suspicious he was of the testimony of eyewitnesses, and, perhaps better than anybody else, he knew how the French legal system allowed, if it did not in fact actively encourage, miscarriages of justice. In several of the writings of his last years, he is concerned with the question of how we may retain capital punishment without executing innocent people. In the *Essai sur les probabilités en fait de justice* (1772), he declares that even the "highest probability of guilt" cannot be sufficient to justify a death sentence, and in an article published at about the same time in his *Questions Concerning the Encyclopedia*, he insists that we must have absolute certainty before sentencing a man to death. He implies that sometimes we do attain such certainty and he thinks that we cannot do without the death penalty because society has to be protected against dangerous people who cannot be controlled in any other way.

Capital punishment is here justified on purely utilitarian grounds. The wickedness of the individual has nothing to do with the matter. He has to be killed as we kill a rabid dog ("un chien enragé"). Some abolitionists insist that we never in fact attain the absolute certainty required by Voltaire, but in this they are clearly wrong. There was no doubt about Charles Manson's guilt, and the same is true of many other ordinary criminals and also, of course, of murderous "magistrates" like the late rulers of Nazi Germany. The proper retort to Voltaire is not that we can never achieve certainty, but that as long as there is capital punishment, people — judges, juries and the public — are liable to *believe mistakenly* that there is certainty and condemn an innocent person. On the question of protecting society against *chiens enragés*, it must be conceded that this is a very real problem. Such rabid dogs exist in profusion in all ages and they are probably more numerous today than in Voltaire's time, but it is doubtful whether capital punishment is the best solution. The United States has capital punishment, whereas England and France do not, but there is no evidence that the American public is any better protected.

APOTHEOSIS

In 1778 Voltaire's latest play, *Irène*, was to be performed in Paris, and he expressed a wish to attend its premiere. He had been banished from the city during the lifetime of Louis XV, but with the accession of Louis XVI and a new ministry that included his friend, the Encylopedist Turgot, Paris was once again open to him.

Voltaire was recognized and hailed by crowds at every stop on the journey from Ferney. In Paris, there were tremendous ovations in the streets, and everywhere he was hailed as "l'homme aux Calas." Voltaire did not lose his head. "What crowds to greet you," somebody said to him. "Alas!" he answered, "there would be just as many to see me on the scaffold." The king ignored his presence, but he was feted at the Comédie Française and the Academy where only the clerical members refused to attend. At the Hôtel de Villette, where he was staying, Voltaire received visitors eager to pay their respects. The callers included Benjamin Franklin and (reportedly) Diderot, with whose writings and activities he was familiar, but neither of whom he had met. Benjamin Franklin brought his grandson and asked Voltaire's blessing for him. Voltaire stretched out his hand and simply said, "God and Liberty." Diderot, it is said, was so eager to impress him with his wit and eloquence that Voltaire had to accept the unaccustomed role of passive listener. After their meeting, Diderot is reported to have described Voltaire as a fairy castle, fallen in ruins, but still inhabited by an old sorcerer. When asked his opinion of Diderot, the "old sorcerer" remarked that there could be no doubt about the man's brilliance, adding that unfortunately "nature had denied him one essential gift, that of dialogue."

In May 1778, Voltaire was seized by a fever. The doctor diagnosed cancer of the prostate. Voltaire died on May 30. There were the usual rumors of agonized shrieks and deathbed confessions. The Marquise de Villette, who was with Voltaire when he died, denied all such assertions. "To the very last moment," she said, "everything showed the goodness and benevolence of his character, everything bespoke tranquility, peace and resignation."

Refused a Christian burial in Paris, Voltaire was buried surreptitiously outside the city. On July 11, 1791, before the Revolution had degenerated into an orgy of violence, his remains were brought back to Paris. A huge parade, led by deputies, city officials, academicians, actors and actresses, and opera singers, passed through the streets of Paris that were lined with enormous crowds. After stopping at the Bastille, the procession moved to the Pantheon, the newly created secular national shrine. Voltaire's coffin stayed there until 1860 when it was opened and found to be empty. It was discovered that fanatics had removed the body many years earlier. The Nazis, quite fittingly, melted down his statue during their occupation of Paris. Voltaire, wrote Lord Morley, "will stand out like the name of the great decisive movements in the European advance like the Revival of Learning or the Reformation. The existence, character and career of this extraordinary person constituted in themselves a new . . . era." The best epitaph came from Thomas Macaulay. "Voltaire possessed a voice," Macaulay wrote, "which made itself heard from Moscow to Cádiz, and which sentenced the unjust judges to the contempt and detestation of all Europe. . . . Bigots and tryants, who had never been moved by the wailing and cursing of millions, turned pale at his name."

GOD, MATTER, AND EVIL

It has been maintained by some reputable scholars that, regardless of his numerous public and private statements to the contrary, Voltaire was an atheist. However, the great majority of commentators agree that he was a sincere and ardent believer in God. It is true that, in one or two places, Voltaire discussed the subject without reaching a definite conclusion. Thus in an essay entitled "On the Existence of God," he simply set out the arguments in favor of God's existence and those against it, and did not declare that he sided with either. There are also passages in his correspondence that dismiss belief in God as absurd. Against this, it must be emphasized that in literally hundreds of books, articles, and letters, he insists, with almost compulsive repetitiveness, that the order of nature and the teleological character of biological systems require us to infer the existence of a "supreme intelligence." Moreover, Voltaire wrote extensively against the atheism of some of his fellow Encyclopedists and of Spinoza, whom he always regarded as an atheist. It seems on balance more reasonable to conclude that, like many other believers, Voltaire occasionally wavered and had spells of doubt and disbelief, than that he engaged in a lifelong deliberate charade, deceiving not only the religious world but also his fellow-philosophers, many of whom he loved and admired.

Voltaire called himself a theist, but the position he advocated is more commonly described as "deism." He believed in the existence of God while opposing revealed religion—miracles, dogmas, and any kind of priesthood. He always made a careful distinction between "true religion" and "superstition," arguing that, unlike superstitious religions, the kind of religion he championed could only do good. In one place he wrote: "The sole religion is to worship God and to be an honorable man. This pure and everlasting religion cannot possibly produce harm." "Superstition," he wrote in the *Treatise on Toleration*, "is to religion what astrology is to astronomy — the mad daughter of a wise mother. These daughters have too long dominated the earth."

In several places he tells us both what we can and what we cannot know about God. The lists of divine attributes supplied in different books are not entirely consistent. In the article "Theist" in the *Philosophical Dictionary*, the theist — the Voltairean believer — is said to be "a man firmly convinced of the existence of a Supreme Being, as good as it is powerful, which has created all the extended, vegetating, feeling, and reflecting beings." To this he characteristically adds that the theist's religion "consists neither in the opinions of an unintelligible metaphysics nor in vain display, but in worship and in justice. To do good — that is his worship; to submit to God — that is his doctrine." It should be noted that the Supreme Being is described as good but not as perfectly good, and as powerful but not omnipotent. In the very late essay "We Must Take Sides" (*Il faut prendre a parti*, 1772), which deals exclusively with the existence and nature of God, goodness is omitted from the list of divine attributes, and the omission is not accidental. This time the emphasis is on the power, the intelligence, and the eternity of God. The Supreme Being is "very powerful" since it "directs so vast and complex a machine," and it is "very intelligent" because "the smallest spring of this machine cannot be equalled by us, who are intelligent beings." Human beings cannot make solar systems, and they also cannot make eyes or ears or stomachs. Since God can produce these things, He must be vastly more intelligent than even the most intelligent men.

As we shall see, Voltaire primarily relies on various forms of the design argument to justify belief in God. However, he realized that, even if it is otherwise unobjectionable, the design argument cannot prove God's eternity. Watchmakers and other "manufacturers" are born and they die; how do we know that the Supreme Designer has no beginning and no end? Voltaire never addresses the latter of these issues, but he has no doubt that he can take care of the former and thus prove God's "infinite duration." To do this, he borrows a version of the cosmological argument found in Locke. God is eternal, Voltaire writes, since He "cannot be produced from nothing, which, being nothing, can produce nothing." Thus, given the existence of something, it is demonstrated that something has existed for all eternity.

The argument is doubly fallacious. Even if it succeeded in proving that there must be an entity that has always existed, it does not follow that this eternal entity is God. Furthermore, the "principle" that something cannot come from nothing does not, in conjunction with the statement that something exists now, yield the desired conclusion that some particular being must always have existed. What does follow is that at all times there must have been something in existence, which is not at all the same as that one and the same thing has always existed. An infinite series of causes, each of whose members is of finite duration, is entirely consistent with the facts that something exists now and that something cannot come from nothing. These objections entirely disregard the vagueness and ambiguity in the principle that something cannot come from nothing.

Not only God, but matter, too, is eternal. Voltaire's God is thus a Demiurge rather than a Creator. "My reason alone proves to me a Being who has arranged the matter of this world." he writes in the article "God-Gods" in the enlarged version in the *Questions Concerning the Encyclopedia*. Reason, however, is "unable to prove that he made this matter—that he brought it out of nothing." In the article "Matter" and also in *The Ignorant Philosopher*, he goes further and maintains that reason requires us to hold that matter is eternal. In one of his customary jabs at the scholastic philosophers, he remarks that "today we are lucky enough to know by faith that God drew matter from nothingness," but this is not a conclusion warranted by the evidence. Nor is it, in fact, the view of most religions, which hold that the "divine hand" arranged the world out of chaos, not out of nothingness. Belief in the eternity of matter has not "injured the cult of the Divinity in any nation." We are not diminishing the majesty of God if we describe him as "the master of an eternal matter." Not even Genesis teaches creation out of nothing. It simply asserts that the gods, *Elohim*, not *Eloi*, "made heaven and earth," leaving it open whether there was any matter out of which heaven and earth were shaped.

Voltaire's pronouncements on the relations between the Demiurge and the rest of the universe are far from clear. In the article "Infinity" in the *Questions Concerning the Encyclopedia*, he writes that the Supreme Being, by "modifying matter," caused "worlds to circulate in space and form animals, vegetables and metals." He approvingly mentions the view of the Romans that "matter, in the hands of God, was felt to be like clay on the potter's wheel," although he adds that such a comparison is no more than a "feeble image" to express divine power. In *The Ignorant Philosopher*, he remarks that "he cannot conceive that the cause that continually and visibly actuates nature" could have been inactive at any time and that an "eternity of idleness" is incompatible with his other properties. He concludes that the world has probably always "issued from a primordial and necessary cause as light emanates from the sun." Voltaire emphatically disagrees with the teaching of non-Christian religions and of Hesiod and Ovid that before the Divinity's intervention, matter was in a state of chaos. "Chaos is precisely contrary to all the laws of nature" and "chaos never existed anywhere but in our heads." As a determinist, Voltaire could have added that, since what goes on in our heads also happens according to laws, chaos never exists even in our heads. If initially there was no chaos, there also was not the order we now find in the world. In the course of replying to the charge that belief in the eternity of matter commits him to Manicheism, Voltaire wrote: "Here are stones an architect has not made; he has raised an immense building with them; I don't accept two architects; brute stones obeyed power and genius."

It appears that Voltaire did believe in one or more datable ordering acts on the part of the Demiurge. Initially, matter was not without order, but the order we now have was imposed on it by the Demiurge. Furthermore, as we shall see later on, Voltaire believed that the Demiurge was and is involved in the production of every biological structure so that, as far as living organisms are concerned, creation is still going on. The similarity of Voltaire's views to those found in Plato's *Timaeus* is obvious, but, according to most of his interpreters, Plato did not believe that the imposition of order by the Demiurge occurred in time.

In his earlier writings, Voltaire did not hesitate to speak of God as good and just. This was in harmony with his generally optimistic view about the prevalence of both virtue and happiness on the human scene. In Chapter 2 of the *Traité de metaphysique*, he offers a fair statement of the problem of evil but does not see in it a serious difficulty for his optimistic deism. His "solution" of the problem is as superficial and evasive as any found in the theologians he came to deride with such zest. He first observes that the materialist, that is, the unbeliever, has as much difficulty in explaining evil as the believer. This entirely misconceives the issue. The believer's difficulty arises from the fact that the evil we find seems incompatible with the assertion that the world was made by a being who is omnipotent, omniscient, and perfectly good. The unbeliever makes no such assertion. Voltaire's main reply is quite conventional and depends on appealing to what later theologians have called the "infinite transcendence of God." We have no ideas of justice, he wrote, except for those we have formed in connection with human relations. We regard actions as just if they conform to laws established for the common good. Such a notion can have no application to God and hence it is as absurd to describe God as either just or unjust as it would be to describe him as blue or square. Voltaire does not realize that this is a suicidal move. For it was he and his fellow deists who initially maintained that God is just, and there would be no problem if that were not their position. If we cannot describe God as just, then Voltaire should not have done so in the first place.

These criticisms of the *Traité* would have been fully endorsed by the later Voltaire. Rousseau was not the only one who saw no obstacle to theological optimism in such events as the Lisbon earthquake. In a sermon on the cause of earthquakes, John Wesley attributed the disaster to "sin," to "that curse that was brought upon the earth by the original transgression of Adam and Eve." Bishop William Warburton, an influential Anglican divine whose main claim to posthumous fame is an attempt to obtain a prosecution of Hume on charges of blasphemy, asserted that the Lisbon earthquake "displayed God's glory in its fairest colors." Voltaire disposed of these and similar "explanations," not only in the *Poem on the Lisbon Earthquake* and *Candide*, but also in a number of articles in the *Philosophical Dictionary* and the *Ignorant Philosopher*. He returned to the subject once more in some powerfully written pages of the above-mentioned essay, "We Must Take Sides." Nobody had shown that there were more sinners in Lisbon than in London or Paris. Yet Lisbon lay shattered while Paris danced. Even if the adult victims of the earthquake had been such dreadful sinners as to deserve their fate, what about the infants that lay crushed and bloody on their mothers' breasts? Moreover, what happened in Lisbon was only an extreme illustration of the suffering that is the inevitable lot of living things. "All the world," Voltaire writes, "in all its members groans, all born for suffering and for mutual death." The "ferocious vulture" darts upon its "timid prey" and "feasts with joy" on its helpless victim. Its triumph, however, is short-lived. For soon an eagle "with sharply cutting beak devours the vulture." The eagle in turn is reached by a deadly shot coming from a man who not long afterward lies dying in the dust of a bloody battlefield. There he serves as the food of voracious birds. Beast and men suffer, almost without ceasing, but men suffer more because, in addition, to all their illnesses and misfortunes, they are conscious of their inevitable extinction. Man is a "very miserable being." The universe, Voltaire addresses optimists, "gives you the lie, and your own heart refutes a hundred times the error of your mind." Pope's "general good" is a "strange thing indeed, composed of the [kidney] stone, the gout, all crimes, all sufferings, death, and damnation."

Voltaire adds the interesting reflection that those writing in support of cosmic optimism have generally been the most miserable of men. He does not even deign to mention the wretched Rousseau whose sensitivity to slights and insults, mostly imaginary, had made Hume describe him as like a man without a skin. He does mention Shaftesbury, Bolingbroke, and Pope, all of whom he admired. Shaftesbury was known to have been a most unhappy man. Voltaire had seen Bolingbroke "torn with grief and rage," and Pope, whom Bolingbroke had induced to "put this miserable joke into verse," was a cripple, unbalanced in temperament, chronically ill, the victim of discrimination because of his Catholicism and harassed by hoards of enemies until his last moment. At least, Voltaire concludes, "let us have happy beings saying that all is well."

Epicurus was right to insist that the existence of evil rules out a God who is both all powerful and perfectly good. The problem of evil is "an abyss whose bottom nobody has been able to see," "an inexplicable chaos for those who search honestly," an "unshakable rock" against which the "arrows fired by a hundred bachelors and doctors of divinity" have been totally ineffective. It is a "terrible shelter" for atheists who are wrong in concluding that there is no God but right in questioning His goodness and justice. The entire situation is a baffling mystery that requires us to confess the limits of our understanding. If my understanding is so weak, he wrote, that I cannot even know "by what I am animated," how "can I have any acquaintance with that ineffable intelligence which visibly presides over the universe?" It should be noted that Voltaire's agnosticism is confined to the moral attributes of God. It does not extend to the intelligence, wisdom, or power of the deity.

VOLTAIRE'S DESIGN ARGUMENTS

Voltaire occasionally had recourse to the cosmological argument, not only in Locke's version mentioned earlier but also in the form in which it is found in Samuel Clarke. Voltaire's statement of the argument is greatly inferior to Clarke's own formulation, and it is evident that he does not have his heart in this argument, which seems to be too scholastic and metaphysical for his taste. On the other hand, he defends numerous versions of the design argument with great enthusiasm. He regards it as a genuinely empirical argument and he finds it adequate to the task of proving the finite Demiurge whose existence he champions. Contemporaries like Holbach who scoff at the argument are castigated at great length. This much despised argument, Voltaire writes, in the article "God-Gods," "is that of Cicero and of Newton. This alone might somewhat lessen the confidence of atheists in their denial." Many sages, "observing the course of the stars, and the prodigious art that pervades the structure of animals and vegetables," have acknowledged "a powerful hand working these continual wonders." The appeal to final causes is "the most natural" and "for common capacities" the most perfect argument to show that an intelligent being "presides over the universe."

As with many other defenders of the argument, both before and after Voltaire, the starting point is what we know or supposedly know about the relation between a watch and its intelligent maker. "When I see a watch whose hand marks the hours," Voltaire wrote, "I conclude that an intelligent being has arranged the springs of this machine in order that the hand may mark the hour." If a clock is not made for the purpose of telling the time, he writes in the expanded version of the article "Final Causes," he is prepared to "admit that final causes are nothing but chimeras," adding that he would be content "to go by the name of a fool" to the end of his life. Needless to say, Voltaire did not think that he had to go by the name of a fool to the end of his life. Unlike those who have "willfully shut their eyes and understanding," he gladly admitted that there is design in nature, and if there is design, then "there is an intelligent cause: there exists a God."

In a passage quoted earlier, Voltaire speaks of "the prodigious art" that pervades the structures of animals and vegetables. This art is displayed in a great variety of ways but most undeniably and impressively in the construction of the bodies of animals and men. "Consider yourself," remarks Freind in *Histoire de Jenni — L'athée et le Sage* ("The Sage and the Atheist," 1775), one of the atheism-bashing pieces of Voltaire's last years, "examine with what art, never sufficiently explored, all is constructed within and without for all your wishes and actions." There is not one "superfluous vessel." The arrangement throughout the body is so artful that "there is not a single vein without valves and sluices, making a passage for the blood." From the roots of the hair to the toes "all is art, design, cause, and effect." It is "audacious madness" to deny that we are here confronted with final causes. A sane person has to admit that the mouth was made to eat and speak with, the eyes "admirably contrived for seeing," the ears for hearing, and the nerves for feeling. Nothing perhaps shows the presence of design more clearly than the arrangement of the reproductive systems in males and females alike and the pleasure associated with the sex act that guarantees the perpetuation of the species. Even Epicurus, the unbeliever, would be obliged to admit that "pleasure is divine" and that pleasure is a "final cause" leading to the incessant introduction of new organisms into the world. "When I see the springs of the human body," Voltaire writes in the relatively skeptical paper "On the Existence of God," "I conclude that an intelligent being has arranged these organs," an intelligent and "superior being" who "skillfully prepared and fashioned the matter." In *The Ignorant Philosopher*, this superior intelligence is referred to as "the supreme artisan" or "workman" who "actuates" the enormous multitude of biological arrangements and who, except for the superiority of his intelligence and skill, is in these respects entirely comparable to human craftsmen.

The order of lawfulness of the universe, especially as it is exemplified in the movements of the heavenly bodies, is just as strong evidence for a supernatural designer as the purposive character of biological structures. The order of the universe, Voltaire writes in the expanded version of "Atheist, Atheism," now that it is better known, "bespeaks a workman; and so many never-varying laws, announce a law-giver." Voltaire was particularly pleased with his dictum that "as a catechist proclaims God to children, so Newton demonstrates him to the learned." In one place he quite correctly attributes this remark to "a philosophical Frenchman who was persecuted in his own country for asserting as much." This theme is developed in detail in "We Must Take Sides," where he writes: "The unvarying uniformity of the laws which control the march of the heavenly bodies and the movements of our own globe" show that there is "a single, universal and powerful intelligence."

There are three possible ways of accounting for the order in the world. One is blind chance; the second is the view that the order was produced by the heavenly and other bodies themselves; and the third is the postulation of an eternal orderer or geometrician. Taking as his illustration one of Kepler's laws, Voltaire dismisses blind chance as "extreme folly." Surely it is preposterous to maintain that blind chance has produced an arrangement in which "the square of the revolution of one planet is always to the squares of the others, as the cube of its distance is to the cubes of the distances of others, from the common centre." Voltaire next rules out the possibility that the planets themselves, or more generally "Nature," are responsible for the order discovered by astronomers. In the "Dialogue Between the Philosopher and Nature," in the *Questions Concerning the Encyclopedia*, Nature remarks that "she" is no mathematician and that yet everything "in and about" her is "arranged agreeably to mathematical laws." The philosopher draws the consequence. If "your great universal system knows nothing of mathematics," the philosopher responds, and if nevertheless the laws by which "you are regulated" are those of the "most profound geometry," there must necessarily be "an eternal geometrician, who directs you, and presides over your operations." Again, in "Atheist, Atheism," we are presented with the disjunction that "either the planets are great geometricians or the Eternal Geometrician has arranged the planets." The former alternative is plainly absurd, and hence we must embrace the latter.

At times Voltaire appeals to the fact, or rather what he takes to be the fact, that the universe is a vast machine. "When we see a fine machine," he writes, "we know that there must be a 'good machinist' with 'an excellent understanding.'" This argument is "old, but is not therefore the worse." It should be remarked that it is not identical with the one appealing to the orderly nature of the universe, but it is doubtful that Voltaire perceived the difference between them.

Another version of the design argument is based on copies or reproductions that human beings make of natural objects or collections of such objects. Since the copy required an intelligent cause, we may affirm the same of the original. In "The Sage and the Atheist," Voltaire offers the illustration of "orreries," the then newly invented devices in which the bodies of the solar system were represented by balls moved by wheelwork. An orrery is "the chef d'oeuvre of the skill of our artisans," and everybody admires Lord Orrery for his invention. Yet it is a very imperfect copy of the solar system and its revolutions. "If the copy indicates genius," how much more must there be in the maker of the orginal! Similar considerations apply to landscape paintings, drawings of animals, or models in colored wax, which are Voltaire's illustrations in "We Must Take Sides." They are the work of "clever artists." If this is true of the copies, it must also be true of the original. "I do not see," Voltaire observed, "how this demonstration can be assailed."

There is also the problem of accounting for intelligence. Even a materialist like Holbach cannot deny that there is "some difference between a clod and the ideas of Newton." Intelligent beings like Newton cannot have been "formed" by something blind, brute, insensible, that is, by matter. It follows that "Newton's intelligence came from some other intelligence." These quotations are from the previously noted article on "Atheist, Atheism." The argument is repeated a short time later in a letter to D'Alembert (July 22, 1770). "It seems to me absurd," writes Voltaire, "to derive intelligence from something like matter and motion which are not intelligent." It may be interesting to note that D'Alembert himself, who eventually became a thoroughgoing atheist, accepted this argument in his earlier years.

After this argument one is prepared for the worst, and the worst does not fail to come. What is the purpose of the sun? Most educated people since Copernicus would find this a senseless question. Not so Voltaire in one of his Panglossian moods. "When the atheist lights a candle," he writes, "he admits that it is for the purpose of giving light." He should then similarly admit that "the sun was made to illuminate our part of the universe." Fortunately, however, such Panglossian outbursts are rare. Most of the time, Voltaire confesses that we do not know the purpose of the universe or presumably that of the sun. In the "Dialogue Between Nature and the Philosopher," the philosopher asks his "beloved mother" why she exists and why, in fact, anything exists. Nature modestly replies that she knows nothing about the matter. The philosopher persists: Why would not "nothing itself" have been preferable to "that multitude of existences formed to be continually dissolved," the animals born to devour others and to be devoured in their turn, the numberless beings whose lives are filled with pain, and the tribes of "reasoning beings" who never or at most rarely listen to reason? For what purpose, he demands, was all this? Leave me alone, Nature replies in effect. "Go and inquire of Him who made me."

The question of the purpose of the universe also arises for Voltaire when he tries to answer the opponents of the design argument who bring up the obvious imperfections in the world as a reason for questioning the wisdom and even the existence of a supernatural designer. Some critics have brought up such phenomena as earthquakes, eruptions of volcanoes, and "plains of moving sands." Others have mentioned frightening and poisonous animals like serpents and sharks. And there is, of course, the problem posed by "the woes and crimes of mankind." Voltaire always gave the same answer to such challenges. The imperfections may show that the designer lacks goodness and concern for the welfare of living things. Perhaps they even show that He is malevolent, but they do not weaken the inference to a designer of *some* kind. "If the naves of your chariot wheel catch fire," he writes, this does not show that "your chariot was not made expressly for the purpose of conveying you from one place to another." Similarly, the existence of serpents and "so many wicked men worse than serpents" does not show that either serpents or men were not designed. If flies could reason, they would undoubtedly complain to God about the existence of spiders, but they would nevertheless admit that the spider's web was arranged in a wonderful manner.

OBJECTIONS TO VOLTAIRE'S ARGUMENTS

Perhaps the most obvious of the many objections to Voltaire's arguments is that, if all of them were valid, they would not establish the existence of a *single* supernatural intelligence. They would establish a "geometrician," an "architect," an "actualizer," and a "lawmaker." In our experience, it is certainly not the case that person having one of these skills invariably also possesses the others. Perhaps all four skills or occupations are rolled into one in the Supreme Intelligence, but that is not immediately evident and requires proof.

Several of Voltaire's arguments are so glaringly invalid that they can be disposed of in a few words. The inference of a supernatural lawmaker from scientific laws involves a fallacy of equivocation. Laws in the sense of legal regulations do indeed require an intelligent lawmaker, but scientific laws are not laws in the same sense. As has often been pointed out since Voltaire's time, legal regulations are prescriptive, while scientific laws are descriptive. Voltaire's "copy" argument is just as threadbare. The fact that a copy like a landscape painting or a model of the solar system is the work of an intelligent being does not show that the original must also have an intelligent cause. If the wind blows bits of paper from a table to the floor and if somebody paints or photographs the resulting scene, the copy is the work of an intelligent cause, but the original is not. In the sense in which "chance" is opposed to design, the original scene is an instance of chance.

Voltaire's argument that intelligent beings can have been produced only by intelligent causes, and that hence the Supreme Being must be intelligent, rests on the well-worn principle of the scholastics and of Descartes that any attribute of an effect must already have been present in its cause. If this proposition were true, the amoeba would have to have been a mathematician. But one does not have to go to evolution to realize that the principle is false. Mill gave the example of the liquidity of water and the gaseous character of its components, and there are countless everyday instances concerning parents and children that conflict with the principle. Even if it were true, it still would not give Voltaire a Supreme Intelligence as distinct from an infinite series of intelligent beings, each the cause of its successor. In one place Voltaire declares that an infinite causal series is impossible, but he gives no reason, and in the present context he does not even mention the issue. One may also question whether Voltaire was sincere in urging this particular argument since he was most emphatic that thought can be produced by organized matter, more specifically, the brains of human beings and animals.

The argument based on the similarities between the watch and biological structures like the eye is much more impressive. Voltaire can hardly be faulted for not knowing the Darwinian explanation of the apparent purposiveness of biological structures, a particularly elegant and persuasive account of which has recently been produced by Richard Dawkins in *The Blind Watchmaker* (1986). However, even before Darwin, several weighty objections, some of them fairly obvious, could be advanced. In the first place, there is a simple but important distinction of which Voltaire shows some awareness but whose full significance he never realized. The distinction is between the notion that something is *used* for a certain purpose and that it was *designed* for that purpose. If we come to a cave and find signs of habitation — beds, cooking utensils, clothes, copies of the Bible and *Candide* — we are entitled to affirm that it is used as a dwelling. We have no right to infer that it was designed for that purpose. This may in fact be the case — the people living in it or somebody in the past may have dug the cave. However, it may also be a "natural" cave produced by purely geological causes. Now it is certainly true that human beings and various animals *use* their eyes for the purpose of seeing, but it does not follow that the eyes were designed for this purpose or, for that matter, that they were designed at all.

Voltaire shows some awareness of another objection, which was stated with great force by Philo in Hume's *Dialogues Concerning Natural Religion* and which has occurred to many other skeptics. Evolution aside, we *know* how eyes and other organs are produced: they are produced by natural reproduction, or what Hume called "generation." Design, so far as our observation goes, has nothing to do with it. This commonsense observation leaves, of course, some important questions unanswered, especially once we realize that species are not immutable. As far as it goes, however, it is absolutely correct and it challenges the design theorists to tell us just where and how the alleged designing and "actuating" by the Demiurge takes place.

Voltaire answers it by declaring that the biological parents are not the true cause of the offspring. All offspring are the work of the "eternal manufacturer." Voltaire cannot very well deny that the biological parents play some role in the production of their children, but they are no more than the "blind instruments" of God. Speaking about the "arrangements" within his own body, he insists that he is indebted for them to God and not to his parents. His parents were not his true cause since, when producing him, "they certainly did not know what they were doing." Voltaire's position here is in effect quite similar in general outline to that of reincarnationists who maintain that the familiar biological processes of conception and gestation are not sufficient to bring about a full-fledged human child and to that of Christian theologians who maintain that God's infusion of the soul into the newly formed embryo is an essential element in the production of a human being. The objections that Voltaire would probably have advanced against the reincarnationists, and some of which he did bring up against theological explanations of the origin of the human soul, are equally applicable to his own contention. What evidence, to begin with, does he have that the natural biological causes are insufficient to produce a complete offspring, eyes included? The answer, of course, is that he has none. He does offer certain arguments, but they beg the question. Thus he argues that the parent organisms, whether they are animals or human beings, do not possess the capacity to "form" their offspring and then concludes that the offspring must have been formed by a superhuman intelligence. Here, "formation" presumably means planning or design followed by "actuation," the way in which a watchmaker designs and actuates a watch. It must be granted that in this sense neither human beings nor animals "form" their children. However, Voltaire's conclusion would follow only if it had been shown that formation is the only means of producing offspring. This assumption is not self-evident, and it is not accepted by the critics of the design argument. Again, as we saw a moment ago, Voltaire writes that parent organisms do not know what they are doing when they produce their offspring, and he takes this to be evidence that the parents are not the true cause. But why does ignorance on the part of the parents prevent them from being the true cause of their offspring? We may assume that parent cats are ignorant of the connection between sexual intercourse and pregnancy and that they know nothing about heredity and embryology. We also know that they cannot "form" their offspring the way a watchmaker assembles a watch. None of this, however, shows that the parent cats are not the true cause of their offspring *by means of generation.*

In the "Chinese Catechism" Voltaire ridicules the theologians who maintain that God sends a soul into the mother's womb at the moment at which the gametes form an embryo. Such a view assigns to the "Creator of the universe" the rather undignified role of "lying continually in wait for men and women to copulate" so as to note the exact moment at which "the seed leaves the body of the man and enters that of the woman." Since, on Voltaire's view, the theologian must also hold that animals have spiritual souls, "the master of the world" has to keep watch not only over the copulations of the human species but also over those of elephants, pigs, owls, fish, and indeed all other animals. What Voltaire does not realize is that his insistence that it is God and not the biological parents who are responsible for new offspring, or at least for the "arrangements' or the "formation" of its parts, opens him to an exactly similar charge. In Voltaire's view, God must "continually lie in wait" over the coupling of men and all other animals to know the precise moment at which He should supply not the soul but the "arrangements" or perform the "actualization" without which a full-fledged offspring could not come into existence.

There are additional difficulties in any attempt to maintain that the existence of organisms is the result of the joint efforts of the observable, embodied parents and a supernatural, unobservable intelligence. Voltaire's claim that the parents are the "blind instruments" of the supreme intelligence *seems* to be perfectly intelligible because we can easily think of situations in which certain things are described as the "instruments" of others who are regarded as the true or at least as the decisive cause. We might say, for example, that Greece's ambassador in Washington, D.C., is little more than an instrument of his government. If he orally presents a message to the Secretary of State, he is not its true cause, even though *he* may have chosen the precise wording. To take a case in which it might be said that the observable agents are merely the instruments of somebody who is not present, let us consider a performance of *Don Giovanni*. We will assume that the singers, the orchestra, and the staging are superb. It could then hardly be denied that the singers, the orchestra, the director, and the conductor play important roles in bringing about the admirable result, but it would still be true that the main credit belongs to Mozart's score. Without singers, conductor, orchestra, and, for that matter, the opera house, the performance could not have taken place or it could not have been so splendid; and they are certainly not "blind" instruments. Nevertheless, in the end, it is Mozart's score that is the basic and most indispensable factor.

Neither this nor any other familiar case of "co-causes," however, provides us with a model on whose basis we could give content to Voltaire's claim about the co-causation of organisms by their parents and God. We know what it is like for a composer to compose a score and we also know how the score can be made available to a conductor, the orchestra, and the singers so that they can put on a performance of the opera. On the other hand, we do *not* know what it would be like for a pure intelligence to produce the plan for a new organism. How can a pure intelligence fashion anything like a blueprint? Does such talk have any sense at all? Furthermore, even if this question could be satisfactorily answered, there remains the problem of realizing the plan in the "instruments," in this case the biological parents. How could this be done? What kind of "imprinting" takes place? Where and how? We have most emphatically not been given a coherent theory unless we are told not only *that* an intelligent being makes eyes and ears and whole animals, but also, at least in outline, *how* this is done. What this objection amounts to is that the word *instrument* has a clear sense only when we are dealing with relations between observable entities and processes. It has lost its sense when one of the entities involved is unobservable. On a few occasions Voltaire himself seemed to recognize as much. In a letter to Mme. du Deffand, which has been cited as evidence that Voltaire was secretly an atheist, he speaks approvingly of the opinion of Epicurus and Lucretius that "nothing is more ridiculous than the notion that an unextended being could govern one which is extended," and he adds, referring presumably to the incarnation of God in Jesus, that "combining what is mortal with what is immortal is something most unsuitable." The same surely applies to any supposed "blending" of the contributions of the biological parents with that of the Divinity to the production of an organism.

Voltaire is aware that, if valid, the design argument gives us an arranger and not a creator, and since he believes in the eternity of matter, this fact does not disturb him. He is not aware, however, that the designer it would give us is one with a body who needs his body for "actuating" or "forming" structures like the eye or whole organisms like a cat. If we followed through the machine-maker analogy without stopping before it became too uncomfortable, we would end up with something like heavenly factories of parts and heavenly places for assembling the parts into the finished biological products. The fact that we need one or more *physical* heavenly arrangers is occasionally but only dimly realized by believers when they talk about "the hand that is divine," as Addison does in his well-known hymn and as Voltaire himself did in the article "God-Gods," in which he refers to the "powerful hand working continual wonders."

The supporter of the design argument is faced with a dilemma, each of whose horns seems to have devastating consequences for his position. If he endows the supernatural arranger with a body, then the arranger could, in principle, "actuate" or "form" biological structures; but educated Western believers find such a position repellent and, what is more, it does seem incredible to almost everybody. It seems incredible because it is so glaringly false. The actuating activities on the part of a *physical* superhuman arranger would surely be observed if they really occurred; but, of course, no such individual ever shows up and engages in any kind of arranging at the moment of conception or at any stage of the mother's pregnancy. If, on the other hand, the supernatural arranger exists without a body, it is not easy to see how he could engage in actuating biological structures; and it is also not the conclusion that the watchmaker argument would authorize. Teleologists and also some of their critics do not see this predicament because they tend to talk in very general terms of "intelligence" rather than "chance" as the cause of living things. It must therefore be emphasized that intelligence in general is not an entity that can produce anything. Only intelligent *beings* can do this, and they need bodies and tools and pre-existing materials.

Turning to the "cosmic" version of the design argument, the first thing to note is that in one obvious respect it is much weaker than the "biological" form just discussed. In any complete teleological argument, we may distinguish two stages. The first consists in identifying something as a teleological system; the second in showing that it is the kind of teleological system that is best explained in terms of conscious design. The biological version does at least get to the first stage, for an organ like the eye may in a broad sense be conceded to be a teleological system. Here we at least have an end, namely that of seeing, to which the various internal mechanisms and adjustments seem to be directed. Discussions of this topic have been bedeviled by the ambiguities of such words as *end* and *goal*. However, if not too much is read into this, we may say, following terminology used by a number of contemporary writers on biology, that the activities of the various parts of the eye are "goal-directed," leaving it an open question whether they are also "goal-intended." Now, the first and most basic trouble with the cosmic version of the argument is that it never gets as far as the first stage. To what common end, corresponding to vision, are all the objects in the universe directed? Except for his one regression to pre-Copernican anthropomorphism, when Voltaire told us that the purpose of the sun is to provide light for human beings on the earth, he himself admitted that there is no answer to this question. Voltaire fudged the issue when he called the universe an "admirable machine." There is a popular sense in which a machine is by definition something that was designed to serve a certain purpose. Machines in this sense are "contraptions" or "devices." If it were known that the universe is a machine in this sense, it would indeed follow that it was designed for a purpose by an intelligent being. However, we most emphatically do not know that the universe is a machine in this sense.

This leaves Voltaire with the claim that the order of the world that is described by scientific laws requires an intelligent cause. It has been questioned by a number of philosophers, including Bertrand Russell, Ernest Nagel, and A. J. Ayer, whether the statement that the universe is orderly has any content. If it did, it should be possible to describe what a disorderly universe, that is, a universe that is not governed by laws, would be like. But, as Leibniz already saw, this is not possible. Not too much weight should be placed on this criticism in the present context because a sympathetic reading shows that Voltaire need not, and much of the time does not, argue from order as such to an intelligent cause. It is rather the simple and beautiful order described by Newton's laws that makes it reasonable and even necessary to invoke a divine geometrician. Stated more fully, the argument says that such a simple and beautiful order is antecedently highly unlikely. Since it cannot be explained by chance, we must infer design. This is quite similar to what Richard Swinburne, perhaps the ablest Christian philosopher writing at the present time, has maintained in his *Existence of God*, and it also has obvious affinities to the "anthropic principle" championed by a number of physicists. "The orderliness of the universe," writes Swinburne, "is a very striking fact about the universe." The universe "might so naturally have been chaotic, but it is not — it is very orderly." This phenomenon, "like the very existence of the world, is clearly something too big to be explained by science." It "seems incredible that there be no cause" of this orderliness. "If there is no explanation in terms of the action of God," this orderliness must be one of "coincidence." Because "the order of the world" would be "very improbable *a priori*," Swinburne concludes that it is evidence for the existence of God. Similarly, the champions of the anthropic principle have pointed to the undeniable fact that if the values of some of the fundamental physical constants were just a little different, life would be impossible. There are so many ways in which the values of the constants could have been different that we must regard the actual values as antecedently highly improbable. The conclusion usually hinted at and sometimes explicitly spelled out is that the value of the physical constants of the actual word must have been fixed by a superhuman intelligence with the emergence of life in view.

All such arguments fail because we *cannot* know that the actual order of the universe was antecedently improbable or for that matter antecedently probable. It is worth reminding ourselves in what kind of situation we *are* faced with such an antecedent improbability. In his unjustly neglected article "Chance" (*Scientific American*, 1965), Ayer offers the following illustration. If a person constantly runs into a stranger for several days in a row, he has grounds for supposing that the stranger is following him and that the meetings are not occurring by chance. The reason for this is something experience has taught us, namely, that when two people live independently in a large city, there are relatively few occasions on which the pursuit of their respective affairs results in their being in the same place. The inference is plausible in such a case only because the number of the meetings constitutes a significant deviation from an empirically established frequency. Now, if, to quote Charles Peirce, universes were as "plentiful as blackberries," we might indeed have reasons for supposing that the actual order of the world was highly unlikely. If all previous ten thousand million universes had been "chaotic" (whatever this means), or if all had exhibited a very different order, then we would have grounds for being astonished at the actual universe and demand an explanation for the departure from the norm. However, the universe occurs only once, and hence we have no means of forming any rational judgments of antecedent probability. We have no ground *whatsoever* for supposing that chaos or some less simple and less beautiful order, or for that matter some simpler and more beautiful order, was antecedently more or less likely.

Neither Voltaire nor Swinburne would like to be compared with Heidegger, but what they are doing is not so different from the astonishment Heidegger repeatedly expressed over the fact that there are things. "Why is there something and not nothing?" is for him the deepest of all questions and *that* there is something and not nothing "the miracle of miracles." But why should there not have been something? If there had been ten thousand million "universes" when there was nothing and then suddenly we have one in which there are things, there would be reason for astonishment, but there have not been ten thousand million such nothing-universes. If there had in fact been nothing, a putative cosmic observer might ask "why isn't there something?" and he could have declared, with as much or as little justification as Heidegger, that the absence of anything is "the miracle of miracles."

Setting aside questions of antecedent probability, does the order of the universe not call for some causal explanation? Many philosophers who do not accept the design argument would go along with Voltaire and Swinburne here. Thus, the Belgian fideistic theologian, Louis Dupré, rejects the design argument because it "gratuitously assumes that the only possible alternative to blind chance is a transcendent design." The real issue for him is between "an order imposed from without and one *emerging* from within" (italics supplied). Dupré opts for the latter alternative. In a famous discussion in his *Pensées philosophiques* (1746), Diderot mentions an argument that would explain the order of the universe on the basis of "chance." The order we find in the world could easily have resulted "fortuitously" from an infinite number of "throws" of atoms just as 100,000 sixes with 100,000 dice would eventually come up if only we are allowed an infinite number of throws. "The mind," Diderot concludes, "ought to be more astonished at the hypothetical duration of chaos than at the actual birth of the universe." Similar arguments were widely discussed in the eighteenth century, with atheists maintaining that the order of the universe could in this way be explained in terms of chance and with believers denying it. The argument appears to be a forerunner of the famous question whether an infinite number of monkeys with an infinite number of typewriters would eventually come up with *Hamlet*. The latter question seems more coherent because, disregarding any difficulties due to the infinite numbers involved, we at least understand the initial conditions — monkeys operating typewriters. The Diderot argument, on the other hand, is hopelessly vague about the initial "chance" distribution of atoms and the "throws" that are supposed to take place.

Voltaire, Swinburne, Dupré, and Diderot, whatever their differences, assume that the order of the universe needs explaining, but this is an assumption that is not at all obvious. When we come to think of it, we really have no reason whatever to suppose that the order that characterizes the universe at present did not always belong to it. On the contrary, we appear to have every reason to maintain that objects have always behaved in accordance with the same laws. We do not hesitate to predict that tomorrow or in the next century or millions of years from now objects will still behave in accordance with the laws of mechanics. We also do not hesitate to extrapolate our laws backward to the time of Julius Caesar or the ice age. What reason is there to suppose that if we were to go still further back in time, the universe would exhibit different laws or no laws at all? As mentioned earlier, Plato and various non-Christian religions teach that originally the universe was in a state of chaos, whatever this might be. Such pronouncements are purely arbitrary. Voltaire did not believe in an original chaos but seems to have thought that his Demiurge was needed to transform the original universe with a different (and presumably less admirable) order into its present state. To suppose that at an earlier time the universe was governed by different laws is just as arbitrary as to suppose that it initially was in a state of pure chaos. Voltaire's confusion on this subject is well illustrated in a speech in the "Dialogues Between Posidonius and Lucretius." "You cannot persuade me," Posidonius tells Lucretius, that "the universe put itself into the admirable order in which we now find it." Indeed, not; but why should *anything* have put the admirable order into the universe? Some contemporary physicists maintain that we cannot extend any of our laws to the period before the "big bang," which they regard as a "singularity." This, too, seems arbitrary, but even if such a view is accepted, it does not show that before the big bang objects behaved in accordance with other laws. It merely raises such a possibility.

It should be pointed out that we do not have any examples in our experience of intelligent causes, or for that matter of anything else, producing the kind of order now under discussion. Experience, therefore, gives us no guidance about the cause of such order, if indeed it has any. If it could really be demonstrated some day that the order exhibited by the universe at an earlier time was different from what it is today, this would be a most interesting discovery, but by itself it would be no evidence for an intelligent cause of such a change. One cannot help feeling that this entire question about the causation of the order or lawfulness found in the world is misguided and the result of the deep-seated belief, even on the part of some of those who have explicitly repudiated it, that the laws discovered by science "regulate" or "control" the world the way legal laws frequently control human behavior.

BODY AND MIND

Voltaire does not discuss the mind-body problem in twentieth-century terminology, but it is fairly clear where he stands. The best way to understand Voltaire here is to see what he is against. To begin with, he is opposed to the kind of materialism associated with Lucretius and Hobbes. Mental states and processes cannot be identified with any physical states and processes. Voltaire does not offer any argument against materialism. He probably believed that the distinctness of the two kinds of reality is intuitively obvious.

Next, Voltaire rejects the parallelism of Leibniz on commonsense grounds. In the *Elements of the Newtonian Philosophy* he discusses the famous illustration of the two perfectly synchronized clocks that Leibniz uses to make his mind-body parallelism intelligible, if not also credible. Let us suppose that we have two clocks that are causally independent but where one strikes whenever the other's hand reaches the end of the hour. Somebody who does not know that the two clocks are independent systems would be liable to believe that there is a causal relation between the movements of the hands of the first clock and the sound made by the second. According to Leibniz, it is the same with the soul and the body. They do not interact, but are like "two clocks made by God, each with its own spring, operating for a certain time with perfect agreement." Voltaire finds this incredible. If Leibniz were right, we would have to believe that the soul of Vergil produced the *Aeneid* and that his hand wrote it down although Vergil's soul did not have the slightest influence on his hand. God "has everlastingly ordained that the soul of Vergil should make verses while a hand attached to Vergil's body should reduce them to written words." No reasonable person can be expected to believe this. What is more, it is not at all clear why the soul of Vergil was attached to Vergil's body since the two have no causal relations to one another. "My soul," writes Voltaire, "might as well have been placed in Saturn as in my body." The union of the soul and body becomes both mysterious and superfluous.

The third view Voltaire opposes is belief in the soul—the spiritual substance of Descartes and of much of the Christian and Jewish tradition. His discussions of this topic invariably begin with an endorsement of Locke's remark that there is no contradiction in the notion that matter can think. In a famous passage in the *Essay Concerning Human Understanding*, Locke had written that there is no contradiction in supposing that "the first eternal thinking being should, if he pleased, give to certain systems of created senseless matter, put together as he thinks fit, some degrees of sense, perception and thought." It is "not much more remote from our comprehension" to conceive that "God can, if he pleases, superadd to matter a faculty of thinking, than that he should superadd to it another substance with a faculty of thinking." Once we agree that there is no contradiction in supposing that matter, or more specifically human bodies, can think, we can proceed to show that this is in fact a highly plausible view that has much to recommend it in opposition to the two-substance view of Descartes and the scholastics. A human being, Voltaire repeatedly affirmed, *is* his body and not a double entity, a body and a soul. Among the attributes of the body, however, are mental states and processes and these, as the aforementioned criticism of Leibniz makes clear, are by no means inefficacious. There is causal interaction from the mental to the physical, and as we shall see when discussing Voltaire's objections to survival after death as pure consciousness, there is also interaction from the physical to the mental. Voltaire is thus an interactionist and a dualist, but his dualism is one of attributes or events and not of substances.

One of Voltaire's favorite arguments against the spiritual soul is based on the undeniable similarities between human beings and animals. The argument is developed most fully in the Letter on Locke and Chapter 4 of the *Traité*. Animals resemble humans in having sense organs and a brain, and we have every reason to believe that they have ideas and feelings though the ideas and feelings of human beings are much more numerous and also far more complex. Voltaire finds it incredible to suppose that animals are "mere machines," that is, beings devoid of ideas and feelings. Only a metaphysician is capable of believing something that so flagrantly contradicts common sense. He could have added that philosophers who professed to believe that animals are mere machines sometimes had pets and were just as concerned as the rest of mankind not to injure them, and for the same reason. There is also a theological reason for denying that animals are mere machines. If God gave them the same sense organs as those he gave to human beings and if they nevertheless do not feel, then God has made something useless. However, it is agreed by all parties that God does nothing in vain, and hence the sense organs of animals produce feelings just as they do in human beings. Now, if the existence of ideas and feelings requires us to postulate a spiritual soul, then animals have one just as much as we do. If people have spiritual souls, then so do dogs and moles and even fleas, worms, and mites. On the other hand, if we deny souls to animals, then we cannot make the possession of feelings and ideas a reason for postulating souls in human beings.

Voltaire nowhere says that the spiritual soul does not exist, but he maintains that it is superfluous. "I am a body and I think," he writes in the Letter on Locke. "Shall I go and contribute to an unknown cause what I can so easily attribute to a secondary cause?" Over thirty years later in "The Chinese Catechism" of the *Philosophical Dictionary*, he asks, "Why postulate two springs for a mechanism when one will do?" A human brain is an observable entity. If it produces thought, why also bring in a mysterious unobservable entity? We tend to believe in the soul even in the absence of any good reason because of our tendency to assume that we are dealing with a real entity just because we have a word "to fix our ideas." In language sounding remarkably modern, Voltaire protests against what some contemporary writers have called the "reification of abstractions." Animals live, but there is no reason to postulate a separate entity called "life" that explains their behavior. People tend to think of passions, memory, and reason as "distinct things," as "little persons who have a separate existence," but this is, of course, not so. Exactly the same applies to the word *soul*. It is useful to help us mark off a certain type of reality, namely feelings and thoughts, from nonmental objects, but it is not something over and above them.

Most contemporary philosophers of mind would regard Voltaire's elimination of the spiritual substance as a step in the right direction, but some of them would prefer to talk of persons rather than bodies as the subjects of mental states, where an essential component of a person *is* his body. This way of speaking avoids certain paradoxes that would arise from Voltaire's assertion that the body is the subject of thought and that is also produces thought.

The writings of Voltaire's last twenty years are full of attacks on materi-

alism, both that found in Lucretius and the version defended by such
contemporaries as Holbach and Diderot. It should therefore be pointed out
that in a very important sense Voltaire was himself a materialist. His
position does indeed significantly differ from that of philosophers who
maintain that thoughts and feelings are themselves material, but it is
identical with the view of the more moderate materialists who assert that
everything without exception has a material foundation. That Voltaire
definitely belongs in this camp will become clear from his views on life
after death.

THE QUESTION OF SURVIVAL

Let us now turn to the question of survival after death. Voltaire discusses
all of the three most familiar forms of survival — reincarnation, the resurrection of the body, and survival as a pure consciousness or disembodied
mind. Reincarnationists have frequently claimed Voltaire as one of their
own, but there is no warrant for such a claim. He quite unambiguously
dismisses reincarnation as a fanciful illusion. "Is this system," he asks in
Chapter 5 of the *Traité*, "any more plausible than the *Thousand and One
Nights?*" And is it not "just the fruit of the lively and absurd imagination of
the majority of Oriental philosophers?"

He devotes much more space to the resurrection of the body. He observes that this would usually not be an easy thing to accomplish. Both the
Egyptians and the Greeks believed in resurrection, but in Egypt the embalmer's first task was to pierce the skull with a small hook and draw out
the brain and to remove the entrails. How, asks Voltaire, "were men to rise
again without intestines and without the medullary part by means of which
they think?" How were they "to find again the blood, the lymph and the
other humors?" It was even more difficult to rise among the Greeks, for
their corpses were frequently burned. How can you be restored to life if
your body has become "a pound of ashes . . . mingled with the ashes of
wood, stuffs and spices?" There is the further problem of children who die
in the womb just after receiving their souls. Will such a being rise again as
an embryo, a child, or an adult? St. Augustine believed that everybody
would be resurrected with a body as it was or would have been at the age of
thirty. This invites the question of how a thirty-year-old body could be
supplied to a child who had died in the womb and who did not go through
the intermediary stages to reach the age of thirty. How, to view it from the
other end, could a man of eighty-five be regressed to the age of thirty? How
could the body at thirty have registered in its brain any of the experiences
that occurred between thirty and eighty-five? Suppose, instead of following
Augustine, we were to say that the person will be resurrected as he was just

before he died. In many cases this might not be a good idea because the individual was decrepit or senile or both.

Contemporary philosophers who believe in the resurrection of the body would maintain that Voltaire is taking the word *resurrection* too literally. They would distinguish a literal and primitive belief in resurrection from a more sophisticated version, which holds that God does not resurrect the original body but a replica or duplicate. Voltaire's criticisms may be just against the primitive version, but their theory is immune to them. This may be true, but the immunity is purchased at a steep price. A replica or duplicate is not the original and this poses serious problems concerning the identity of the person possessing the duplicate body with the one whose body died. Aside from this, however, believers in the sophisticated version have two of the same ticklish problems on their hands as the primitive believers. In the first place, nobody has ever observed the creation of a duplicate body any more than the resurrection of dead bodies. This is a simple commonsense objection that has presented an insuperable difficulty to many reflective persons and one that is brushed aside rather too speedily by some contemporary theologians. Second, Augustine's regression problem equally bedevils both versions.

What about survival as a disembodied mind? In his published writings Voltaire occasionally allows a character in a dialogue to defend the negative answer on the ground that consciousness is so closely dependent on the body that it cannot continue to exist once the body has died. "The effect at last ceases with the cause," remarks Lucretius in the *Dialogues Between Lucretius and Posidonius*, "and the soul vanishes like smoke in the air." Voltaire does not defend this view in the first person in any of the writings published in his lifetime, but he does so, and with great vigor, in Chapter 5 of the *Traité*. "Reason has taught me," he writes, that "all the ideas of men and animals come to them through the senses" and it is surely preposterous that men will still have ideas after they have lost their senses. Thinking and feeling are caused by the senses and the brain and it is "a little strange" to suggest that "the results of the organs" continue after the organs themselves have perished. One might as well say that a man will go on eating and drinking without a mouth and stomach. God has connected our capacity for thinking with a certain area of the brain, and it is no more possible for thinking to continue without this organ than it is for the song of a bird to continue after its throat has been destroyed in death. God could indeed have supplied both animals and men with an immortal soul, and he could have arranged matters in such a way that this immortal soul could exist independent of the body, just as he could have made human beings with two noses and four hands, and with wings and claws. God *could* have given us an immortal soul, but all indications are that he did not. Should I, Voltare writes, who know that human beings have a beginning, affirm that there is in them "a part which is eternal by its nature," while I refuse immortality to "whatever animates the dog, the parrot or the lark?" Shall I award this prize to man just because he desires it? Voltaire concedes that he does not possess conclusive proofs, but "all probable evidence" goes against immortality.

These were Voltaire's real and considered views on the subject, but they were not published by him. In his early works like the *Philosophical Letters*, he professes a complete theoretical agnosticism accompanied by facetious remarks about our duty to be guided by revelation. Later, in the 1760s and 1770s, when he had become alarmed by the spread of atheism, the agnosticism is accompanied by a ringing pragmatic defense of the affirmative position. One of the best-known statements occurs in his polemic against Holbach's *System of Nature*. Holbach's philosophy is accused of "snatching consolation and hope" from suffering mankind. Voltaire grants that "philosophy furnishes no proof of a happiness to come" but insists that it also does not demonstrate the contrary. He then adds a reflection that sounds strange, coming from somebody who had always made fun of the philosophy of Leibniz, including the latter's theory of monads. "There may be in us an indestructable monad," Voltaire wrote, "which feels and thinks, without our knowing anything at all of how that monad is made." He then proceeds to argue, in the spirit of William James's "Will to Believe," that belief in an afterlife has a "prodigious advantage" over unbelief. It is "useful," while unbelief is "baneful." "We are all swimming in a sea of which we have never seen the shore." The unbeliever is like a man who cries out, "You swim in vain, there is no land;" and with his cry he "disheartens me and deprives me of all my strength." It should be noted that Voltaire himself did not believe that there was "land," and yet he was not disheartened in the least and did not lose any of his formidable strength.

The notion of an indestructible monad "inside of us" must have appealed to Voltaire's imagination. It appeared repeatedly in his writings of this period, each time with new embellishments. In one of the "Homilies" that he wrote in the 1760s, advocating natural religion in opposition to both Christianity and atheism, he begins by declaring once again that we are ignorant of "the principle which thinks in us." It follows that we cannot be certain that this "unknown principle" will not survive death. The indestructible monad is now described as a "hidden flame" and "a particle of divine fire." It is entirely "possible" that this divine particle does not die but merely "changes its form" when the body disintegrates. This "possibility" is transformed into a "probability" in the dialogues between Cu-Su, a wise disciple of Confucius, and the skeptical Prince Kou, the son of the King of Lou, which are included as "Chinese Catechism" in the *Philosophical Dictionary*. A thought, Cu-Su begins reasonably enough, "cannot be regarded as something material." It then should not be so difficult to believe that God has placed an "immortal and indissoluble principle" inside all of us. Surely this is not impossible. But if it is possible, "is it not also highly probable? Can you reject so noble a system and one which is so necessary to mankind?" David Friedrich Strauss, in a highly sympathetic discussion of Voltaire's philosophical views, addressed himself to this wretched argument in which Voltaire moves from possibility to probability. "Somebody who cannot defend immortality in a better way," Strauss wrote, "would edify us more if he openly denied it." In defense of Voltaire, it might be noted that Cu-Su is at once answered by Prince Kou in a most convincing fashion. Although Prince Kou ultimately surrenders, most readers are likely to be far more impressed by his skeptical arguments, than by the pious declarations of the ostensible victor.

Rejecting belief in life after death is harmful not only because it "disheartens" people and deprives them of their strength. It is even more damaging by removing one of the most powerful sanctions against vice and crime. A small number of philosophical unbelievers with a peaceful disposition may not need hellfire as a deterrent. The same, however, is not true of the world's rulers, nor unfortunately of most ordinary men and women. "Eternal hell" may be an illusion, we read in the article "Hell" in the *Philosophical Dictionary*, "but it is a good thing for your servant, your tailor and even your lawyer to believe in it." The "fear of men" is not enough. "Shall we give ourselves up to fatal passions," asks Freind, the sage in *The Sage and the Atheist*, "and live like brutes, with no other restraint upon us than the fear of men, rendered eternally cruel to each other by their mutual dread?" A man who fears no divine retribution in the hereafter is going to become a "God to himself," and he will sacrifice the whole world to his caprice. A poor and needy atheist "would be a fool if he did not assassinate or steal to get money." If atheism and its companion belief that death is final became common, all the bonds of society would be "sundered," "secret crimes" would inundate the world, and "like locusts" they would "spread over the earth." One cannot help feeling that in these and countless similar passages, Voltaire expressed some deep-seated and largely irrational fear. The facts do not seem to bear him out at all. It may be granted that, just as in Voltaire's day, the world is filled with "knaves," with "persons addicted to brutality, intoxication and rapine," and generally with individuals who are cruel and callous. Experience shows that, within rather severe limits, their destructive impulses can be controlled by secular restraints. Fear of punishment in a hereafter seems to be totally ineffective. A cruel believer does not greatly differ in his conduct from a cruel unbeliever. The difference lies largely in the kind of rationalization he will offer.

That the views Voltaire expressed in the *Traité de métaphysique* were his real ones is shown beyond all doubt by remarks about death made to his friends and in his correspondence. That Voltaire believed death to be final and that nothing whatever awaits us afterward is evident both when he consoles himself and others by the thought that the absence of our consciousness, since it involves no suffering of any kind, is not something to be dreaded, and when during fits of depression he likens man to a prisoner awaiting his death sentence. "When the hour arrives," he wrote in one of these moods, "it becomes clear that we have lived to no purpose, that all reflections are vain and all reasoning . . . only wasted words." Such fits of depression were rare, and more commonly Voltaire admonishes us to think about death as little as possible and to get on with the job of living. People who announce death ceremoniously "are the enemies of the human race; we must keep them from ever approaching us." "To cease to love and be lovable," he wrote in a short poem addressed to Mme. du Châtelet, "is a death unbearable; to cease to live is nothing," and in a letter he repeated that "death is nothing at all — the idea alone is sad."

Some of the earlier statements about death were taken from letters to Mme. du Deffand, an exceptionally sensitive old lady who had become blind. In one of his letters to her, Voltaire told of a man who compared us with a musical instrument that cannot produce a sound after it has been broken. This man held it as evidence that human beings had a beginning and an end just like all other animals, like plants, and probably everything else in the world. He also taught that our best consolation concerning aging and death consists in our knowledge that they are inevitable. This man greatly admired the laughing Democritus, and when he became as old as Democritus he followed his master in laughing about everything. It goes without saying that this man was Voltaire himself.

THE FOUNDATIONS OF MORALITY

It is hardly surprising that Voltaire objects to deriving moral judgments from theological premises. The simple reason for this is that we do not possess any such premises. If God had said to me, he writes in the final chapter of the *Traité*, "I want so many kingdoms on earth and not one republic; I want the youngest son to inherit all the father's estate, and the eating of turkeys and pigs punishable by death," these laws "will become the unalterable rules of good and evil." Unfortunately, God has not condescended to supply us with any such information and hence we have to use our own resources to discover the rules of morality. Voltaire equally opposed any theory maintaining that there are moral qualities and relations existing independently of the needs and emotions of human beings or, more generally, of organisms capable of experiencing pleasure and pain. Locke had shown to Voltaire's satisfaction that the so-called secondary qualities like hot and cold, colors and smells lack objective existence. Exactly the same is true of moral qualities. A person claiming that "moral good exists independently of us" would be as "poor" a reasoner as somebody maintaining that the secondary qualities have independent existence.

At the same time Voltaire was very much opposed to moral skepticism, especially in the form given to it by Hobbes. It is true that in one flippant passage in the *Traité* he himself seems to be a Hobbist. Pointing to the mutually contradictory laws of different countries, he observes that "it hardly matters by which laws a state governs itself—the only thing that matters is that once the laws are established, they should be enforced." This lapse did not escape Condorcet and his associates when they brought out the Kehl edition of Voltaire's works. In a sternly worded footnote, Condorcet insists that it matters a great deal by which laws a state governs itself. This correction was quite unnecessary since a few pages later Voltaire offers his considered position, which is quite opposed to moral skepticism; and several years later in the *Ignorant Philosopher* he devoted a whole section to Hobbes's mistake. Hobbes taught that "there are no laws in the world but the laws of convention" and that "there is no justice and injustice but what has been agreed upon as such in a country." To refute this view Voltaire appeals to our moral feelings or intuitions. Suppose Hobbes had been alone with Cromwell on an island and suppose Cromwell attempted to kill Hobbes because of Hobbes's royalism. Would such an attempt not be as unjust on that island as in England?

Voltaire would probably maintain that his imaginary example not only shows that Hobbes's theory is wrong but also that some form of utilitarianism must be correct. The word *utilitarianism* had not been coined in the eighteenth century, but there can be no doubt that, like several of the other Encyclopedists, Voltaire was in fact a utilitarian. In spite of all the variation in the laws and moral rules in different regions, "there are natural laws which men throughout the universe are obliged to acknowledge, whatever they might say." Examples of such "natural laws" are that people should respect their fathers and mothers and that "perjury, calumny and homicide are abominable crimes." Not only is everybody obliged to acknowledge these and other laws, but in fact everybody does so, at least on reflection and when not consumed by passions like rage.

These "natural laws" have the same status as any true empirical proposition. They are, "one and all," statements about the useful or harmful effects on society. "The well-being of society" is the "sole standard for measuring moral good and evil." Voltaire offers numerous illustrations meant to show that the well-being of society is in fact the standard to which human beings appeal in judging the morality of various practices. In general we regard telling the truth as a good thing because it is *generally* in the interest of society that people do not tell lies. However, in certain special situations the survival of society may depend on a lie and then we regard lying as morally justified. Similarly we regard sexual relations between a father and his daughter as morally wrong in most ordinary situations. However, in a colony in which there was only a father, his son, and daughters, we would regard incest as morally justified so that the species should not perish. Voltaire was well aware that many people do not act in ways calculated to advance the well-being of society, but as we shall see later, he maintains that such behavior is not necessarily an index of what the individual believes in calm and reflective moments.

An important element in Voltaire's position that is logically distinct from his utilitarianism is his belief in a natural sentiment of "benevolence." It is ironic that his first and fullest description of this sentiment occurs in the *Traité* in the very chapter in which the influence of Bernard Mandeville is most apparent. Mandeville (ca. 1670–1733) was a Dutch physician and philosopher who had emigrated to England at the age of twenty-one and who is noted primarily for *The Fable of the Bees, or Private Vices: Public Benefits*, perhaps one of the most cynical works about the nature of man ever written. Following Hobbes and Machiavelli, Mandeville maintained that individual self-seeking is the only spur to action. Between 1735 and 1739 both Voltaire and Mme. du Châtelet read and discussed Mandeville and evidently accepted a good deal of his teaching. Mme. du Châtelet translated parts of the *Fable* into French and several of the ideas in Chapter 8 of the *Traité*, especially those about the role of pride, ambition, and vanity in the formation and cementing of society, are derived from a section of the final edition of the *Fable* entitled "An Enquiry into the Origin of Moral Virtue." On the question of psychological egoism, however, neither of them followed Mandeville. "If one should see an infant being destroyed, he would endeavor to save it," Mandeville wrote, but this would not be due to genuine sympathy, but "to prevent his own *amour-propre* from being revolted." Voltaire maintained the exact opposite. We would try to save the child because we are so constructed as to feel pity for it. This pity is part of the "bienveillance naturelle," the natural benevolence that is just as much part of our innate constitution as our self-interest. "If . . . the most savage man saw a sweet child being devoured by some animal," Voltaire writes in reply to Mandeville, he would feel "an anxiety born of pity, and a desire to run to his aid." It is true that this feeling of pity is often overwhelmed by purely selfish impulses, and it is not deplorable that this should be so. Otherwise we might fail to take steps to protect our own lives. However, the benevolence is very real; it is one of the basic ties in any society and it helps the preservation of our species.

Not only do human beings possess a natural sentiment of benevolence, but they also have an innate sense of justice. This topic is discussed in many places, perhaps most interestingly in one of the earliest of the letters to Frederick (October 1737, see pp 208 ff). Suppose there were only four men on earth and suppose that one of them eats his companion's supper. The others will surely revolt because their sense of justice would be outraged. Voltaire realizes that what he says here may seem incompatible with his rejection of innate ideas. He concedes that nobody "carries with him at birth" the idea that we must be just, but God has so constructed us that at a certain age everybody comes to acknowledge this truth. He compares the situation with our ability to walk. When we are born we cannot walk, but we are born with feet and legs and when we are strong enough we learn to walk. "At what age do we become acquainted with what is just and unjust," he asks in *The Ignorant Philosopher*, and he answers "at the age when we realize that two and two make four."

Voltaire is concerned to show, in opposition to the more extreme relativists, that on really basic moral issues human beings take the same position. At times what he claims is quite modest. Thus in the article on "Beauty" in the *Philosophical Dictionary*, or rather in the section that was added in the *Questions Concerning the Encyclopedia*, he points out that people of different national backgrounds whose aesthetic tastes are radically different nevertheless agree on moral issues. The Algonquins, the French, and the Chinese will react quite differently to a play or a musical composition, but they will agree in admiring the devotion of a son to his father or the loyalty of one friend to another. A black man "with round eyes and flattened nose" would not give the ladies of the French court the name of beautiful, but he will pronounce as beautiful the same moral deeds that are so regarded by Frenchmen who have quite different criteria of female beauty. There are, Voltaire observes, two kinds of beauty — "the beautiful which only strikes the senses and the imagination" and "the beauty which strikes the heart." The latter, unlike the former, is "not uncertain," by which Voltaire means that people from the most diverse backgrounds will reach the same conclusion.

In the article "Beauty," Voltaire does not go so far as to maintain that on basic moral issues the *whole* of mankind has the same opinion, but this is the claim made in the *Ignorant Philosopher*. He realizes, of course, that people often *seem* to disagree and that many human beings violate even very basic moral principles in their conduct. All these facts, he thinks, can be reconciled with what he fondly speaks of as the "universal morality." To show that there are no innate moral ideas, Locke had referred to Mohammedan saints who have sexual relations with asses in order to avoid the sin of fornicating with women, to the "Mengrelians," a people professing Christianity, who bury their children alive without scruple," and to cannibals who fatten their children in preparation to eating them. Voltaire dismisses these and similar stories as not based on reliable evidence. Locke's prize illustration, which could not be dismissed in the same way, concerns the plunder, rapes, and wanton killing practiced by conquering armies. "View but an army at the sacking of a town," Locke wrote, "and see what sense of moral principles, or what touch of conscience they exhibit for all the outrages they do." To this Voltaire replies that the behavior of the soldiers is excusable or at least comprehensible since they were prepared to risk their lives for the sake of the spoils and since they believe that if they had lost the battle they and their families would not have been treated any more kindly by the enemy. However, the same soldiers would reject with horror the proposal to "cut the throats of their king, his chancellor and his secretaries of state" in exchange for more money and handsomer women. Voltaire sounds incredibly naive here. Probably most soldiers would not be induced to kill their own sovereign in such circumstances, but, as A. J. Ayer has pointed out, instances of treachery, and not only by mercenaries, cast doubt on Voltaire's historical judgment. And there is, of course, much which we know today and which Voltaire could hardly have known that makes any attempt to defend a "universal morality" in his sense quite ludicrous. Psychopaths, for one thing, are devoid of all moral sentiments and there are numerous sadists who do not feel the slightest compunction about their cruel acts and who lust for ever new victims, the more vulnerable, the better. In certain circumstances they pay lip service to the moral principles accepted by other human beings, but their behavior shows that they believe nothing of the kind.

Suppose that there is no universal agreement even on basic moral questions. Would this undermine Voltaire's other claims about morality? Lack of agreement would hardly be fatal to utilitariansim if this is put forward not as an account of the criterion everybody always uses in making moral judgments but as a normative theory about the criterion that people ought to use. Such a recommendation could, of course, be accompanied by the observation that in actual fact many people do employ utilitarian criteria in deciding many important issues. Neither lack of agreement nor the widespread and often horrible cruelty of human beings would refute Voltaire's claims about natural benevolence. He clearly allows for other motives and he need not and does not dispute that these frequently overcome our benevolence. Voltaire could also have quite consistently observed that the natural benevolence of human beings is in many instances eroded over the years as a result of suffering, disappointments, and attachment to cruel ideologists; and much the same would no doubt apply to the innate sense of justice postulated by Voltaire.

MIRACLES

Voltaire was rarely more amusing than when writing about miracles. Nothing else, not even the fatuous optimism of Panglossian metaphysicians, provoked so much ridicule. He was evidently having a great good time so that one can almost hear his chuckles. The purpose, however, was serious. Miracles are completely at variance with what we know about the working of the world. Belief in miracles is also theologically unsound, and it degrades religion into a form of magic. The miracles reported throughout history are a mixture of fraud and nonsense. Moreover, the nonsense is usually not innocent, because it is used by priests and rulers to keep the common people in ignorance and subjection. Several philosophers, notably the English deists, and also Bayle, Middleton, and Hume, had written against miracles before Voltaire. Bayle, and Hume had raised subtle difficulties that Voltaire ignored, but it was Voltaire's attack that had the most devastating impact. Voltaire had a wonderful eye for the absurd, and he also had vast learning in the history of religions, especially that of Christianity, which supplied him with an endless stream of hilarious illustrations. By the 1760s he had perfected his tongue-in-cheek style, and it was nowhere used to greater effect than in his treatment of miracles.

Voltaire's various discussions are deliberately chaotic. Case is piled on case, each more absurd than the one before, and yet all of them miracles at one time widely accepted on the basis of supposedly unimpeachable evidence. Voltaire's general objections are mentioned almost as asides, and they are usually accompanied by pious declarations that, although reason may cause philosophers to spurn miracles, revelation and faith are superior guides. Philosophers may exalt "the immutability of the Supreme Being" and the eternity of his laws, but they are clearly mistaken since the histories of most nations are as full of miracles as of natural events. "I do not know of a county," Voltaire writes, "where incredible prodigies have not been performed, especially at a time when the people could hardly read or write." It might in fact be laid down as a law that there is an inverse relationship between frequency of miracles and the level of education in any given nation. The number of miracles increases as the level of education declines, and it decreases as the people become more educated.

Voltaire was particularly amused by stories about animals that could talk. Not only could many animals talk in past ages, but they could also make the most accurate forecasts of fateful happenings. No less an authority than Titus Livius reported that one day in the marketplace in Rome an ox cried out to the crowds: "Rome, take care of yourself!" Pliny wrote that when the tyrant Tarquin was driven from the throne, a dog commented on the event; and Suetonius vouched for the fact that a crow said — in Latin, of course —"All is well" when Domitian was assassinated. A horse by the name of Xante told its master, Achilles, that he would be killed before Troy. The gift of speech was also occasionally bestowed on fish. The fish Oannes made it a practice to come out of the Euphrates every day to deliver a sermon on its banks. Voltaire laconically observed that fish did not preach any more in his time, although St. Anthony of Padua had preached to the fish. However, that was not a miracle, and in any event "such things happen so rarely nowadays, that most people pay no attention to them." The fish, incidentally, listened attentively to St. Anthony's admonitions, but after the sermon they all went their merry ways, much as human beings who ignore the advice of their spiritual guides.

Among both the Romans and the Christians, many people were miraculously cured of illnesses that did not respond to more natural methods.

Perhaps the most impressive and best-attested of these cures were performed in Alexandria in the first century B.C. by the Roman emperor Vespasian, who is otherwise best remembered for building the Coliseum and for banishing the Stoic philosophers from Rome. Voltaire thought that this case was particularly illuminating and mentions it in several places, for example, in his correspondence with Frederick and most fully in Chapter 33 of *The Philosophy of History* (1765), which is one of his most extended discussions of miracles. During his visit to Alexandria, two men, one blind and the other paralyzed, presented themselves before the emperor, imploring him to restore them to health. Vespasian modestly replied that he possessed no such healing powers. The two unhappy individuals then told the emperor that the god Serapis had appeared to them, announcing that they would be cured by Vespasian. Moved by their plight, the emperor consented to touch both men, but he warned them that success was most improbable. "Favoring his modesty and virtue," Voltaire writes, "the Divinity communicates to Vespasian his power and that instant the blind man sees and the lame one walks." This twin miracle was performed in the presence of innumerable spectators, Roman, Greek, and Egyptian. It has been preserved in the archives of the empire and is mentioned in all contemporary histories. And yet, Voltaire adds, it has in the course of time come to be universally disbelieved because nobody has an "interest" in the acceptance of its authenticity.

With relish Voltaire enumerates other miraculous cures, including that of a blind man by St. Ambrose. In a dream, Ambrose had been informed by St. Gervasius and St. Prostasius where their corpses were lying. He promptly dug them up and used the holy relics to cure a blind man in the presence of numerous witnesses. This remarkable event occurred in Milan and is vouched for by no less an authority than St. Augustine, who was in the city at the time. In more recent times the kings of England, right up until William III, daily performed medical miracles. William III finally refused to continue the practice and his successors have followed his example. If England should "undergo a great revolution" so that the country once again slides into barbarism and ignorance, we may be confident that miracles will again be performed every day.

Many alleged miracles have an inner lack of logic that makes it quite unnecessary to investigate the supposed evidence. One of these, St. Polycarp's last-minute rescue from the flames, is related in the article on "Miracles" in the *Philosophical Dictionary*. This miracle took place in the second century, when Polycarp, the Bishop of Smyrna, had been condemned by the Romans to be burned at the stake. Several eyewitnesses heard a heavenly voice calling out to the bishop. "Courage Polycarp! Be strong, show yourself a man!" Polycarp showed himself a man, whereupon the flames were diverted from his body, and a dove, the symbol of the Holy Ghost, flew out of the midst of the stake. The jubilations of Polycarp's partisans were, however, premature. Almost immediately after his deliverance from the flames, the luckless bishop had his head cut off. Philosophers will wonder why the executioner's axe was not also deflected.

Another of Voltaire's favorite miracles, which is mentioned in the *Treatise on Toleration*, concerns King Robert, who had been excommunicated by Pope Gregory V for marrying his godmother, Princess Bertha. After the king was excommunicated, his servants threw his dinner out of the window. This disrespectful treatment of the monarch, though strange enough, does not qualify as a miracle. The miraculous punishment for the incestuous marriage occurred when Queen Bertha was delivered of a goose. "I doubt," Voltaire observed, "if in our time the waiters of the King of France would, if he were excommunicated, throw his dinner out of the window and whether the Queen would give birth to a gosling."

The Romans did not show much interest in bringing the dead back to life. In other countries and among Christians, resurrections have been common. Among the Greeks the resurrections were usually carried out by gods. Hercules, Alcestis, and Pelops were all brought back by the gods. Pelops had been hacked to pieces by his father, and it has not been disclosed how the gods put the pieces of his body back together. Athalide, Mercury's daughter, had the gift of coming back to life at will and repeatedly made use of it. Er, made famous for later generations by Plato, came back to the world after spending two weeks in hell. Aesculapius, who was chiefly noted for his miraculous treatment of illness, brought Hippolytus back to life. It should be remembered that the Greek gods were physical and that their activities, miraculous or otherwise, could be observed by human beings. In the case of Aesculapius, Voltaire tells us that "we still have documents containing the names of eyewitnesses."

Not being a friend of the Jesuits, to put it mildly, Voltaire turned with delight to resurrections attributed to St. Francis Xavier, one of the founders of the Jesuit order. Xavier had been noted for the vast number of conversions he achieved in his missionary travels to India and the Far East. He was also spectacularly successful as a resurrector. In Japan, between 1549 and 1551, Xavier resurrected no less than eight bodies. This feat was altogether remarkable, not only because, as Voltaire rightly notes, eight is quite a number, but also because Xavier had lost, or else had never possessed, the gift of tongues, a supernatural gift of a much lower order than that of resurrecting the dead. In his letters from Japan, he complained that he felt like a "mute statue" since he could not understand or speak the language of the natives. In the case of Xavier's resurrections, it is important to remember — Voltaire tells us — that they were carried out 15,000 miles from home. Some people, he wryly adds, regard the expulsion of the Jesuits from France as a much greater miracle.

Xavier's resurrections are dealt with in the previously mentioned article on "Miracles" in the *Philosophical Dictionary*. Jesus himself is left alone there, but this omission is rectified in the section added in the *Questions*, published approximately ten years later. Voltaire here poses as a pious Christian who reports, with a sense of outrage, the heresies of the English deist, Thomas Woolston (ca. 1669–1733), who was one of the first writers to offer a critical, indeed a highly critical, examination of the miracles attributed to Jesus.

It is "only with regret and even with trembling" that Voltaire quotes such blasphemies, which are certain to "shock every Christian ear" and "fill every Christian soul with indignation." "Let us hope," he concludes the section, that Woolston "repented on his death-bed and that God has shown him mercy." In fact, of course, Voltaire greatly admired Woolston, not only for his "daring" opposition to Christianity but also for repeated and eloquent defenses, to quote Woolston himself, of "a universal and unbounded toleration of religion without any restrictions or impositions on men's consciences." Between 1727 and 1730, Woolston had published six *Discourses on the Miracles of Our Saviour*, whose purpose it was to expose "the absurdities, improbabilities and incredibilities" of the miracles worked by Jesus if the New Testament stories are interpreted literally. Woolston had examined every last miracle related in the New Testament, but Voltaire confined himself to the three resurrections attributed to Jesus —of the daughter of Jairus, the son of the widow of Naim, and, of course, Lazarus, who had been dead four days. For Christians these miracles have always been "decisive and resplendent" evidence for the divinity of Jesus, and if the rest of the world had known about them it would surely have been instantly converted to Christianity. Unfortunately, the rest of the world did not hear about them for at least two hundred years. This is as amazing as it is regrettable. Neither the historian Josephus nor the scholarly Philo nor any of the Greek or Roman historians of the time mention so much as one of these resurrections. What is more, if these sensational events had really occurred, we may rest assured that the Jewish magistrates and especially Pontius Pilate would have undertaken the most minute investigations and obtained the most detailed and authentic depositions. Tiberius had ordered all proconsuls, prefects, and governors of provinces to inform him with exactness of all significant events, and Lazarus as well as the other two beneficiaries of Jesus' supernatural powers would have been interrogated. In the case of Lazarus, Voltaire notes in passing, "not a little curiosity would have been excited" about the fate of his soul during the four days when his body was dead. Suppose that God in our time should send an ambassador to London and that this ambassador succeeded in raising several men from the dead; would not everybody be talking about such remarkable occurrences and would not contemporary histories be filled with descriptions of these events and their repercussions? Not only did the world at large not hear about these miracles for two hundred years, but fully a hundred years had passed before "some obscure individuals" showed one another writings that contained any mention of these events. It may be of interest to point out that tolerant England was not so tolerant in its treatment of Woolston. In 1729, at the instigation of Anglican clergymen, he was tried and convicted on the charge of blasphemy. He was sentenced to a year's imprisonment and a fine of a hundred pounds. He was unable to pay the fine and also refused to promise to abstain from further writings on religion. As a result he remained in prison until his death. To his great credit, Samuel Clarke interceded on Woolston's behalf, but without success.

Voltaire was no admirer of the Jews of the Old Testament or, for that matter of the Jews of any age; but, since the main enemy was Christianity and not Judaism, he delighted to point out that the miracles performed by God on behalf of the Jews were much more stupendous than any of those performed by Jesus. Who would not be impressed by such spectacles as the ten plagues of Egypt, the stopping of the stars in their course over Gibeon and Ajalon, and the sea's opening a passage and suspending its waves so that the Jews could safely go through! Compared to divine interventions on such a scale, miracles like that of the Gadarene swine or the fig tree or even the admittedly mind-boggling resurrection of Lazarus after his brain must already have been totally decayed are paltry. Voltaire approvingly quotes a heretical writer who compared the differences to that between a grand concert and a rustic ditty. Such dangerous reflections have "enchanted" not a few Christians who rashly and audaciously concluded that Judaism and not Christianity was the true religion. Instead of showing the miracles of Jesus "the respect to which they are entitled," these unfortunate men trusted their deceitful reason and maintained that, if God for many ages worked a train of "astonishing and tremendous miracles" in favor of what He himself had pronounced to be the true religion, He would not suddenly cause it to become a false one. For their own good, and for the good of the world, most of the admirers of Judaism have carefully concealed their apostasy from the public, but some misguided priests made no bones about their preference and openly derided the miracles of the New Testament. Suspending his tongue-in-cheek manner, Voltaire relates the case of Nicholas Anthony of Pont-à-Mousson in Lorraine. He first switched to Calvinism, becoming for a short time a minister in Geneva, and then, not long afterward, was received as a Jew in Venice. He returned to Geneva and proclaimed to the judges and magistrates as well as to the people in the street that the Jewish religion was true, declaring that there was only one god and that Jesus was an impostor. Nicholas Anthony was put in chains and burned at the stake in Geneva on April 20, 1632.

Voltaire does offer some general arguments against the possibility of miracles. A miracle is a violation of a law of nature, but this is impossible because by definition a law cannot have exceptions. Here Voltaire displays a lamentable inability to put himself into the position of the opponent. In relation to a believer in miracles, this argument clearly begs the question. The believer does not admit that laws cannot have exceptions or, to avoid a pointless fight over words, that there are full-fledged laws. Voltaire also uses a theological argument. Believing in miracles is an insult to God. It implies that, like a watchmaker who bungled his work, God is required to make repairs in the "immense machine of the universe." If God is infinitely intelligent, then he foresaw all the unfortunate events that inspire men to pray for the suspension of His laws; and if He too had regarded the events in question as undesirable, He would have fashioned different laws. If it is argued that He failed to foresee the unfortunate events, then He is not infinitely intelligent and hence "He is no longer God." This is not unreasonable, but it is not clear that Voltaire, as a believer in a limited deity, can avail himself of this argument. The request for a miracle addressed to an omniscient, omnipotent, and perfectly good god does not make any sense, but the request for a miracle here and there might not be unreasonable when addressed to a finite deity of the kind favored by Voltaire himself. For in that case God may not know everything and informing Him of some unintended mishap might be the signal for rectification.

Voltaire is on much firmer ground in his reflections about the unreliability of the witnesses who have vouched for the miracles recorded in various holy books. What Voltaire said here resembles Hume's critique, but his challenge is less sweeping and not open to some of the objections leveled at Hume. "In order to believe in a miracle," Voltaire opens one discussion, "it is not enough merely to have seen it." The reason for this is that even careful observers can be deceived. Many "excellent persons" who are in general quite trustworthy "think that they have seen what they have not seen and heard what was never said to them." They thus become witnesses of miracles that did not take place or, if they are suggestible and especially if they have a touch of madness, they may even become the subjects of miracles, for example, miraculous cures. Before paying the slightest attention to such a claim, it is necessary that "the miracle should have been seen by a great number of very sensible people, in sound health, and perfectly disinterested in the affair." When "interest mixes with the transaction," as it almost invariably does in the case of religious believers, "you may consider the whole affair worth nothing." This is so even if a whole nation testifies to the occurrence of the miracle. Above all, the witnesses should have solemnly sworn in writing to what they supposedly witnessed. Voltaire points out that in everyday transactions of a very simple kind, such as the purchase of a house, a marriage contract, or a will, we require "minute cautionary formalities" in writing. How much more necessary is the execution of such documents in order to verify "things naturally impossible on which the destiny of the world is to depend"! Not one of the miracles described in the Old or the New Testament is supported by anything even remotely approximating such evidence. However, even this kind of evidence is not sufficient. For the sake of being fully verified, it would be desirable that a miracle "should be performed in the presence of the Academy of Sciences in Paris, or the Royal Society in London, and the Faculty of Medicine." This is not an unreasonable demand; for surely, if somebody can really transform water into wine or resurrect a corpse, he should be able to do this regardless of who is in the audience. In view of the credulity of many scientists and their insufficient experience in detecting fraud, one may fault Voltaire for not requiring that the observers should include skeptical magicians like Houdini or the Amazing Randi.

Both Hume and Voltaire occasionally thought that they had knock-out arguments against the possibility of miracles. This is not something that an empiricist should ever try for. The best he can do is insist that all past cases are seriously defective and that even those that appear the strongest invariably collapse when they are carefully examined. They collapse either because in the end the testimony does not hold up or because a natural explanation cannot be ruled out. The empiricist can add that there is no good reason for supposing that things will be different in the future.

As a postscript to the story about Vespasian's miraculous cures, it may be of some interest to note that Voltaire was in all probability mistaken about the facts. Hume also discusses these alleged miracles and rejects them out of hand, but Antony Flew went to the trouble of checking the account in the *Histories of Tacitus* and discovered that neither Voltaire nor Hume had been aware of all the relevant information. Tacitus explains that when the two sufferers appealed to Vespasian for help, the emperor asked for medical advice, receiving a prognosis that was not unfavorable in either case. "In the one case," Tacitus wrote, "the power of sight was not destroyed, and with the removal of obstruction would return; and in the other the crippled joint could be healed, given an access of healthy strength." It was only after he obtained this report that Vespasian decided to proceed with his cures, which, according to Tacitus, were instantaneous and dramatic. Although Hume and Voltaire were probably wrong about the facts of the case, it is evident that the cures achieved by Vespasian are not promising candidates for miracles. It is not at all obvious that the conditions that *really* troubled the two men cannot respond to psychological influences. We do not know exactly where the limits of psychological effects on physical illnesses are to be placed, but we do know that their possible range is vastly greater than was generally believed before the twentieth century. Anatole France once visited Lourdes where he was shown a room full of crutches, canes, wheelchairs, eyeglasses, and other implements left behind by people who had been miraculously cured of their ailments. "What," asked France, "no wooden legs?" This was one of Bertrand Russell's favorite stories, and we may be sure that Hume and Voltaire would also have greatly enjoyed it because it so neatly captures the essence of their case.

Note on the Translations

"On Mr. Locke," translated by Ernest Dilworth, reprinted by permission of the Macmillan Company from *Philosophical Letters*, published in 1961.

A Treatise on Metaphysics was translated by June Burnham for the present volume.

"How We Know Distance, Size, Shape and Position" was translated by the editor from the text of *The Elements of the Newtonian Philosophy* as it appears in the Kehl edition of Voltaire's *Works*.

"Dialogue Between Lucretius and Posidonius" is reprinted from the 1763 edition of the Works of *M. de Voltaire*, edited by Tobias Smollett, T. Francklin, and others.

Extracts from *A Treatise on Toleration* and *We Must Take Sides* are reprinted from *Selected Works of Voltaire*, translated by Joseph McCabe, first published in London by Watts and Co. as one of their *Cheap Reprints* in 1911 and then in the *Thinker's Library* in 1935. These extracts are reprinted with the approval of the *Rationalist Press Association Ltd.*

All articles from the *Philosophical Dictionary*, except the one on "Self Love," are reprinted with the permission of the publisher in the translation by Peter Gay, published in 1962 by Basic Books.

The article "Self Love" from the *Philosophical Dictionary*, the extracts from *A Commentary on the Book of Crimes and Punishments*, and the letter to Frederick the Great of October 1737 were translated by Haskell M. Block and are reprinted with the permission of Random House from *Candide and Other Writings*, published in 1956.

The translation of the extracts from *The Ignorant Philosopher* and *Questions Concerning the Encyclopedia* is attributed to William F. Fleming.

The letter on sorrow to an unknown correspondent is reprinted from S. G. Tallentyre's *Voltaire and His Letters* published in 1919. The remaining three letters—to Diderot, Rousseau and Tronchin—were translated by the editor. Rousseau's letter to Voltaire on providence was translated for the present volume by Barbara Gerber.

The translations of the "Dialogue Between Lucretius and Posidonius" and of the extracts from *The Ignorant Philosopher* and *Questions Concerning the Encyclopedia* have been substantially revised. Spelling and grammar have been modernized and numerous errors corrected. In *The Ignorant Philosopher* several sexually explicit passages were either bowdlerized or completely omitted by the translator. These have been restored.

Letter on Locke

This selection is Chapter XIII of the *Philosophical Letters*, published in English in 1733 and in French a year later. There was an earlier less cautiously worded version of this *Letter*, which Voltaire prudently decided to replace by the chapter as we now have it. Parts of the earlier version were incorporated in the article "Soul" in the *Philosophical Dictionary*.

Unless otherwise indicated, the footnotes are by the translator.

——————

Perhaps there has never been a wiser, more orderly mind, or a logician more exact, than Mr. Locke; and yet he was no great mathematician. He never could submit to the drudgery of calculations, nor to the dryness of mathematical truths, which in themselves offer nothing concrete to the understanding; at the same time no one has better demonstrated than he that one may have a geometrical intellect without the help of geometry. Great philosophers before his time had positively determined what the soul of man is; but since they knew absolutely nothing about the matter, it is quite proper that they should all have been of different opinions.

In Greece, the cradle of arts and errors, where the grandeur and foolishness of the human mind were carried so far, people reasoned about the soul as we do.

The Divine Anaxagoras, to whom an altar was raised for teaching mankind that the sun is larger than the Peloponnesus, that snow is black, and that the heavens are made of stone, declared that the soul is an airy spirit but nevertheless immortal.

Diogenes—another than the one who became a cynic after having been a counterfeiter—asserted that the soul is a portion of the very substance of God, and that idea at least was a brilliant one.

Epicurus saw it as composed of parts, like the body; Aristotle, who has been explicated in a thousand ways because he was unintelligible, believed—if we can trust some of his disciples—that the human understanding is a single universal substance.

The divine Plato, master of the divine Aristotle; and the divine Socrates, master of the divine Plato, called the soul corporeal[1] and eternal. No doubt the *daimon* of Socrates had told him all about it. It is true there are people who maintain that a man who bragged of having a familiar spirit was without question either a madman or a knave, but such people are too hard to please.

As for our Fathers of the Church, several of them in the earlier centuries believed the human soul, the angels, and God himself to be corporeal.

The world is getting subtler every day. St. Bernard, as Father Mabillon admits, taught that after death the soul did not see God in heaven but conversed only with the humanity of Jesus Christ. This time they did not take his word for it; the adventure of the Crusade had somewhat discredited his oracles. A thousand scholastic philosophers came after him, such as the Irrefragable Doctor, the Subtle Doctor, the Angelic Doctor, the Seraphic Doctor, the Cherubic Doctor,[2] all of whom have been quite sure they knew the soul through and through, but have never failed to discuss the subject as if they wanted nobody to understand a word of it.

Our Descartes, born to bring to light the errors of antiquity and to put his own in their place, being led astray by that spirit of system which blinds the greatest of men, imagined he had demonstrated that soul is the same thing as thought, just as matter, according to him, is the same as extension. He maintained that we are perpetually thinking, and that the soul makes its arrival in the body already provided with every possible metaphysical notion, knowing God, space, and infinity, as well as the whole range of abstract ideas, and filled, in other words, with splendid knowledge all of which it unfortunately forgets as it leaves its mother's womb.

M. Malebranche, of the Oratory, in his sublime hallucinations, not only allowed the existence of innate ideas but was certain that all we perceive is in God and that God, so to speak, is our soul.

After so many deep thinkers had fashioned the romance of the soul, there came a wise man who modestly recounted its true history; Locke has unfolded to man the nature of human reason as a fine anatomist explains the powers of the body. Throughout his work he makes use of the torch of

[1]This is surely a very strange reading of Plato and may at first suggest a typographical error in the translation or in Voltaire's original text. It is nothing of the kind. The only one of Voltaire's editors to comment on this passage is Gustave Lanson who, in his scholarly two-volume edition of the *Philosophical Letters* (1909), remarks that Voltaire always thought that for Plato the soul is "nothing but a most subtle and light kind of matter." This does not seem to be true of later discussions in which Voltaire endorses the more usual view that Plato believed and was indeed the first champion of the *in*corporeal soul. In a section of the article "Soul," which appeared in the *Questions Concerning the Encyclopedia* in 1770, Voltaire first repeats his view that "all antiquity" regarded the soul as corporeal, but then adds that "at last Plato so refined this soul" that it "became doubtful whether he had not entirely separated it from matter." (Ed.)

[2]Alexander Hales, John Duns Scotus, St. Thomas Aquinas, St. Bonaventura, and, fifth, a joke borrowed from Rabelais.

science. He dares sometimes to affirm, but he also dares to doubt. Instead of defining at once what we know nothing about, he examines, bit by bit, that which we want to understand. He takes a child at the moment of birth, he follows step by step the growth of its understanding, he marks what it has in common with animals, and in what ways it is superior to them. Above all, he consults his own experience, the consciousness of his own thoughts.

> But whether (he says) the soul be supposed to exist antecedent to, or coeval with, or some time after the first rudiments of organization, or the beginnings of life in the body, I leave to be disputed by those who have better thought of that matter. I confess myself to have one of those dull souls, that doth not perceive itself always to contemplate ideas; nor can conceive it any more necessary for the soul always to think, than for the body always to move....[3]

As for me, I am proud of the honor of being in this respect as stupid as Locke, for no one will ever convince me that I am always thinking. And I am no more disposed than he is to imagine that a few weeks after my conception I was an exceedingly learned soul, knowing a thousand things that I later forgot in being born, having quite fruitlessly arrived *in utero* at mental attainments that were swept away as soon as I could have any use for them, and that I have never since been able to recover.

Having done away with innate ideas, having altogether renounced the vanity of believing that we are always thinking, Locke proves that all our ideas come to us through the senses, examines our ideas both simple and complex, follows the human mind in all its operations, and shows the imperfections of all the languages spoken by man, and our constant abuse of terms. He comes at last to consider the extent, or rather the nothingness, of human knowledge. It is in this chapter that he humbly ventures to suggest that "possibly we shall never be able to know whether any mere material being thinks or no."[4] These sage words struck more than one theologian as a scandalous declaration that the soul is material and mortal.

Certain Englishmen, pious in their way, gave the alarm. The superstitious are in society what cowards are in an army: they are seized by, and they spread, panic terror. The cry went up that Locke was trying to overturn religion.[5] This was not a religious matter, though; it was a purely philosophic one, quite independent of faith and of revelation. All people had to do was to consider without bitterness whether there is any contra-

---

[3] *Essay Concerning Human Understanding*, Book II, Chapter I, Section 10.

[4] Book IV, Chapter III, Section 6. For "any mere material being" Locke had first written "matter."

[5] See, for instance, Thomas Burnet, *Remarks upon an Essay Concerning Humane Understanding* (London, 1697–99); Henry Lee, *Antiscepticism, or Notes upon Each Chapter of Locke's Essay* (London, 1702).

diction in saying, "Matter can think," and whether or not God is able to infuse thought into matter. But theologians have a bad habit of complaining that God is outraged when someone has simply failed to be of their opinion. They are too much like the bad poets who, because Boileau was making fun of them, accused him of speaking offensively of the King.

Doctor Stillingfleet[6] acquired the reputation of a moderate theologian by not saying anything positively abusive to Locke. He entered the lists against him but was beaten; for he argued as a man of learning, and Locke as a philosopher who was acquainted with the strength and weakness of the human mind and fought with weapons whose temper he knew.

If I were so bold as to speak after Mr. Locke on so ticklish a subject, I should say: Men have been wrangling for a long time over the nature and immortality of the soul. As for its immortality, that is impossible to prove since we are still arguing over its nature, and since, in order to determine whether something that exists is immortal or not, we surely must first be thoroughly familiar with it. The human reason is so little capable of proving by its own means the immortality of the soul that religion has been obliged to reveal it to us. The common good of mankind requires that we believe the soul immortal; faith commands it; nothing more is necessary, and the question is settled. The nature of the soul is a different matter; religion cares little what the soul is made of so long as it is virtuous. It is a clock we have been given to regulate; but the craftsman who made it has not told us the composition of the spring.

I am a body, and I think; that is all I know. Shall I go and attribute to an unknown cause what I can so easily attribute to the only secondary cause I know? Here all the philosophers of the School interrupt and say, "The body has only extension and solidity, and it is capable only of movement and of figure.[7] Now movement, figure, extension, and solidity cannot produce an idea, and thus the soul cannot be material. This great piece of reasoning, which has been so often repeated, may be reduced to these words:

> I am totally ignorant of the nature of matter; I make imperfect
> conjectures as to some of its properties. Now I am totally ignorant
> as to whether there is any possible connection between these
> properties and idea or thought. Thus, because I know nothing
> whatsoever, I positively affirm that matter is incapable of thought.

There, plainly, is the School's way of reasoning. Locke would say to these gentlemen with perfect simplicity, "Confess at least that you know as little

---

[6]Edward Stillingfleet (1635–99), Bishop of Worcester, published three pamphlets (1696–97) in a controversy with Locke on the doctrine of the Trinity.

[7]Cartesian, Voltaire, the reader may have guessed, admired "Our Descartes who was the greatest philosopher in Europe, before Sir Isaac Newton appeared . . ." (Dedication of *La Henriade* to the Queen of England, 1728), and wished that Descartes had more often followed his own Method, as laid down, for instance, in the first precept, "never to accept anything as true unless I know it certainly to be so."

as I. Your imagination no more than mine can conceive how it is that a body should have ideas; do you understand any better how any substance whatever should have them? You comprehend neither matter nor spirit; how then do you dare affirm anything?"

Then, in his turn, comes the superstitious man, and he says that those who suspect that thought is possible with the sole aid of the body ought to be burnt for the good of their souls. But what would such people say if it were they themselves that were guilty of irreligion? In fact, what man could venture to assert, without an absurd impiety, that it is impossible for the Creator to give thought and feeling to matter! See now, if you please, to what straits you are reduced, you who thus limit the power of the Creator! The animals have the same organs as we, the same feelings, the same perceptions; they have a memory, they combine certain ideas. If God has been unable to animate matter and to give it feeling, then one of two things is true: either animals are mere machines, or else they have a soul.

It appears to me almost certain that animals cannot be mere machines. Here is my proof: God made for them precisely the same sense organs as our own, and so if they do not feel, God has made a useless work. Now even you acknowledge that God does nothing in vain, and so He has not manufactured all those organs of feeling in order that no feeling should be done with them, and therefore animals are not mere machines.

Since according to you the animals cannot have a soul, there is, like it or not, nothing for you to say but that God gave to the organs of animals, which are matter, the faculty of feeling and perceiving, which in them you call instinct.

Well now, who can prevent God from imparting to our more subtle organs that faculty of feeling, perceiving, and thinking which we call human reason? Wherever you turn you are obliged to confess your ignorance and the boundless power of the Creator; cease then to struggle against the wise and unassuming philosophy of Locke. Far from being opposed to religion, it would serve as proof if religion had need of it. For what philosophy is more religious than that which, affirmingly only what it clearly understands, hand able to own to its weakness, tells us that no sooner do we examine first principles than we must have recourse to God.

Besides, we should never fear that any philosophical opinion could harm the religion of a country. Let our Mysteries be contrary to our demonstrations, they are no less revered for it by Christian philosophers, who know that matters of reason and matters of faith are different in nature. Never will philosophers set up a religious sect. Why? Because they do not write for the people, and because they are without enthusiasm.[8]

---

[8]Voltaire, in following Locke, is using the word "enthusiasm" in the then popular sense of "Fancied inspiration: 'a vain confidence of divine favour or communication,.'" if not of "Ill-regulated or misdirected religious emotion, extravagance of religious speculation." (O.E.D.)

Divide the human race into twenty parts. Nineteen of them are composed of those who work with their hands, and will never know if there is a Locke in the world or not. In the remaining twentieth part how few men do we find who read! And among those who do read there are twenty who read novels for every one who studies philosophy. The number of those who think is exceedingly small, and they are not aiming to disturb the world.

It is not Montaigne, nor Locke, nor Bayle, nor Spinoza, nor Hobbes, nor Lord Shaftesbury, nor Mr. Collins, nor Mr. Toland, and so on, who have carried the torch of discord in their native country; it is theologians, for the most part, who having first had the ambition of being leaders of their sect, have soon afterward desired to be heads of parties. Why, all the books of the modern philosophers put together will never make as much noise in the world as once was made just by the dispute of the Cordeliers[9] over the shape of their sleeve and their hood.

[9]Greyfriars, Franciscans.

Treatise on Metaphysics

There is compelling evidence that Voltaire composed three versions of the *Traité de métaphysique*, the first in 1734, which consisted of only seven chapters, a second in 1736, which is the only one that has been preserved in its entirety and is offered here in translation, and a third in 1737. One chapter of the last version survived because a copy of it was sent to Frederick the Great, then Crown Prince, together with Voltaire's letter of October 1737 (see pp. 208–210). It corresponds to Chapter 7 of the second version. Although the basic views are identical, the arrangement is much tighter and several of the arguments are presented in a clearer form. There is reason to believe that Voltaire was never fully satisfied with his *Traité* even in its third version. It is probable that his dissatisfaction with the work was one of the reasons for not attempting to publish it.

INTRODUCTION—DOUBTS ABOUT MAN

Few people concern themselves with acquiring a clear understanding of what man is. The peasants of one part of Europe have hardly any other conception of our species than that man is a two-footed animal with a swarthy skin, speaking a few words, cultivating the land, paying—without knowing why—certain dues to another animal they call "king," selling their produce at the highest price they can, and gathering together on certain days of the year to chant prayers in a language they do not understand at all.

A king views almost the whole human species as beings made to obey him and his kind. A young Parisian girl, entering fashionable society, sees only those who can be useful to her vanity; the confused idea she has of happiness, and the bustle of all that surrounds her, prevent her from hearing the voice of all the rest of nature. A young Turk, in the silence of the seraglio, sees men as superior beings, obliged by a certain law to sleep every Friday with their slaves, and his imagination goes no further than that. A priest divides the whole world into ecclesiastics and laymen, and he

This translation of the *Treatise on Metaphysics* is copyright 1988, Paul Edwards.

has no difficulty considering the ecclesiastic part as nobler and made for leading the other.

If one thought that the philosophers had more fully developed ideas on human nature, one would be very mistaken: for if you leave out Hobbes, Locke, Descartes, Bayle, and a very small number of wise minds, all the others have constructed for themselves their particular view of man, which is as narrow as the common man's view, but more obscure. Ask Father Malebranche what man is; he will tell you that man is a substance created in God's image, and though much blemished since he first sinned, is joined more closely to God than to his own body, seeing all things in God, thinking and feeling all things in God.

Pascal regards the universe as a collection of the wicked and the unfortunate, created only to be damned; God has, however, chosen a few souls from this infinite number — that is, one in five or six million — to be saved.

One of these philosophers says: Man is a soul joined to a body; when the body dies, the soul lives forever. The other states that man is a body which necessarily thinks. But neither one nor the other proves what he asserts.

In this research on man I want to behave as I do when I study astronomy: sometimes I imagine myself to be outside the earth's globe, from whose surface all celestial movements appear irregular and confused. And after having observed the movements of the planets as though I were on the sun, I compare the apparent movements that I see from the earth with the real movements I would see if I were on the sun. In the same way, I shall try in my study of man to stand at first outside his sphere and concerns and to cast off all my preconceptions formed by education, country, and especially philosophers.

I suppose, for example, that born with the faculty of thought and sensibility which I have now, but not in human shape, I come down to earth from the planet of Mars or Jupiter. I can cast my eyes rapidly over all the centuries, all the countries, and, consequently, all the stupidities of this little globe.

This supposition is as easy to make, to say the least, as the one I make when I imagine myself on the sun examining from that viewpoint the sixteen planets which regularly revolve in the space around that star.

CHAPTER 1 — ON THE DIFFERENT SPECIES OF MEN

Once down on this small lump of mud, and having no more idea of man than man has of the inhabitants of Mars or Jupiter, I land near the oceanic coasts, in the Cape country, and I set off at once to find a *man*. I see monkeys, elephants, and negroes, who all seem to have a glimmer of reasoning abilities. All the species have languages which I cannot understand, and all their activities seem equally related to particular ends. If I judged things by their immediate effect on me, I would tend to think at first that of all these beings, it is the elephant which is the animal who can reason; but so as not to decide anything too lightly, I catch the young of these different beasts; I examine a six-month-old negro child, a baby elephant, a baby monkey, a baby lion, and a young dog; I see, with no possible doubt, that the young animals have incomparably more strength and dexterity, more ideas, more emotions, and a better memory than the baby negro and that they can express much more clearly all their desires; but a little while later, the young negro has quite as many ideas as all the others put together. I also notice that these negro animals speak among themselves a language which is much better articulated and much more varied than that of the other animals. I spent some time learning this language. Finally, because of this small degree of superiority which they had in the long term over the monkeys and the elephants, I ventured to decide that this was indeed *man*, and I constructed the following definition for myself: Man is a black animal with wool on his head, who walks on two paws, is almost as skillful as a monkey, not as strong as other animals his size, with a few more ideas than they have, and more ability to express them; he is subject, moreover, to all the same forces, being born, living, and dying just like them.

After spending some time among this species, I move on to the maritime regions of the East Indies. I am surprised by what I see: the elephants, monkeys, lions, parrots here are not exactly the same as those in the Cape, but men here seem to be absolutely different: they are of a handsome yellow color, have no wool, their heads being covered with great black manes. Their ideas on everything appear quite different from those of the negroes. I am therefore forced to change my definition and to sort humanity into two species: yellow with manes and black with wool.

But in Batavia, Goa, and Surat, which are the meeting places of all nations, I see a great number of Europeans who are white and have neither manes nor wool, but very fine blond hair and a beard on the chin. I am also shown many Americans, who have no beard at all; now my definition and my list of human species have really expanded.

At Goa I meet a type even more extraordinary than all those before; it is a man wearing a long black cassock, who claims he was made for instructing the others. All these different men, he says, are born from the same father, and he goes on to tell me a long story. But that this animal says seems very unlikely to me. I enquire whether a negro man and a negro woman, with their black wool and flattened noses, ever have white children with blond hair, aquiline noses, and blue eyes; if beardless nations have come from bearded people; or if white men and women have ever produced yellow people. I am told no, that negroes transported to Germany, for example, only have negroes, unless the Germans take it upon themselves to change the species. And it is added that no man with some learning has ever asserted that unmixed species might degenerate and that hardly anyone but the Abbé Dubos would have said such a foolish thing in a book entitled *Reflections on Painting and Poetry*[1]

It seems to me then that I have fairly good grounds for believing that in this respect men are like trees; just as firs, oaks, pear trees, and apricot trees do not come from the same tree, white men with beards, negroes with wool, yellow men with manes, and men without beards do not come from the same man.

CHAPTER 2—WHETHER THERE IS A GOD

We have to examine the faculty of thought in these different species of men; how his ideas come to him, if he has a soul distinct from his body, if this soul is eternal, if it is free, if it has virtues and vices. But most of these ideas depend on the existence or nonexistence of a God. We must start, I think, by sounding the depths of this great principle. Here, more than ever, we must rid ourselves of every emotion and all preconceptions and see in good faith what our reason can teach us on this question:

"Is There or Isn't There a God"

I note first of all that there are some tribes who have no knowledge of a creator God; these tribes are in truth barbarians, and they are very small in number, but after all they are men. If the knowledge of a God were necessary to humanity, the Hottentot savages would have as sublime an idea of a supreme being as we do. Even more noteworthy, there is not one child among the civilized communities who has the least idea of a God in his head. It is impressed on children with difficulty; they will often pronounce the word "God" all their lives without giving it any fixed meaning; moreover, you see that men's ideas about God differ as much as their religions and laws, so that I cannot resist this thought: is it possible that knowledge of a God, our creator, our preserver, our All, might be less necessary to man than a nose and five fingers? All men are born with a nose and five fingers, and no one is born with knowledge of God: whether that should be deplored or not, it is certainly the human condition.

Let us see then if we acquire knowledge of a God with the passage of time, in the same way that we acquire some elementary mathematics and a few metaphysical ideas. What could we do better, in such an important piece of research, than weigh the possible arguments for and against and make up our minds as to which seems to us to be more consistent with reason.

[1]The reference is to Vol. II, Section 15 of *Réflexions sur la peinture et sur la poèsie* by the Abbé Jean-Baptiste Dubos (1670–1742).

Summary of Arguments in Favor of the Existence of God

There are two ways of acquiring the notion of a being who directs the universe. The more natural and perfect for those of ordinary ability is by considering not only the order which there is in the universe, but the end to which each thing appears to be directed. Many large books have been written about this idea alone, and all these large books taken together contain nothing more than this argument: when I see a watch with a hand marking the hours, I conclude that an intelligent being has designed the springs of this mechanism, so that the hand would mark the hours. So, when I see the springs of the human body, I conclude that an intelligent being has designed these organs to be received and nourished within the womb for nine months; for eyes to be given for seeing; hands for grasping, and so on. But from this one argument, I cannot conclude anything more, except that it is probable that an intelligent and superior being has prepared and shaped matter with dexterity; I cannot conclude from this argument alone that this being has made the matter out of nothing or that he is infinite in any sense. However deeply I search my mind for the connection between the following ideas — *it is probable that I am the work of a being more powerful than myself, therefore this being has existed from all eternity, therefore he has created everything, therefore he is infinite, and so on.* — I cannot see the chain which leads directly to that conclusion; I can see only that there is something more powerful than myself and nothing more.

The second argument is more metaphysical, less easily grasped by untrained minds, but it leads to a much greater understanding. Here is a summary of it: I exist, therefore something exists. If something exists, something has therefore existed from all eternity, since he who is, either is of himself or has received his being from another. If he is of himself, he necessarily is, he has necessarily always been, and so this is God. If he has received his being from another, and this second from a third, he from whom the last received his being must necessarily be God. For you cannot conceive that a being could give being to another unless he had the power to create; moreover, if you state that a thing receives, I am not saying its form, but its existence, from another thing, and the latter from a third, this third from yet another, and so on back to infinity, your statement will be nonsense. For then none of these beings would have any cause of their existence. Taken together as a group, they would have no external cause of their existence; taken each one individually, they would have no internal cause; that is to say, taken together, they do not owe their existence to anything; each one considered separately, none exists of itself; therefore none can necessarily exist.

I am thus compelled to acknowledge that there is a being who exists necessarily of himself from all eternity and who is the origin of all other beings. From that it must follow that this being is infinite in time, space, and power; for who could set limits on him? But, you will tell me, the material world is precisely that being for whom we are looking. Let us examine in good faith if that is probable.

If this material world exists of itself of absolute necessity, it would be a contradiction in terms to suppose that the smallest part of this universe could be other than as it is; for if it is at this moment of absolute necessity, that phrase alone would exclude any other manner of being. Yet, this table on which I am writing, this pen I am using, have certainly not always been what they are now; these thoughts I am setting down on paper did not even exist a moment ago, so they cannot necessarily exist. Now, if each part does not exist of absolute necessity, it is therefore impossible for the whole to exist of itself. I can produce motion, thus the motion did not exist previously; so motion is not essential to matter; so matter receives it from elsewhere; so there is a God who gave it the motion. In a similar way, intelligence is not essential to matter, for rocks and wheat cannot think. From whom then did those parts of matter, which can think and feel, receive the faculty of thought and sensibility? It cannot be from themselves, because they feel in spite of themselves; it cannot be from matter in general, because thought and sensation are not the essence of matter; they have therefore received these gifts from the hand of a supreme being who is intelligent, infinite, and the original cause of all beings.

So there in a few words are the proofs for the existence of a God, and the summary of several volumes: a summary which each reader can expand at his will.

And following, just as briefly, are the objections which can be made to that system.

Problems Concerning the Existence of God

1. If God is not this material world, he created it (or, if you prefer, he gave some other being the power to create it, which comes to the same thing), but to make this world, he had either to draw it out of nothing or draw it from his own divine self. He cannot have drawn it out of nothing, which is nothing; he cannot have drawn it from himself, because in that case this world would in essence be part of the divine essence. Thus I cannot have an idea of the creation, so I must not acknowledge its creation.

2. God would have made this world either necessarily or freely; if he made it of necessity, he must always have made it, for this necessity is eternal; in which case the world would be both eternal and created, which implies a contradiction. If God made it freely by pure choice, without any antecedent reason, that would still be a contradiction; for it is inconsistent to assume an infinitely wise being making everything without any reason

for it and an infinitely powerful being spending an eternity without making the slightest use of his power.

3. If it appears to the majority of men that an intelligent being was stamped the seal of wisdom on all nature and that each thing seems to have been made for a certain end, it is even more true in the eyes of some philosophers that everything happens in nature according to the eternal, independent, and unchanging laws of mathematics; the construction and course of life of the human body are a consequence of the equilibrium of fluids and the force of levers. The more discoveries we make about the structure of the universe, the more we find it arranged according to mathematical laws, from the stars down to the smallest mite. It is therefore permissible to believe that these laws, having worked according to their nature, result in necessary effects which are taken to be the arbitrary decisions of an intelligent power. For example, a field produces grass, because such is the nature of its soil when watered by rain, and not because there are horses which need hay and oats.

4. If the design of some parts of this world, and all that happens to those beings who think and feel, was evidence for a creator and master, it would be even better evidence for a barbaric being; for if one assumes there are final causes, one will be obliged to say that an infinitely wise and infinitely good God has given life to all creatures in order that some should be devoured by others. In fact, if one considers all the animals, one can see that each species has an irresistible instinct to destroy another species. As to man's miseries, there is enough of those with which to reproach the deity throughout our lives. However much we are told that the wisdom and goodness of God are not shaped like ours, this argument will have no effect on the minds of a good many people, who will reply that they can only judge God's justice by that idea of justice which God is supposed to have given them, that they can only measure with the gauges they have, and that it is as impossible not to consider barbaric a being who behaves like a barbaric man as it is impossible not to think that someone is six feet tall, when we measure him with a six-foot ruler and he seems to us to be just that size.

If someone were to reply to us, he could say that our gauge was faulty. In that case he would be telling us something which seems to imply a contradiction; for it is God himself who must have given us that false idea, thus God would have made us only to deceive us. Now, that means that a being who can have nothing but perfection is casting his creatures into error, which is, properly speaking, the one imperfection; that is obviously a contradiction. Finally, the materialists will complete this by saying: We have fewer absurdities to swallow in the system of atheism than those in the system of deism; for in the former it is necessary to believe that this world we see is eternal and infinite, but in the latter it is necessary to imagine another being who is infinite and eternal, and then add to that the creation, of which we can have no notion. It is therefore easier, they conclude, not to believe in God than to believe in him.

Reply to These Objections

The arguments against creation reduce to showing that it is impossible for us to conceive of it; that is to say, to conceive the manner of it, but not that it is impossible in itself; for to prove that the creation was impossible, it would be necessary to prove first of all that it was impossible for there to be a God; but far from proving this impossibility, one is obliged to recognize that it is impossible that he does not exist. This argument that it is necessary for there to be an infinite, eternal, boundless, all-powerful, free, and intelligent being beyond us, and the darkness which accompanies this light, only serves to show that the light exists; for that argument, even as it demonstrates an infinite being to us, also demonstrates that it must be impossible for a finite being to comprehend him.

It seems to me that one can commit only fallacies or state absurdities if one strives to deny the necessity that a being exists of itself or if one tries to maintain that matter is that being. But when it involves establishing and discussing the characteristics of that being whose existence has been demonstrated, that is quite a different thing.

The masters of the art of reasoning like Locke and Clarke, tell us: *This being is an intelligent being, for he who produced everything must have all the perfections which he placed in those he produced, or the effect would be more perfect than the cause*; or, put differently: *There would be a perfection in the effect which would have been produced from nothing, which is obviously absurd. Thus, since there are intelligent beings, and matter could not have given itself the faculty of thought, then the being which exists of itself, God, must be an intelligent being.* But could not this argument be turned around to say: *God must be material*, because there are material beings; for otherwise, the material would have been produced from nothing, and a cause would have produced an effect whose principle was not contained in the cause? Some had hoped to avoid this argument by slipping in the word "perfection." Clarke seems to have anticipated it, but he did not dare bring it right out into the open; he posed only this objection to his argument: *Someone will say that God has managed to impart divisibility and form to matter, even though he is without form and is indivisible.* And then he has a very easy and very solid answer, which is that divisibility and form are negative qualities and limitations, and that although a cause cannot pass on to its effect any perfection which it does not have itself, the effect can and must necessarily have limitations and imperfections which the cause does not have. But what would Clarke have replied to someone who said to him: "Matter is not a negative being, a limitation, an imperfection; it is a real, positive being which has properties just like the mind; now, how could God have produced a material being if he is not material?" So you must admit that the cause can communicate something positive which it does not have or that matter has no cause of its existence or, finally, that matter is pure negation and limitation. Or if all three positions are absurd, you must admit that the existence of intelligent beings no more proves that the being existing of himself is an intelligent being than the existence of material beings proves that the being existing of himself is material; for the case is absolutely identical; one could say the same thing about movement. With regard to the word "perfection," it is obviously being misused here; for who would dare to say that matter is an imperfection and that thought is a perfection? I cannot believe that anyone would dare to make that sort of a decision about the essence of things. And then what does perfection mean here? Is it perfection in the sight of God or according to us?

It might be said that this argument would bring us back to Spinoza's view. To this I would reply that I cannot help that, and that my reasoning, if it is good, cannot become false just because of the inferences which follow from it; but in any case, nothing would be more wrong than that inference, for it would only prove that our intelligence no more resembles God's intelligence than our manner of extension resembles the manner in which God occupies space. God is not the same kind of cause as the causes which we know; he was able to create mind and matter without being either mind or matter; neither one nor the other derives from him but are created by him. I do not know the *quomodo*, the way in which it was done, it is true; I prefer to stop there than to err. His existence has been demonstrated to me; but as to his attributes and essence, it has been demonstrated to me, I believe, that I am not made for understanding them.

To say that God has made this world neither necessarily nor of his free will is nothing but a fallacy which fails of its own accord as soon as it has been proved that there is a God, and that the world is not God. This objection can be reduced to the following: I cannot understand why God created the universe at one particular time rather than another; therefore he could not have created it. That is just like saying: I cannot understand why such a man or such a horse did not exist one thousand years earlier; therefore their existence is impossible. Moreover, the free will of God is a sufficient reason for the time at which he willed the creation of the world. If God exists, he is free, and he would not be if he were always determined by a sufficient reason and if his free will could not serve him as one. Also, is this sufficient reason inside him or outside him? If it is outside him, then he cannot decide freely; if it is inside him, what is it other than his free will?

Mathematical laws are unchanging, it is true; but it was not necessary that such laws be preferred to others. It was not necessary that the earth be placed where it is; no mathematical law can act by itself; none can operate without movement; movement does not exist by itself; therefore one must resort to a prime mover. I admit that the planets, placed at such a distance from the sun, must revolve in their orbits according to the laws which they observe, that even their distance can be regulated by the quantity of matter they contain. But can one then say that it was necessary that there should be a particular amount of matter in each planet, that there should be a certain number of stars, that this number could not be increased or decreased, and that on earth there should be a certain number of beings by an absolute and inherent necessity in the nature of things? No, without question, because this number changes every day; thus all nature, from the furthest star to a blade of grass, must be subordinate to a prime mover.

As to the objection that a meadow is not essentially made for horses and other animals, it cannot be concluded from this argument that there is no final cause, but only that we do not know all the final causes. Here, above all, we must reason in good faith and not seek to deceive ourselves; when we see a thing which always has the same effect, and only that effect, which is made up of an infinity of organs, in each of which there is an infinity of movements, all contributing to the same result, it seems to me that we cannot, without a secret reluctance, deny a final cause. The embryo of all plants, all animals is such a case; would it not be rather imprudent to say that none of these bore any relation to an end?

I acknowledge that there is no proof, properly speaking, that the stomach is made for digesting, just as there is no proof that it is daylight; but the materialists are very far from being able to prove that the stomach is not made for digesting. Let us just decide with natural impartiality, as we decide things in everyday life, whose opinions are the more likely.

As to the criticisms of God on the grounds of injustice and cruelty, my first reply is that supposing there were a moral evil (which seems pure fantasy to me), this moral evil is just as impossible to explain in the system of matter as in the system of a God. Next, I reply that we have no other ideas about justice than those we have formed for ourselves about any action useful to society and which conform to laws established by us for the common good; now this idea being only an idea about relations among men, it cannot have any analogy with God. It is just as absurd to say about God, in this way, that God is just or unjust, as to say that God is blue or square.

It is therefore senseless to reproach God if flies are eaten by spiders, if men only live eighty years or abuse their freedom to destroy each other or are ill or have cruel emotions, and so on; for we certainly have no idea that men and flies ought to be eternal. To be really sure that something is evil, one would have to see at the same time that one could do better. We can only judge with certainty that a machine is imperfect by the idea of the perfection which it lacks; for example, we cannot judge that the three sides of a triangle are unequal if we have no idea of an equilateral triangle; we cannot say that a clock is bad if we have no distinct idea of a certain number of equal spaces which the hand of this clock must traverse in equal times. But who will ever have an idea by which to judge that this world does not conform to divine wisdom?

There are problems to be found in the view that there is a God; but in the opposite view there are absurdities; and this is what one must examine carefully, by making a little summary of what a materialist is obliged to believe.

Necessary Consequences of the Materialists' Views

It is necessary for them to say that the world exists necessarily and of itself, such that it would be a contradiction in terms to say that one part of the matter could not exist or could exist other than as it is; it is necessary for them to say that the material world has thought and feeling essentially in itself; for it cannot acquire them, since then they would come to the world from nothing; it cannot receive them from elsewhere, because it is assumed to be all that there is. It is therefore necessary that this thought and feeling are inherent in the material world, like extension, divisibility, and capacity for movement are inherent in matter; but then it would be necessary to admit that only a very small number of the parts of the world have this feeling and thought essential to the whole world and that these feelings and thoughts, even though inherent in matter, are, however, perishing all the time; or alternatively, one would need to assert that there is a world soul which distributes itself among the organisms, and then this soul would need to be something other than the world. So whichever way we turn, we find nothing but fantasies, which demolish themselves.

The materialists must also maintain that movement is essential to matter. That obliges them to say that movement never could and never will increase or diminish, they would be forced to assert that a hundred thousand men marching and a hundred cannons firing would produce no new movement in nature. They would also need to affirm that there is no liberty, and in that way destroy all social ties, and to believe in an inevitable fate which is quite as difficult to understand as liberty, but which they themselves deny in practice. Let an impartial reader see, after mature consideration of the arguments for and against the existence of a creator God, on which side probability lies.

Having thus followed our trail from doubt to doubt, and from conclusion to conclusion, until we could regard the proposition "there is a God" as the most probably true thing that men could think, and having seen that the contrary proposition is one of the most absurd, it seems natural to discover what relationship exists between God and ourselves, to see if God has set up laws for thinking beings corresponding to the mechanical laws governing material things, to examine if there is a moral law and what that might be, and to find out if there is a religion established by God himself. These questions are without doubt of overwhelming importance, and the topics with which we concern ourselves much of our lives are quite frivolous in comparison; but these questions will be more in place when we come to consider man as a social animal.

Let us examine first how man comes by his ideas and how he thinks before seeing what use he makes or ought to make of his thoughts.

CHAPTER 3—THAT ALL IDEAS COME THROUGH THE SENSES

If anyone were to give a faithful account of all that had happened in his mind, he would affirm without difficulty that his senses had provided him with all his ideas, but some philosophers who have misused their reasoning have claimed that we have innate ideas; they have asserted this on the same grounds which they used to state that God took cubes of matter and rubbed one against another to form the visible world. They have fabricated systems with which, they flatter themselves, they can venture some apparent explanation of natural phenomena. This method of philosophizing is even more dangerous than the despicable jargon of the scholastics. Since their jargon was devoid of all sense, it only needed a little bit of attention by an honest mind to see its ridiculous nature immediately and to look elsewhere for the truth; but an ingenious and daring hypothesis, which has at first sight some glimmer of probability, tempts human pride to believe it; our mind rejoices in these subtle principles and uses all its ingenuity to defend them. It is clear that one must never form hypotheses; one must not say: let us start by inventing some principles with which we shall try to explain everything. But what one must say is: let us analyze things exactly, and then we shall try to see with much caution if they correspond to some principles. Those who write novels about innate ideas flatter themselves that they have explained ideas of infinity, immensity, God, and certain metaphysical notions which they assume are common to all men. But if, before embarking on this system, they had endeavored to reflect that many men go through life without the least smattering of these notions and that children have them only when given them and that even when the ideas have finally been acquired, one has only some very imperfect perceptions and some purely negative ideas, these philosophers themselves would be ashamed of their views. If there is anything that has been demonstrated, outside mathematics, it is that there are no innate ideas in man; if there were, all men would have the idea of a God at birth, and they would all have the same idea; they would all have the same metaphysical notions; add to that the ridiculous absurdity some bring on themselves by asserting that God gives us in our mother's womb the notions we must be taught completely as children.

Thus it is undeniable that our first ideas are our sensations. Little by little we receive composite ideas from that which strikes our organs; our memory retains these perceptions; then we arrange them into general ideas. From this one faculty we have of combining and arranging our ideas in this way follows all of man's vast knowledge.

There are those who raise the objection that the notions of infinity of time, extension, and number cannot come from our senses. They should reflect for a moment. They will see that they have no complete, or even only a positive, idea of the infinite; it is only by adding material things together, one after another, that they recognize that they will never reach the end of their calculation; this impossibility has been named "infinity"; but it is really more an affirmation of human ignorance than an idea beyond the reach of our senses. If someone raises the objection that a real infinity exists in geometry, I reply: no, one proves only that matter is always divisible; one proves that all possible circles will pass between two lines; one proves that an infinity of areas has nothing in common with an infinity of cubes; but that gives no more an idea of infinity than the proposition "there is a God" gives us an idea of what God is.

But it is not enough for us to be convinced that our ideas all come to us via our senses; our curiosity makes us want to know how the ideas come. It is on this that all the philosophers have written such fine romances; it was easy to save ourselves from those by considering in good faith the limits of human nature. Where we cannot be guided by the compass of mathematics or the torch of experience and physics, it is certain that we cannot take one step. Until we have eyes sufficiently sharp to distinguish between the constituent parts of gold and the constituent parts of a grain of mustard, it is quite certain that we cannot argue about their essence; until man is of a different nature and has organs with which to perceive his own substance and the essence of his ideas, like the organs he has for various sensations, it will certainly be impossible for him to understand them.

To ask how we think and how we feel, how our movements obey our will, is to ask the Creator's secret; our senses no more provide us with the paths to that knowledge than they give us wings when we wish we could fly. That well proves, in my opinion, that all our ideas come via our senses, because when we lack the senses, we lack the ideas. So it is impossible to know how we think for the same reason that it is impossible for us to have the idea of a sixth sense; it is because we lack the organs which would inform us of those ideas. That is why those who were rash enough to invent a system based on the nature of the soul and our conceptions have been obliged to conjecture the absurd notion of innate ideas, deluding themselves that among the metaphysical ideas assumed to descend from the sky into our minds would be some which would uncover this impenetrable secret.

Of all those rash reasoners who become lost in the depths of their research, it was Father Malebranche who seems to have erred most splendidly. Look at what his system, which caused so much stir, boils down to: our perceptions, which come to us in the presence of objects, cannot be caused by those objects themselves, which certainly do not have in themselves the power to produce sensations; they do not come from us, for we are in this respect as impotent as those objects; therefore it must be God who gives them to us. Now, God is the link between minds, and the minds have their existence in him; therefore, it is in him that we have our ideas and see all things.

Now I ask any man who is not convinced by this system, what clear idea are we given by the argument above? What can it mean by "God is the link between minds"? Even if the words "feeling and seeing all things in God" stood for a distinct idea in our minds, I ask, what would we have gained and in what way would we be wiser than we were before?

Certainly, to reduce Father Malebranche's system to something intelligible, we would have to resort to Spinoza's system and imagine that God is the whole universe, that God acts in all beings, senses in all animals, thinks in all men, grows in all trees, is thought and stone, has all the parts of himself destroyed at every moment, and, in short, all the absurdities which necessarily follow from that principle.

The aberrations of all those who wanted to examine the depths of what for us is impenetrable ought to teach us not to desire to go beyond the limits of our nature. The true philosophy is to know where to stop and never to travel without a sure guide.

There is enough ground still to be covered without voyaging in imaginary space. Let us be content therefore to know from experience supported by reasoning, the sole source of our knowledge, that our senses are the doors through which all ideas enter our understanding; let us remember well that it is absolutely impossible for us to know the secret of this mechanism, because we do not have suitable instruments for examining its working.

CHAPTER 4—THAT THERE ARE IN FACT EXTERNAL OBJECTS

One would not have considered dealing with this question if the philosophers had not tried to doubt the clearest things, just as they flatter themselves that they know the most doubtful.

Our senses give us ideas, they say, but perhaps our understanding is receiving perceptions without there being any object outside ourselves. We know that during sleep we see and feel things which do not exist; perhaps our life is a continual dream, and death will be the moment of our awakening or the end of a dream with no awakening. Our senses sometimes deceive us even when we are awake; the least deterioration in our organs makes us sometimes see objects and hear sounds whose cause is only a disorder of our body. It is thus very possible that something which happens to us sometimes is happening always.

They add that when we see an object, we perceive a color, a shape, and we hear sounds, and it has pleased us to name all of that the "modes" of the object. But what is the substance of this object? That is, in fact, where the object escapes our understanding. What we so boldly call the "substance" is, in fact, none other than the combination of these modes. Strip this tree of that color, that shape which gave you the idea of a tree, and what would remain of it? Now, what I called "modes" is nothing more than my perceptions; I can well say that I have an idea of a green color and of a body with a certain shape, but I have no proof that this body and this color exist. That is what Sextus Empiricus said and to which he could find no answer.

Let us for a moment grant these gentlemen more than they ask. They claim that one cannot prove to them that there are bodies. Let us assume they succeed in proving that there are no bodies. What would follow from that? Would we conduct our lives differently? Would we have different ideas about anything? We would just have to change one word in our conversations. When, for example, battles took place, one would have to say that ten thousand men appeared to have been killed, that a certain officer seems to have a broken leg, and that a surgeon will seem to cut it off. In the same way, when we are hungry, we shall ask for the appearance of a piece of bread, so that we can pretend to eat it.

But here is a more serious reply:

1. You cannot in a strict sense compare life to the state of dreaming, because while asleep you dream only about those things of which you had an idea while awake; you are sure that your dreams are nothing more than a feeble recollection. And in contrast, if we have a sensation while awake, we are never able to conclude that it was through recollection. If, for example, a stone fell and broke our shoulder, it would seem fairly difficult for that to be done by an effort of memory.

2. It is very true that our senses are often deceived; but what does one mean by that? We have only one sense, properly speaking, which is that of touch; sight, hearing, and smell are only the touch of intermediary bodies between us and the distant body. My only idea of stars comes through contact; as this contact with the light which strikes my eyes from a thousand million leagues away is not tangible, like the contact of my hands, and depends on the medium through which these bodies have passed, this contact is what one wrongfully calls *deceitful*, it does not let me see the objects in their real place; it gives me no idea of their size; not one of these nontangible contacts gives me a positive idea of the body. The first time that I sense a smell without seeing the object from which it comes, my mind finds no relation between a body and that smell; but the contact, or

properly put, the proximity of my body to another, independently of my other senses, gives me the idea of matter; for when I touch a rock, I sense that I cannot put myself in its place and that something must be there which has extension and is impenetrable. So, supposing (for why not suppose it!) that a man had all the senses save that of touch, properly called, this man could quite well doubt the existence of external objects and even perhaps be without an idea of them for a long time; but a man who was deaf and blind and yet had the sense of touch could not doubt the existence of things whose hardness he had experienced; that is because the essence of matter is not that a body has color or makes a sound, but that it has extension and is impenetrable. But what would outraged sceptics reply to these two questions:

1. If there are no external objects, and my imagination does everything, why am I burnt when I touch fire, and not burnt when in a dream I think I touch fire?

2. When I write my ideas down on paper and another man reads to me what I have written, how can I hear the same words which I wrote and thought if this other man is not actually reading them to me? How can I even find them again if they are not there?

In short, whatever effort I make to doubt, I am more convinced of the existence of bodies than I am of several truths of geometry. This may seem astonishing, but I can do nothing about it. If an all-powerful being came and told me that of the two propositions, "there are bodies" and "an infinity of curves pass between the circle and its tangent," one proposition was false and asked me to guess which one, I would guess the latter; for knowing how ignorant I was for a long time of that proposition and how I had needed all my attention to understand its proof, and then found difficulties with it, and knowing, finally, that geometric truths have reality only in my mind, I would suspect that I had erred. There are no geometric demonstrations to prove I have a mother and father; but the truth of this proposition is nevertheless evident.

Be that as it may, as my principal aim here is to examine man as a social being, and as I cannot be a social being unless there is a society and consequently objects outside ourselves, the Pyrrhonians must allow me to start by believing firmly that there are bodies, otherwise I shall have to deny existence to these gentlemen.

CHAPTER 5—WHETHER MAN HAS A SOUL, AND WHAT IT MIGHT BE

We are certain that we are matter, that we feel, and that we think. We have been persuaded of the existence of a God whose work we are, by reasons our minds will not rebel against. We have proved to ourselves that this God has created what exists. We are convinced that it is impossible for us, and that it must be impossible for us, to know how he has given us being. But can we know what does the thinking in us? What is this faculty which God has given us? Is it matter which feels and thinks? Is it an immaterial substance? In a word, what is a soul? Here, it is more than ever necessary to put myself back into the state of a thinking being, descended from another planet, having none of the preconceptions of this planet, and having the same abilities as myself, though without being what we call man, and considering man in an impartial way.

If I were a superior being to whom the Creator had revealed his secrets, I would be able to tell as soon as I saw man what this animal was; I would be able to define his soul and all his capabilities from knowledge of the facts with as much boldness as all those philosophers who defined him while knowing nothing about him; but acknowledging my ignorance and trying out my feeble reasoning powers, the only thing I can do is use the analytical process, which is the stick that nature gave to the blind; I shall examine it all, section by section, and then see if I can judge the whole.

I shall assume therefore that I have arrived in Africa and am surrounded by negroes, Hottentots, and other animals. I notice first of all that the organs of life are the same as ours, the actions of their bodies are based on the same principles as ours; they all have, as far as I can see, the same desires, the same emotions, the same needs, although they express them in their own languages. The language I understand first is that of the animals; it could not be otherwise. The sounds they make do not seem arbitrary, they are living symbols of their emotions; these signs bear the imprints of the emotions they are expressing: the cry of a dog who wants food, taken with his whole posture, has a reasonable relationship to its object; I can pick out straightaway the cries and movements he uses to please another animal or those he uses to hunt or those he uses to complain; I can even discern whether his complaint expresses the anxieties of solitude, the pain of a wound, or the impatience of love. So, after some observation, I can understand the language of all the animals; they have no feeling which they do not express; perhaps it is not the same with their ideas, but as it seems that nature has given them few ideas, it also seems to me that it would be natural for them to have a limited language, in proportion to their perceptions.

What differences do I encounter in the negro animals? What can I see there, except a few extra ideas and combinations of ideas in their heads, expressed in a language pronounced differently? The more I examine all these beings, the more I have to suspect that they are different species of the same genus; this admirable faculty they have of retaining ideas is common to them all; they all have dreams and faint images during sleep of ideas that they received while awake; their faculty of sense and thought grows with their organs, becomes weak with them, perishes with them; if a monkey and a negro lose blood, they are both soon in such a state of exhaustion that they are beyond recognizing me; soon afterwards, their senses no longer function, and finally they die.

I ask then what gave them life, sensation, thought; it was not their own work nor that of matter, as I have already proved to myself, therefore it is God who gave all these bodies the power to feel and to have ideas to different degrees, suited to their organs. That, I am sure, is what I shall at first suspect.

Finally, I see some men who seem to me to be superior to these negroes, as the negroes are to monkeys, and as monkeys are to oysters and other animals of that kind.

Some philosophers will tell me: Do not deceive yourself, man is entirely different from other animals; he has a spiritual and immortal soul; for (note this well) if thought were a product of matter it would necessarily be the same as that from which it is made — it would be divisible, capable of movement, etc. Now, thought cannot be divided, thus it is not a product of matter; it has no parts, it is single, it is immortal, it is the work and the image of a God. I listen to these masters, and I reply, as mistrustful as ever of myself but with no trust in them: if man has a soul, such as you assert, I must believe that the dog and the mole have exactly similar ones. They all swear to me that it is not so. I ask them what difference there is between the dog and them. Some reply: the dog is a substantial form. Others say: don't believe it — substantial forms are a myth; this dog is a machine like a skewer and nothing more. I ask the inventors of substantial forms again what they mean by the term, and as the reply is sheer nonsense, I go back to the inventors of skewers and say to them: If these beasts are pure machines, you are without doubt in relation to them, only what a watch which sounds the hour is in relation to a skewer; so if you have the honor of possessing a spiritual soul, the animals have one as well, for they have all that you have, they have the same sense organs as you do. If these sense organs are not used by them to the same ends, God has performed a useless task in providing them, and God, according to you, does nothing in vain. Choose therefore either to award a spiritual soul to a flea, to a worm, to a mite, or to be an automaton like them. All that these gentlemen can say in response is that they presume that the mechanisms in the animals which appear to be sense-organs are necessary to life, and in animals are nothing but mechanisms of life; but this reply is only an unreasonable assumption.

It is certain that one needs neither nose nor ears nor eyes to live. There are animals which do not have these senses and still live; therefore these sense-organs are only given for producing sensation; therefore the animals sense like us; therefore it can only be from excessively ridiculous vanity that men award themselves a soul of a different kind from that which animates the beasts. So, it is clear that up to now neither the philosophers nor I know what the soul is; all I have proved for myself is that it is something common to the animal called "man" and the animal called "beast." Let us now see if this faculty common to all these animals is matter or not.

It is impossible, I am told, for matter to think. I cannot see this impossibility. If thought were a product of matter, as they tell me, I would affirm that thought would have to be extended and divisible; but if thought is an attribute of God, given to matter, I cannot see that it is necessary for this attribute to be extended and divisible; for I see that God has transmitted other properties to matter which have neither extension nor divisibility; movement, gravitation, for example, which acts without intermediary bodies and which acts in direct proportion to the mass, not the surfaces, and in inverse square proportion to distance, is a real and demonstrated property whose cause is as hidden as that of thought.

In a word, I can only judge from what I can see, and according to what appears to me to be the most probable; I see that everywhere in nature the same effect implies the same cause. Thus I judge that the same cause acts in beasts and men, but in proportion to the capacity of their organs; I believe that this element common to men and beasts is an attribute given by God to matter. For if what one calls *soul* were a separate type of being, whatever the nature of this being, I would have to believe that its essence was thought, otherwise I could have no idea of this substance. Likewise, all those who have assumed an immaterial soul have been obliged to say that this soul is always thinking; but I appeal to the consciences of all these men: Do they think all the time? Do they think while soundly asleep? Do beasts constantly have ideas? Does an unconscious man have many ideas while in that state, which is really a temporary death? If the soul is not always thinking, then it is absurd to attribute to man a substance whose essence is to think.

What could we conclude from this except that God has arranged the body for thinking as well as for eating and digesting? By informing myself on the history of the human species, I learn that men have long held the same opinion as mine on this subject. I read the world's most ancient book, preserved by those who claim to be the most ancient people; this book even tells me that God seems to think like me; it teaches me that God gave to the Jews long ago the most detailed laws that a nation has ever received; it even instructs them on how they should go to the toilet, but it does not say one word to them about their soul; it tells them only of earthly sorrows and rewards. This proves at the very least that the author of this book did not live in a nation which believed in the spirituality and immortality of the soul.

I am indeed told that two thousand years later God came to teach men that their souls are immortal; but, coming myself from another planet, I cannot help being astonished at this disparity being attributed to God. It seems strange, to my way of reasoning, that God would have made men believe both sides of the argument; but if it is a point of revelation where my reason cannot see at all, then I shall hold my tongue and adore in silence. It is not for me to examine what has been revealed; I note only that these books of revelation do not say that the soul is spiritual; they say only that it is immortal. I do not find that hard to believe; for it seems just as possible for God to form the soul (whatever nature it has) to be preserved as to be destroyed. The God who can preserve or annihilate the movement of a body as he pleases can surely make the faculty of thought in one part of that body last forever; if he has indeed told us that this part is immortal, then we have to be convinced it is so.

But what is this soul made of? That is what the supreme being has not judged appropriate to teach men. Therefore, although the only guides in my research are my own insights, the desire to know things, and the sincerity of my heart, I shall seek honestly whatever my reason by itself can discover for me; I shall try out its strength, not to make it think it can carry all these immense burdens, but to improve it by exercise and to teach myself how far its power can reach. Thus, although always ready to give in as soon as revelation puts up its barriers in front of me, I shall continue my reflections and my conjectures solely as a philosopher until my reason can advance no further.

CHAPTER 6—WHETHER MAN IS IMMORTAL

This is not the place to examine whether God has, in fact, revealed the immortality of the soul. I am still assuming that I am a philosopher from another planet, who judges only according to my reason. This reason has taught me that all the ideas of men and animals come to them via their senses; I confess that I cannot help laughing when I am told that men will still have ideas when they no longer have senses. When a man loses his nose, the lost nose is no more a part of him than the pole star. When he loses all his parts and is no longer a man, isn't it then a little strange to say that he keeps the results of the organs which perished? I might just as well say that he eats and drinks after his death as say that he keeps his ideas after death; one is no more illogical than the other, and it certainly needed a fair number of centuries before anyone dared to make such an astonishing proposition. I know very well, I repeat, that as God has connected the ability to have ideas to a part of the brain, he can preserve this faculty only if he preserves this part of the brain; for preserving this faculty without the part would be as impossible as preserving a man's laugh or a bird's song after the death of the man or the bird. God could also have given men and animals a plain, immaterial soul, which he preserves independently of their bodies. For him, that is just as possible as creating a million worlds more than he did or giving me two noses and four hands, wings and claws; but if we are to believe that he has, in fact, done all these possible things, it seems to me that we would have to see them.

Seeing then no more than the extension and the feelings of man, let us assume he has something immortal. Who will prove to me that it is immortal? What! Me, even though I do not know its nature, I shall affirm that it is eternal! Me, though I know man did not exist yesterday, I shall affirm that there is in this man a part which is eternal by its nature! And while I shall refuse immortality to whatever animates the dog, the parrot, the lark, I shall award it to man just because he desires it!

It would indeed be very sweet to survive one's own self, to keep forever the most excellent part of one's being, while the other is destroyed, to live eternally with one's friends, etc. This fantasy (considered in that one sense) would be a consolation among real miseries. That is perhaps why the system of transmigration of souls was invented in earlier times; but is this system any more probable than the *Thousand and One Nights*? And is it not just the fruit of the lively and absurd imagination of the majority of oriental philosophers? But I shall assume, in spite of all probability, that God preserves what one calls man's "soul" after his death and that he abandons the soul of brute beasts to the way of ordinary destruction of all things. I shall ask what man gains by that; I shall ask what the spirit of Jacques has in common with Jacques when he is dead?

What forms Jacques as a person, what makes Jacques himself and the same self that he was yesterday in his own eyes is that he remembers the ideas he had yesterday and that he associates, in his mind, his existence yesterday with his existence today; for if he had lost his memory entirely, his past existence would be as unknown to him as that of any other man; he would no more be the Jacques of yesterday, the same person, than he would be Socrates or Caesar. Now, supposing Jacques, during his final illness, totally lost his memory, and as a consequence, died without being the same Jacques who had lived. Would God give back to his soul that memory which was lost? Would he create afresh those ideas which no longer existed? And in that case, wouldn't he be a new man, as different from the one who existed before as an Indian is from a European?

But one can also say that if Jacques entirely lost his memory before dying, his soul could recover it again just as one recovers it after fainting or after a fever, because a man who entirely loses his memory when gravely ill does not cease to be the same man when he recovers his memory. Thus, Jacques' soul, if he has one, and which should be immortal by God's will, as one assumes, could recover his memory after death, just as it recovers his memory after a fainting spell during life; thus Jacques will be the same man.

These difficulties are well worth the trouble of suggesting them, and whoever finds a sure way of solving the equation for this unknown quantity, will be, I think, a clever man.

I shall not advance further into the darkness; I shall stop here where the light of my candle ceases to reach, it's enough for me that I can see the limits of where I can go. I do not assert that I have proofs against the spirituality and the immortality of the soul; but all the probabilities are against it; it is equally unjust and unreasonable to demand proof from an enquiry in which only conjectures are possible.

One must, however, anticipate the attitude of those who believe that the mortality of the soul would be contrary to the well-being of society and remind them that the ancient Jews, whose laws they admire, believed that the soul was material and mortal, not to mention the great schools of ancient philosophers who regarded the Jews highly and who were very honorable men.

CHAPTER 7—WHETHER MAN IS FREE

Perhaps there is no simpler question than that about liberty; but there is none which men have made more complicated. The difficulties which philosophers have raised over this issue and the foolhardy desire of some people to wrest God's secret from him and reconcile his foreknowledge with free will have caused the idea of liberty to become obscured by the efforts of those who claimed to clarify it. We are so unaccustomed to pronouncing the word *freedom* without remembering all the problems which accompany it, that now we scarcely know what we mean when we ask if man is free.

This is not the place to imagine a being endowed with reason who is not human and who can examine man impartially. On the contrary, it is here that each man must look within himself and testify to his own experience.

Let us immediately strip the problem of all the fantasies with which we are accustomed to surround it and define what we mean by this word *freedom*. Freedom is solely the power to act. If a stone moved by its own choice, it would be free; animals and men have this power; therefore they are free. I can with great effort dispute the right of animals to this faculty; I can imagine, if I don't mind misusing my reason, that the beasts who resemble me in every other respect differ from me on that sole point. I can conceive of them as machines without sensations, or desires or will, even though they appear to have all these. I shall invent systems, that is to say, errors to explain their nature; but, finally, when I come to examine myself, I shall really have to admit that I have a will and that I have within me the power to act, to move my body, and to apply my thoughts to this or that matter, etc.

If someone comes and says to me: You think you have a will, but you haven't; you have an experience which is deceiving you, just as you think you see the sun as two feet wide, yet its size, in proportion to the earth, is about a million to one. I shall reply to this person: But that's different; God did not deceive me by making me see the size of something far away in proportion to its distance; the mathematical laws of optics are such that I can and must see objects only in direct proportion to their size and distance; the nature of my organs are such that if my eyes could perceive the real size of a star, I would not be able to see any object on earth. It is the same with the sense of hearing and the sense of smell. The sensations I receive vary in strength, other things being equal, according to the distance I am from the loud or fragrant objects. In that case there is no error, but if I had no will and though I had, God would have purposely created me to deceive me; just as if he had made me believe there were bodies outside myself, although there were not; the only result of this deception would be a foolish act by a supreme being with infinite wisdom.

And let no one say that it is unworthy of a philosopher to appeal here to God as proof. For, first of all, accepting this God as proven, it is also proven that he is the cause of my liberty if I am free; that he is the foolish author of my error, if after making me into a being who merely endures without will, he then makes me think that I am an agent and free. Secondly, supposing there is no God, who would have led me into this error? What would have given me this feeling of freedom while subjecting me to slavery? Would it be matter, which cannot of itself have intelligence? I cannot be informed or deceived by matter nor receive the ability to will from it; I cannot have received from God the feeling that I have a will unless I have one; therefore I really have a will, therefore I am my own agent.

To will and to act, that is precisely the same as to be free. God himself can only be free in this sense. He has willed and has acted according to his will. If one assumed that his will was necessarily determined, if one said: he necessarily willed what he did, it would be as ridiculous as saying; there is and there isn't a God; for if God were necessity, he would no longer be an agent, he would be passive, and he would no longer be God.

We must never lose sight of these fundamental and interconnected truths. There is something which exists; therefore some being exists from all eternity; therefore this being exists by his own means of an absolute necessity; therefore he is infinite; therefore all other beings come from him, although we do not know how; therefore he was able to transmit freedom to them just as he transmitted movement and life; therefore he gave us this freedom which we feel within us, as he gave us the life we feel within us.

The freedom within God is the power always to think all that he wants to think and always to make happen all that he wants to happen. The freedom given by God to man is the weak, limited, and temporary power to consider a few thoughts and make certain movements happen. The freedom of children who have not yet begun to think and of animals who will never think consists simply in being able to will and bring about movements. On what basis could one imagine that there was no freedom? Here are the causes of that error. It was seen from the first that we often have violent emotions which lead us astray in spite of ourselves. A man would prefer not to love his unfaithful mistress and yet desires stronger than reason drive him back to her; we are led to take violent action in bouts of temper which we cannot master; we would like to lead a quiet life, yet ambition throws us into the excitement of business.

So many visible chains burden us nearly all our life that we think we are tied down everywhere else, too; it has been said: sometimes man is carried away rapidly with violent tremors whose shakings he senses, and sometimes he is led by a gentle movement of which he is no more the master; he is a slave who does not always feel the weight and dishonor of his chains, but he is always a slave.

That reasoning, which is only the logic of human weakness, is similar to this: Men are sometimes ill, thus they are never well. Now, who cannot see the absurdity of that conclusion? Who, on the contrary, cannot see that to feel ill is an irrefutable proof that one has been well and that to feel one's slavery and impotence is invincible proof that one has had power and freedom?

When you were in that furious temper, your will was no longer obeyed by your senses; you were no more free then than when a paralysis stops you moving the arm you wish to move. If a man were dominated all his life by violent tempers or if his brain were always possessed by certain thoughts, he would lack that part of his humanity which consists of being able to think sometimes what one wants to think; that is the situation of several madmen whom we lock up and even a good many others whom we don't.

What is really certain is that there are some men who are freer than others for the same reason that we are not all equally enlightened, equally strong, etc. Freedom is the health of the soul; in few people is this health complete and unchanging. Our liberty is weak and limited, like our other faculties. We strengthen it when we habitually reflect on our actions; this exercise of the soul makes it a little more vigorous. But whatever effort we make, we could never manage to make our reason rule our desires; there will always be involuntary movements in our soul as there are in our body. We are only free, wise, strong, healthy, and witty to a very small degree. If we were always free, we would be what God is. Let us be content with a share suitable to the rank we hold in nature. But let us not believe that we lack those things we feel we possess; just because we do not have the attributes of God, we do not surrender our claims to the faculties of man.

In the middle of a ball or during a lively conversation or when the pains of illness made my head heavy, I would try in vain to calculate the thirty-fifth part of ninety-five thirds and a half, multiplied by twenty-five nineteenths and three quarters; I would not have the freedom to do such a sum. But a little rest would soon give me back that power I had lost in the excitement. The most determined enemies of freedom are thus forced to allow that we have a will which is sometimes obeyed by our senses: "But this will," they say, "is necessarily determined, just as a pair of scales is moved by the greater weight; man only wills what he judges to be the better; his understanding is not an authority which can decide something is bad which to him appears good. The understanding works necessarily; the will is determined by the understanding; thus the will is determined, thus man is not free."

This dazzling argument, which in reality is only a fallacy, has seduced many people, because men rarely do more than glance at the ideas they examine. Let us see where the fault in this argument lies. Man can certainly only will those things of which he has some idea. He could not want to go to the opera if he had no idea of the opera; he would not wish to go there and would not choose to go there if his understanding did not represent this opera to him as something agreeable. Now, that it what his freedom is; it is the power to choose for himself to do what appears to him to be good; to will what would not give him pleasure is a contradiction in terms and an impossibility. Man chooses that which seems to him the best and that is indisputable; but the point of the question is to know whether he has within himself that motive force, that original power to choose or not. Those who say: "The assent of the mind is necessary and determines the will necessarily," assume that the mind acts in a physical way on the will. They are talking obvious nonsense; for they are assuming that a thought is a small real being who really acts upon another being called the will; it does not occur to them that these words "will," "understanding," etc. are only abstract ideas, invented to add clarity and order to our discussion and which mean nothing except man "thinking" and man "willing." The "understanding" and the "will" therefore do not exist really as different beings, and it is irrelevant to say that one acts upon the other.

If they do not assume that the mind acts physically upon the will, they must say either that man is free or that God acts for man, determines man's actions, and is eternally busy deceiving man; in which case they must at least admit that God is free. If God is free, freedom is therefore possible, and man can therefore have it. So they have no reason for saying that man is not free. They have tried to say that man is determined by pleasure; that acknowledges that there is freedom, although without them realizing it; because to do what gives pleasure is to be free.

God, I say again, can only be free in this way. He can only work according to his pleasure. All the fallacious arguments against the freedom of man also attack the freedom of God.

The last refuge of the enemies of freedom is in the following argument: "God knows with certainty when a thing will happen; thus it is not in man's power not to do it."

First, notice that this argument again attacks that freedom which we are obliged to recognize in God. One can say: God knows what will happen; it is not in his power not to do what will happen. What does this oft-repeated argument prove? Nothing, except that we do not know and cannot know what God's foresight is and that all his attributes are, for us, impenetrable abysses.

We know by demonstration that if God exists, God is free; we know at the same time that he knows all; but this foresight and omniscience are as incomprehensible to us as his greatness, his infinite existence in the past, his infinite existence in the future, the creation, the conservation of the universe, and so many other things that we cannot either deny or understand.

This dispute over God's foreknowledge has caused so many quarrels because we are ignorant and conceited. What would it cost us to say: I do not know what the attributes of God are, and I am not constructed for grasping his essence? But that is what a Bachelor or Graduate cannot bring himself to assert; that is what has made them the most absurd of men and turned a holy science into miserable charlatanism.

CHAPTER 8—MAN CONSIDERED AS A SOCIAL BEING

The grand design of nature's author seems to be to preserve each individual for a certain time and to perpetuate his species. Each animal is always attracted by an unconquerable instinct toward all which can lead to his own preservation; yet, there are moments when he is carried away by an instinct which is almost equally strong to unite with another and propagate his species, without us ever being able to say exactly how all this happens.

The wildest and most solitary animals leave their lairs when love calls them and for a few months feel themselves tied by invisible chains to the females and the young which they bear; after which they forget this temporary family and return to their savage solitude until the spur of love forces them out once again. Other species are formed by nature to live always as a group, some, such as bees, ants, beavers, and a few species of birds in a truly organized society; others, such as cattle on earth and herrings in the sea, gather together only through a blind instinct, which unites them with no apparent design or purpose.

Man is certainly not driven by instinct to form an organized society such as that of the ants and bees; but if we consider his needs, emotions, and reason, it is easy to see that he would not have stayed for long in a wholly savage state.

For the universe to be what it is today, all it needed was for one man to be in love with one woman. The mutual care they had for each other and their natural love of their children would soon have stimulated their ingenuity and given birth, at first in a rough way, to certain skills. Two families would have needed each other as soon as they were formed, and their needs would have created new articles of trade.

Man is unlike the other animals which have only the instincts of self-interest and procreation. Not only does man have the self-interest which is necessary for his preservation but he also has a natural benevolence toward others of his species which we do not observe in the beasts. If a dog saw another dog, born of the same mother, torn into a thousand pieces and all bloody, she would take a morsel without feeling the least pity and continue on her way; however, this same dog would defend her own young and die fighting rather than let them be taken away.

If, on the other hand, even the most savage man saw a sweet child nearby being devoured by some animal, he would feel, in spite of himself, some disquiet, an anxiety born of pity, and a desire to run to his aid. It is true that this feeling of pity and benevolence is often suppressed by a fierce self-interest; wise nature did not need to give us more love for others than ourselves; with this benevolence we already have much to encourage us to unite with other men.

But benevolence is still too weak an aid to have made us live in society; it could never have served as a foundation for the great empires and flourishing towns if we had not had strong emotions.

These emotions, which, when badly used, have caused so much harm, are, in fact, the principal cause of the order we see on earth today. Pride, especially, is the principal tool used to build the splendid structure or our society. Men had hardly been brought together by mutual need than the cleverest of them noticed that all these men had been born with an ungovernable pride as well as an unconquerable regard for their own welfare.

It is not difficult to persuade them that if they did something for the common good of society which cost them a small amount of their own well-being, their pride would be amply rewarded for it.

Men were thus divided into two classes from early on: the first, those saintly men who sacrifice their self-interest for the public good; the second, wretches who love only themselves. Everyone wanted and still wants to be in the first class, although everyone at heart is in the second; the men who were the meanest and most self-indulgent shouted more loudly than the others that everything should be sacrificed for the public good. The love of being in authority, which is an offshoot of pride and which can be seen as clearly in a schoolmaster or village sheriff as in a pope or an emperor, was an even more powerful stimulus to man's skill at persuading some men to obey others; one only needed to make it clear to them that one knew more than they did and that one would be useful to them. It was necessary, above all, to use men's greed to buy their obedience. The frantic acquisition of worldly goods added daily improvement in all skills.

This machine would still not have gone very far if it had not been helped by envy, a very natural emotion which men always disguise by calling it emulation. This envy woke up the idle and sharpened the ingenuity of anyone who saw that his neighbor was powerful or prosperous. Thus, by degrees, emotions by themselves grouped men together and extracted all the skills and pleasures from the earth. By this means, God, whom Plato called "the eternal geometer," but whom I shall call here "the eternal machine-maker," gave life and beauty to nature; emotions are the wheels which drive all these machines.

Our modern logicians who are trying to prove their fantasy that man was born without emotions and was only given them because he disobeyed God might just as well have said that man was at first a beautiful statue, formed by God, and was later brought to life by the devil.

Self-interest and all its ramifications are as necessary to man as the blood coursing through his veins; those who want to take away a man's emotions because they are dangerous resemble someone wanting to take away all his blood, in case he has a stroke.

What would we say about someone who claimed that the winds were an invention of the devil, because they make some ships sink, and didn't imagine them to be a kindness from God so that commerce could join together all the places on earth divided by enormous seas?

It is quite clear therefore that we owe the order and the useful inventions, with which we have enriched the universe, to our emotions and our needs; it is very likely that God only gave us the needs and the emotions so that our ingenuity would use them to our advantage. Even if so many men have abused them, it is not for us to complain about a benefit which some have misused. God kindly put a thousand delicious foods on earth for man; the gluttony of those who turned this food into a poison which can kill them cannot be used to criticize Providence.

CHAPTER 9—CONCERNING VIRTUE AND VICE

In order for a society to exist, laws were needed — rules are needed for every game. Most of these laws seem to be arbitrary; they depend on the concerns, emotions, and opinions of those who invented them, and on the type of climate of the place where the men gathered together as a social group. In a hot country, where wine makes people wild, drinking is considered a crime; in colder climates, it is respectable to become drunk. In one place a man must be content with one wife; in another he is allowed to have as many as he can support. In some countries, fathers and mothers beg strangers to sleep with their daughters; everywhere else, a girl who gives herself to a man is disgraced. In Sparta adultery was encouraged; in Athens it was punishable with death. Among the Romans, fathers had the right of life and death over their children. In Normandy, a father cannot deprive his most disobedient son of the least part of his estate. The king's name is sacred for many nations and detested in others.

But all these peoples, who conduct their affairs so differently, are united on this point: that they call "virtuous" whatever conforms to their established laws and "criminal" whatever is contrary to them. Thus, in Holland a man who resists arbitrary power will be a very virtuous man; in France a man who wants to set up a republican government will be condemned to death. The same Jew who in Metz would be sent to the galleys if he had two wives would be able to have four wives in Constantinople and would be more highly esteemed by Muslims for it.

Most of these laws are so obviously contradictory that it hardly matters by which laws a State governs itself; but what really matters is that once the laws are established, they are enforced. In the same way, it is of no importance whether there are these rules or those rules for games with dice or cards; but one could not play for a single moment if the arbitrary rules which had been agreed upon were not strictly followed.

Virtue and vice, moral good and moral evil, are then in every country, whatever is useful or harmful to society. In every place and in every age whoever sacrifices the most for the public good is the one who will be called the most virtuous. It seems then that good actions are nothing other than actions from which we all benefit, and crimes are the opposite. Virtue is the habit of doing those things which please men, and vice is the habit of doing things which displease them.

Although what is called virtue in one climate may be precisely what is called vice in another, and although the majority of rules on good and evil vary as much as languages and clothes, nevertheless, it seems certain to me that there are natural laws which men are obliged to acknowledge throughout the universe, whatever they might say. It is true that God did not say to men: Look, here are laws which I am giving you directly from my mouth, by which I want you to govern yourselves; but he has done for men what he has done for many other animals. He gave bees a powerful instinct which makes them work and feed together, and he gave man certain feelings which he can never shake off and which are the permanent ties and first laws of society in which he foresaw that men would live. Our benevolence toward our own species, for example, is born with us and is always working within us, unless it conflicts with self-love, which must always prevail. So a man is always inclined to help another man when it doesn't cost him anything. Even the most barbaric savage returning from slaughter, and dripping with the blood of the enemies he has eaten, will be moved by the sight of a comrade's suffering and will give him all the help in his power.

Adultery and homosexuality may be allowed by many nations, but you will not find any place where breaking one's word is allowed; because a society can well exist among adulterers or homosexuals, but not among people who boast of deceiving one another. Petty theft was in favor in Sparta because all goods were held in common; but as soon as you institute "yours" and "mine," it will be impossible for you not to regard theft as contrary to society and consequently as unjust.

It is so true that the well-being of society is the sole standard for measuring moral good and evil, that we are forced to change, according to need, all the ideas we have formed for ourselves on justice and injustice.

We are horrified by a father sleeping with his daughter, and we also brand as incestuous the brother who abuses his sister; but in a new colony where there was only a father with his son and two daughters, we would consider it a very good action if this family took care not to let the species perish. A man who kills his brother is a monster; but a man who had no other means to save his country than by sacrificing his brother would be an admirable man.

We all love truth, and we make it into a virtue because it is in our own interest not to be deceived. We have attached all the more disgrace to lying because it is the easiest of all wrong acts to hide and the one which is the least costly to commit; yet look how often the lie turns into a heroic deed! When it's a matter of saving a friend's life, someone who told the truth on that occasion would be covered in shame; we would not see much difference between a man who slandered someone who was innocent and a man who, although he could have saved his brother's life by lying, preferred to abandon him by telling the truth. M. de Thou who had his head cut off because he would not reveal the conspiracy of Cinq Mars is held in blessed memory by the French; if he had not lied, he would be remembered with disgust.[1]

But, someone will tell me, in that case crime and virtue, moral good and evil, will only exist in relation to us; will there be no good which exists by itself, independent of man? I shall ask those who put that question whether cold and hot, sweet and sour, good and bad smells exist except in relation

[1]Voltaire here refers to the trial and execution of François-Auguste de Thou (1607–1642) for his involvement in the so-called Cinq Mars conspiracy. The ringleaders of this conspiracy, which was primarily directed against the harsh rule of Cardinal Richelieu, were Louis XIII's brother and the Marquis de Cinq Mars. De Thou was not only not one of the conspirators, but when he was told about the plot he tried to persuade Cinq Mars to abandon his plan. De Thou was nevertheless condemned for *not* informing the authorities about what he knew. Voltaire discusses the case at some length in Chapter XV of the *Commentary on the Book Crimes and Punishments*, which is a scathing indictment of the absurd and unjust laws relating to high treason in England as well as in France. Françoise-Auguste de Thou should not be confused with Jacques-Auguste de Thou (1553–1617), his much more famous father. The elder de Thou, as president of the Paris *parlement*, faithfully served Henry IV and the cause of religious toleration. It was he who negotiated the Edict of Nantes of 1598, which brought religious

to us? Isn't it true that a man who claimed that heat exists all by itself would be a very poor reasoner? So, would a person who claimed that a moral good exists independently of us be reasoning any better? Our physical state can only be good or bad in relation to us; why should our moral state of good or bad be any different?

Aren't the aims of the Creator, who wanted men to live in society, adequately fulfilled? If some law had fallen out of the sky and taught men really clearly what was God's will, then the moral good could only be conformity to that law. If God were to say to men: "I want so many kingdoms on earth, and not one republic; I want the younger son to inherit all the father's estate, and the eating of turkeys and pigs punishable by death," then these laws will certainly become the unalterable rules of good and evil. But as God has not condescended, as far as I know, to interfere in that way in our arrangements, we shall have to be content with those gifts he has given us. Those gifts are reason, self-love, benevolence toward our own species, needs, emotions, all the means by which we have set up society.

Lots of people are ready to say to me here: If it adds to my well-being to upset your society, to kill, to steal, to slander, there will be nothing now to restrain me, and I can give way to all my emotions without scruple! The only thing I have to say to those people is that they will probably be hung, just as I shall kill wolves which carry off my sheep. It is precisely for those men that the laws were made, like tiles were invented to protect us from hail and rain.

As to the princes who posses force and abuse it to devastate the globe, who send some men to their death and reduce the rest to poverty, it is men's own fault that they suffer this abominable destruction, which they often even honor with the name of virtue. They have no one to blame but themselves for the bad laws they have made or the feebleness which stops them from having good laws enforced.

All these princes who have done so much harm to men are the first to proclaim that God has given rules on good and evil. There isn't one of these scourges of the earth who doesn't participate in the solemn rites of religion; so I cannot see that much is gained by having such rules. It is a misfortune associated with human nature that, in spite of our desire for self-preservation, we mutually destroy each other in anger and madness. Almost all animals devour one another, and among the human species the males

---

peace to France for several decades. He was also noted for his *Historia sui Temporis,* a vast history of the sixteenth century, which has been praised by subsequent historians as a model of exact scholarship. Voltaire knew and admired this work calling de Thou "the only good historian of which France can boast." In the article "Julian the Philosopher," this praise is qualified. "From Titus Livius up to including de Thou," Voltaire there writes, "all histories are infected with miracles."

exterminate themselves by war. It even seems as if God has anticipated that disaster by causing more males to be born than females; in fact, the peoples who have thought most carefully about the interests of humanity and who keep exact records of births and deaths have noticed that, on the average, one twelfth more males than females are born each year.

From all this it will be easy to see that it is very likely that all these murders and robberies are disastrous for society, without it concerning God in the least. God has put men and animals on earth, but it is up to them to conduct themselves there as well as they can. It is unfortunate for the flies who are trapped by spiders' webs, it is unfortunate for the bull that is attacked by a lion, and for the sheep which encounter wolves! But if a sheep were to say to a wolf: You lack moral worth, and God will punish you; the wolf would reply: I'm doing what is good for my body, and it appears that God does not care very much whether I eat you or not. All that the sheep has to do to improve things is not to wander from the shepherd or the dog that can defend him.

If only the supreme being had been pleased to give us laws and to recommend the punishments and rewards! If only he had said to us: This is vice in itself, this is virtue in itself. But we are so far from having rules about good and evil that all those who have dared to give men laws on God's behalf, there isn't one who has given one ten-thousandth part of the rules we need to conduct our lives.

If someone were to infer from all this that he has only to give in unreservedly to all the frenzy of unbridled desire, and since he has no virtue or vice in himself, he can do anything without fear of punishment, then that man must first of all ensure that he has an army of one hundred thousand soldiers very keen to serve him; otherwise he will be taking a great risk by thus declaring himself as an enemy of the human race. But if he is just an ordinary individual, if he has the least bit of reason, he will see that he has chosen a very poor course and that he will certainly be punished, either by the punishments which men have so wisely devised for enemies of society or just by the fear of punishment, which is cruel torture in itself. He will see that the life of those who defy the law is usually the most miserable.

It is morally impossible that a wicked man will not be found out; as soon as there is the least suspicion about him, he will be forced to realize that he is the object of contempt and hatred. Now, God has wisely endowed us with a pride which can never bear other men hating or despising us; being despised by those we live with is something which no one ever could or will be able to endure. Perhaps that is the greatest restraint nature has placed on the unjust acts of men; it is by this mutual fear that God has considered it appropriate to bind men. So any reasonable man will conclude that it is obviously in his own interest to be honorable. The understanding he will have of the human heart and the conviction he will have that there is neither virtue nor vice in itself will never stop him from being a good citizen or from fulfilling all life's duties. But then one can see that philosophers (who are branded as unbelievers and libertarians) have through the ages been the most honorable men in the world. Without drawing up a list here of all the great men of antiquity, we know that La Mothe le Vayer, tutor to Louis XIII's brother, Bayle, Locke, Spinoza, Lord Shaftesbury, Collins, etc., were men of strict virtue; it was not only the fear of men's scorn which made them virtuous, it was their liking for virtue itself. A rational individual is honest for the same reason that a clear palate prefers the excellent wine from Nuitz to the wine from Brie, and partridges from Le Mans to horse meat. A healthy education perpetuates these feelings among all men, and from that comes the universal sentiment we call "honor," which the most corrupted men cannot shake off and which is the pivot of society. Those who need the help of religion to be honorable are really to be pitied; they would need to be monsters if they could not find within themselves the social sentiments necessary for their society and were obliged to borrow from elsewhere what they ought to find in their own nature.

How We Know Distance, Size, Shape, and Position

As explained in the introduction, Voltaire wrote two books on Newton, *The Elements of the Newtonian Philosophy* (1738) and *The Metaphysics of Newton* (1740), which were combined into one book in 1741. A second edition was published in 1748 and a third in 1756. The present selection consists of most of Chapter VI of the original edition of 1738, which became Chapter V of Part II of the book in its later form. It is of some interest to note that Voltaire reprinted the major portions of this chapter under the title "Distance" in his *Questions Concerning the Encyclopedia* (1772). He added one paragraph, which I have inserted as a footnote in the appropriate place. Voltaire habitually misspelled English words and names. Bishop Berkeley is referred to as "Dr. Barclay," and Dr. Cheselden, the surgeon who performed the celebrated operation on the blind man, as "Chiselden." I have substituted the correct spellings. Two paragraphs that did not seem to advance Voltaire's argument have been omitted. The subheadings are Voltaire's own. He put them at the head of the chapter, but I have inserted them in the text.

DISTANCE NOT KNOWN FROM THE OPTIC ANGLES AND LINES

Let us begin with distance. It is plain that it cannot itself be immediately perceived; for distance is no more than a line from an object to us. This line terminates in a point; we therefore perceive only this point; and whether the object be a thousand miles or only a foot from us, the point is still the same. We do not therefore have any immediate means of knowing distance instantly, as we have by touch, of distinguishing whether a body is hard or soft; by taste, whether it is sweet or bitter; and by the ear, whether of two sounds one is low and the other high. The idea of distance must therefore be attained by means of some other intermediate idea; but I must at least have that intermediate idea at the same time; for an idea that I do not have will certainly never occasion my having another. I say a house is a mile from a certain river; but if I don't know where the river is, I certainly don't know where the house is. A body that easily receives an impression from my hand I immediately conclude to be soft; another resists and I immediately perceive its hardness. It would therefore be necessary that I perceive the angles formed in my eyes, in order to determine immediately the distances of objects. But the greatest part of mankind do not so much as know that such angles exist. It is evident therefore these angles cannot be the immediate cause of our knowing distances.

The person who for the first time in his life hears the noise of a cannon, or the harmony of a concert, would not be able to judge whether the cannon was discharged, or the concert performed at the distance of a league or at that of thirty paces. Only experience can accustom him to judge of the distance between him and the place from which those sounds came. The vibrations, the undulations of the air, convey sounds to his ears, or rather to his mind, but they apprize him no more of the place where the sounds commenced than they instruct him about the shape of the cannon, or of the instruments that produced the music. It is exactly the same thing with respect to the rays of light transmitted from an object: they do not inform us at all of the distance of that object.

SIZE AND SHAPE NOT KNOWN BY THESE OPTIC LINES

Nor do they afford us any more information with regard to size and shape. I see at a great distance what seems to be a small round tower. I advance, I look, and touch a large quadrangular building. Certainly what I now see and touch is not what I saw before. The little round object which was before my eyes is not this large square building. The measurable and tangible object therefore is one thing, and the object of vision another. I hear in my room the noise of a coach: I open my window and see it; I go down and get into it. Now this coach, which I have heard, this coach which I have seen, and this coach I have touched, are three absolutely distinct objects of three of my senses, which have no immediate relation to one another.

But it is demonstrated, as I have observed before, that an angle is formed in my eye twice as large (or to speak more precisely that the apparent diameter is double the size) when I see a man at four feet from me, as when I see the same man at a distance of eight feet. However, I always see this man as having the same size. Why should my perception thus contradict the mechanism of my organs? . . . The geometrical lines and angles are no more the cause why we see objects in their proper positions than that we see them of a certain size and at a certain distance. The mind does not consider that, if a certain part were to be painted at the bottom of the eye, it could collect nothing from lines it did not see. The eye turns downward only to see what is near the ground, and upwards to see what is above it. All this could only be explained, and made incontestable by a person born blind, and restored to the sense of sight. For if this blind person, at the moment he received sight, judged correctly of distances, sizes, and positions, it would follow that the optic angles, formed that instant in his retina, were the immediate causes of his thoughts. Dr. Berkeley accordingly has assured us, after Mr. Locke (and indeed has gone beyond Locke in this particular) that neither position, size, distance, nor shape would be at all discerned by a blind person, at the instant his eye should behold the light.[1]

PROOF BY AN EXPERIMENT ON A PERSON BORN BLIND, CURED BY DR. CHESELDEN

But where was the blind person to be found, on whom the indisputable decision of this question depended? In the year 1729, Mr. Cheselden, one of those famous surgeons who combine great knowledge with dexterity in operations, having imagined that sight might be given to a person born blind by removing the cataracts which he believed to have been formed in his eyes almost at the moment of his birth, he proposed an operation.[2] The blind person was reluctant to consent. He could not very well conceive that the sense of sight would contribute greatly to his happiness. He definitely would not have consented if a desire to learn to read and write had not been instilled in him. His indifference in this matter sufficiently proves that *it is impossible to be unhappy by the privation of the good of which we have no idea*, a truth of the last importance. However that be, the operation was performed and succeeded. The youth, then about fourteen years of age, saw the light for the first time and his experience confirmed all that Locke and Berkeley had so ably foreseen. For a long time he distinguished neither size, distance, position, nor even shape. An object of an inch placed before his eyes, that concealed a house from his sight, appeared to him as big as the house.

---

[1]Voltaire here refers to the famous Molyneux problem, which was posed by Locke's friend William Molyneux in the following words:

> Suppose a man born blind, and now adult, and taught by his touch to distinguish between a cube and a sphere of the same metal, and nighly of the same bigness, so as to tell when he felt one and the other, which is the cube, which is the sphere. Suppose then the cube and the sphere placed on a table, and the blind man made to see; query, Whether by his sight, before he touched them, he could now distinguish and tell which is the globe, which the cube? (*Essay Concerning Human Understanding*, II, ix, 8)

To this question Molyneux gave the following answer, which Locke fully endorsed:

> Not. For though he has obtained the experience of how a globe, how a cube, affects his touch, yet he has not yet attained the experience, that what affects his touch so or so, must affect his sight so or so . . .

Everything he saw seemed at first to be upon his eyes, and to touch them, as the objects of the sense of touch are in contact with the skin. He could not distinguish what he had judged round by the help of his hands from what he had judged angular; nor discern with his eyes whether what his hands had perceived to be above or below were really above or below. He was so far from knowing dimension that after having at length conceived by sight that his house was larger than his room, he could not conceive how sight could give him that idea. He could not comprehend, until two months' experience, that pictures are only representations of solid bodies. And when, after so long a trial of his new sense, he though that bodies, and not surfaces only, were painted in the pictures, he applied his hand to them, and was amazed that he did not feel those solid bodies, of which he began to perceive the representations. He asked which deceived him: the sense of touch or that of sight.

This was an indisputable decision, that the manner in which we see objects is no immediate consequence of the angles formed in our eyes; for the same mathematical angles were in the eyes of the youth, as in ours, and were of no manner of use to him without the aid of experience, and the other senses.[3]

HOW WE KNOW SIZE AND DISTANCE

How then do we represent to ourselves size and distance? In the same manner as we imagine the passions of men, by the colors which those passions paint in their faces, and the alteration they make in their features. There is nobody who does not immediately read sorrow or anger in another's countenance. This is the language which nature speaks to every eye; but a language to be learned only by experience. It is experience only that also teaches us, that when an object is too remote, we see it in a confused and faint manner: from this we form ideas, which always accom-

---

Several eighteenth-century philosophers were particularly interested in this question. References to the older as well as to contemporary literature are found in the Bibliography, pp. 237–238.

[2]William Cheselden (1688–1752) was an eminent surgeon and anatomist. The correct date of the operation is 1728, and Voltaire elsewhere remarks that he was in England when it was performed. Cheselden published a paper on this case in the *Philosophical Transactions*, Vol. XXXV, entitled "An Account of Some Observations Made by a Young Gentleman Who Was Born Blind and Was Couch'd Between Thirteen and Fourteen Years of Age."

[3]In the article "Distance," Voltaire at this stage inserts the following paragraph: "The adventure of the man born blind was known in France around the year 1735. The author of *The Elements of the Newtonian Philosophy* who had seen a great deal of Cheselden mentioned this important discovery, but did not take much notice of it, and even when the same cataract operation was performed in Paris on a young man who was said to have been deprived of sight from his cradle, one neglected to follow the daily development of the sense of sight in him. The fruit of this operation was therefore lost to philosophy."

pany the sensation of sight. Thus every man who, at the distance of ten paces, has seen a horse five foot high, if, some minutes later, he sees the same horse no bigger than a sheep, immediately concludes by an involuntary judgment that the horse is at a greater distance.

It is certain that when I see my horse of the size of a sheep, a much smaller picture is formed in my eye — a more acute angle, but that is what attends, not what causes, my thought. In like manner my brain is affected differently when I see a man red with shame, and when I see him red with anger; but those impressions would suggest nothing to me of the passions which agitate the soul of that man, without experience, which alone imparts that knowledge to me.

So far from the angle being the immediate cause of my judgment that a horse is far off when I see it very small, I see my horse equally large at ten, twenty, thirty, or forty paces, though the angle may be double, treble, or quadruple. I see at a great distance, through a little hole, a man on the top of a house; the distance and small number of rays prevent me from distinguishing at first whether it is a man or not. The object seems very small, and I take it for a statue of two feet at most; the object moves and I judge it to be a man, and from that moment he appears to me of his usual height. What is the source of two judgments so different? When I believe I see a statue, I imagine it two feet high, because I see it under such an angle; no experience inclines my mind to contradict the rays impressed upon my retina; but as soon as I judge it a man, the connection implanted in my brain by experience between the idea of a man and the idea of a height from five to six feet obliges me, without thinking of it, to imagine, by an instant judgment, that I see a man of a certain height, and, in effect, to see that height.

WE LEARN TO SEE AS WE LEARN TO READ

From all this we must absolutely conclude that distance, size, and position are not, properly speaking, visible things, that is to say, the proper and immediate objects of sight. The proper and immediate object of sight is nothing but colored light; all the rest we only discover by time and experience. We learn to see exactly as we learn to speak and read. The difference is that the art of seeing is easier and that we are all equally nature's pupils in learning it.

EXTENSION NOT KNOWN BY SIGHT

The spontaneous and almost uniform judgments, which every mind forms at a certain age, of distances, sizes and positions, makes us think it only necessary to open the eyes, in order to see things as they are. But this is a mistake; it requires the help of the other senses. If men had only the sense of sight, they would have no means of knowing the length, breadth, and depth of things; and a pure spirit could never know them, unless God revealed them to him. It is very difficult to separate in our understanding the extension of an object from its colors. We never see anything that is not extended, and from this we are led to the belief that we actually see extension. We can scarcely distinguish in thought the yellow, which we see in a piece of gold, from the piece of gold of which we see the yellow. Thus when we hear the word "guinea" pronounced, we cannot help annexing the idea of that coin to the sound we hear spoken.

If all men spoke the same language, we should always be ready to believe that there is a necessary connection between words and ideas. Now in relation to the imagination all men do in fact have the same language. Nature says to them all: when you have seen colors for a certain time, your imagination will represent to you, in the same manner, all the bodies to which those colors appear attached. That spontaneous and involuntary judgment, which you shall form, shall be useful to you during the course of your lives; for to estimate the distance, size and position of all that surrounds you, it were necessary to examine the angles and rays of vision, you would die before you knew, whether the things you had occasion to use were at the distance of ten paces from you, or at that of a hundred million of leagues, whether they were of the size of a mite or a mountain. In such circumstances it would be better for you to be born blind.

We are therefore very wrong to say that our senses deceive us. Each of them performs the function for which nature intended it. They assist each other, in conveying to our mind by means of experience the measure of knowledge which our condition permits. We demand of our senses what they were not intended to give us. We would have our eyes acquaint us with solidity, size, distance, etc., but touch must unite in this with sight, and experience with both. . . .

Dialogue Between Lucretius
and Posidonius

This selection is the first of two dialogues between Lucretius and Posidonius published in 1756 in Voltaire's *Mélanges de littérature, d'histoire et de philosophie*. Voltaire greatly admired Lucretius (99/96–55/51 B.C.) and his opposition to supernaturalism, but he frequently criticized the materialism expounded in *De Rerum Natura*. It was not unnatural for him to make Lucretius the spokesman for atheism in this dialogue. Some of the statements put into the mouth of the character bearing this name are literal quotations from *De Rerum Natura*. Posidonius (c. 135–c. 51 B.C.) was a Stoic philosopher who is known to have made contributions to Stoic physics and ethics. None of his writings has been preserved and there is no evidence that he held the views advanced by the Posidonius of Voltaire's dialogue. There is also no evidence that he invented the armillary sphere.

POSIDONIUS. Your poetry is sometimes admirable; but the philosophy of Epicurus is, in my opinion, very bad.

LUCRETIUS. What! Will you not allow that the atoms, of their own accord, disposed themselves in such a manner as to produce the universe?

POSIDONIUS. We mathematicians can admit nothing but what is proved by incontestable principles.

LUCRETIUS. My principles are so.

Ex nihilo nihil, in nihilum nil posse reverti.

Tangere enim et tangi nisi corpus nulla potest res.[1]

POSIDONIUS. Should I grant you these principles, and even your atoms and your vacuum, you can no more persuade me that the universe put itself into the admirable order in which we now behold it, than if you were to tell the Romans that the armillary sphere[2] composed by Posidonius made itself.

LUCRETIUS. But who then could make the world?

---

[1] "From nothing nothing is produced, nothing can return to nothing. Nothing can touch and be touched except a body."

[2] An ancient astronomical device consisting of an arrangement of interlocking rings representing the main celestial circles (equator, ecliptic, tropics, etc.) rotating on an axis.

POSIDONIUS. An intelligent Being, much more superior to the world and to me than I am to the brass of which I made my sphere.

LUCRETIUS. How can you, who admit nothing but what is evident, acknowledge a principle of which you have not the least idea?

POSIDONIUS. In the same manner as, before I knew you, I judged that your book was the work of a man of genius.

LUCRETIUS. You allow that nature is eternal, and exists because it does exist. Now if it exists by its own power, why may it not, by the same power, have formed suns, and worlds, and plants, and animals, and men?

POSIDONIUS. All the ancient philosophers have supposed matter to be eternal, but have never proved it to be really so; and even allowing it to be eternal, it would by no means follow that it could form works in which there are so many striking proofs of wisdom and design. Suppose this stone to be eternal if you will, you can never persuade me that it could have composed the "Iliad" of Homer.

LUCRETIUS. No; a stone could never have composed the "Iliad," any more than it could have produced a horse: but matter organized in process of time, and become bones, flesh, and blood, will produce a horse: and, organized more finely, will produce the "Iliad."

POSIDONIUS. You suppose all this without any proof; and I ought to admit nothing without proof. I will give you bones, flesh, and blood, ready made, and will leave you and all the Epicureans in the world to make your best of them. Will you only consent to this alternative: to be put in possession of the whole Roman Empire, if, with all the ingredients ready prepared, you produce a horse, and to be hanged if you fail in the attempt?

LUCRETIUS. No; that surpasses my power, but not the power of nature. It requires millions of ages for nature, after having passed through all the possible forms, to arrive at last at the only one which can produce living beings.

POSIDONIUS. You might, if you pleased, continue all your lifetime to shake in a cask all the materials of the earth mixed together, you would never be able to form any regular figure; you could produce nothing. If the length of your life is not sufficient to produce even a mushroom, will the length of another man's life be sufficient for that purpose? Why should several ages be able to effect what one age has not effected? One ought to have seen men and animals spring from the bosom of the earth, and corn produced without seed, before he should venture to affirm that matter, by its own energy, could give itself such forms; but no one that I know of has seen such an operation, and therefore no one ought to believe it.

LUCRETIUS. Well! men, animals, and trees must always have existed. All the philosophers allow that matter is eternal; and they must further allow, that generations are so likewise. It is the very nature of matter that there should be stars that revolve, birds that fly, horses that run, and men that compose "Iliads."

POSIDONIUS. In this new supposition you change your opinion; but you always assume the point in question, and assert something for which you have not the least proof.

LUCRETIUS. I am at liberty to believe that what is to-day was yesterday, was a century ago, was a hundred centuries ago, and so on backwards without end. I make use of your argument: no one has ever seen the sun and stars begin their course, nor the first animals formed and endowed with life. We may, therefore, safely believe that all things were from eternity as they are at present.

POSIDONIUS. There is a very great difference. I see an admirable design, and I ought to believe that an intelligent being formed that design.

LUCRETIUS. You ought not to admit a being of whom you have no knowledge.

POSIDONIUS. You might as well tell me that I should not believe that an architect built the capitol because I never saw that architect.

LUCRETIUS. Your comparison is not just. You have seen houses built, and you have seen architects; and therefore you ought to conclude that it was a man like our present architects that built the capitol. But here the case is very different; the capitol does not exist of itself, but matter does. It must necessarily have had some form; and why will you not allow it to possess, by its own energy, the form in which it now is? Is it not much easier for you to admit that nature modifies itself, than to acknowledge a being that modifies it? In the former case you have only one difficulty to encounter, namely, to comprehend how nature acts. In the latter you have two difficulties to surmount: to comprehend this same nature, and the invisible being that acts on it.

POSIDONIUS. It is quite the reverse. Is see not only a difficulty, but even an impossibility in comprehending how matter can have infinite designs; but I see no difficulty in admitting an intelligent being, who governs this matter by his infinite wisdom, and by his almighty will.

LUCRETIUS. What? Is it because your mind cannot comprehend one thing that you are to suppose another? Is it because you do not understand the secret springs, and admirable contrivances, by which nature disposed itself into planets, suns, and animals, that you have recourse to another being?

POSIDONIUS. No; I have not recourse to a god, because I cannot comprehend nature; but I plainly perceive that nature needs a supreme intelligence; and this reason alone would to me be a sufficient proof of a deity had I no other.

LUCRETIUS. And what if this matter possessed intelligence of itself?

POSIDONIUS. It is plain to me that it does not possess it.

LUCRETIUS. And to me it is plain that it does possess it, since I see bodies like you and me who reason.

POSIDONIUS. If matter possesses, of itself, the faculty of thinking, you must affirm that it possesses it necessarily and independently: but if this property be essential to matter, it must have it at all times and in all places; for whatever is essential to a thing can never be separated from it. A bit of clay, and even the vilest excrement would think; but you will surely not say that dung thinks. Thought, therefore, is not an essential attribute of matter.

LUCRETIUS. Your reasoning is a mere sophism. I hold motion to be essential to matter; and yet this dung, or that piece of clay, is not actually in motion; but they will be so when they are impelled by some other body. In like manner thought will not be an attribute of a body, except when that body is organized for thinking.

POSIDONIUS. Your error proceeds from this, that you always assume the point in question. You do not reflect that, in order to organize a body, to make it a man, to render it a thinking being, there must previously be thought, there must be a fixed design. But you cannot admit such a thing as design before the only beings in this world capable of design are formed; you cannot admit thought before the only beings capable of thinking exist. You likewise assume the point at issue, when you say that motion is necessary to matter; for what is absolutely necessary always exists, as extension, for instance, exists always and in every part of matter; but motion does not always exist. The pyramids of Egypt are surely not in motion. A subtle matter, perhaps, may penetrate between the stones which compose the pyramids; but the body of the pyramid is immovable. Motion, therefore, is not essential to matter, but is communicated to it by a foreign cause, in the same manner as thought is to men. Hence it follows that there must be a powerful and intelligent being, who communicates motion, life, and thought to his creatures.

LUCRETIUS. I can easily answer your objections by saying that there have always been motion and intelligence in the world. This motion and this intelligence have been distributed at all times according to the laws of nature. Matter being eternal, it must necessarily have been in some order; but it could not be put into any order without thought and motion; and therefore thought and motion must have always been inherent in it.

POSIDONIUS. Do what you will, you can at best only make suppositions. You suppose an order; there must, therefore, have been some intelligent mind who formed this order. You suppose motion and thought before matter was in motion, and before there were men and thoughts. You must allow, that thought is not essential to matter, since you dare not say that a flint thinks. You can oppose nothing but a *perhaps* to the truth that presses hard upon you. You are sensible of the weakness of matter, and are forced to admit a supreme intelligent and almighty being, who organized matter and thinking beings. The designs of this superior intelligence shine forth in every part of nature, and you must perceive them as distinctly in a blade of grass, as in the course of the stars. Everything is evidently directed to a certain end.

LUCRETIUS. But do you not take for a design what is only a necessary

existence? Do you not take for an end what is no more than the use which
we make of things that exist? The Argonauts built a ship to sail to Colchis.
Will you say that the trees were created in order that the Argonauts might
build a ship, and that the sea was made to enable them to undertake their
voyage? Men wear stockings: will you say that legs were made by the
Supreme Being in order to be covered with stockings? No, doubtless; but
the Argonauts, having seen wood, built a ship with it, and having learned
that the water could carry a ship, they undertook their voyage. In the same
manner, after an infinite number of forms and combinations which matter
had assumed, it was found that the humors, and the transparent horn which
compose the eye, and which were formerly separated in different parts of
the body, were united in the head, and animals began to see. The organs of
generation, dispersed before, were likewise collected, and took the form
they now have; and then all kinds of procreation were conducted with
regularity. The matter of the sun, which had been long diffused and
scattered through the universe, became concentrated into a ball, and
formed the star that gives light to our world. Is there anything impossible in
all this?

POSIDONIUS. In fact, you cannot surely be serious when you have recourse to such a system: for, in the first place, if you adopt this hypothesis,
you must, of course, reject the eternal generations of which you have just
now been talking: and, in the second place, you are mistaken with regard to
final causes. There are voluntary uses to which we apply the gifts of nature;
and there are likewise necessary effects. The Argonauts need not, unless
they had pleased, have employed the trees of the forest to build a ship; but
these trees were plainly destined to grow on the earth, and to produce
fruits and leaves. We need not cover our legs with stockings; but the leg
was evidently made to support the body, and to walk, the eyes to see, the
ears to hear, and the parts of generation to perpetuate the species. If you
consider that a star, placed at the distance of four or five hundred millions
of leagues from us, sends forth rays of light, which make precisely the same
angle in the eyes of every animal, and that, at that instant, all animals have
the sensation of light, you must acknowledge that this is an instance of the
most admirable mechanism and design. But is it not unreasonable to admit
mechanism without a mechanic, a design without intelligence, and such
designs without a Supreme Being?

LUCRETIUS. If I admit the Supreme Being, what form must I give Him?
Is He in one place? Is He out of all place? Is He in time or out of time?
Does He fill the whole of space, or does He not fill it? Why did He make
the world? What was His end in making it? Why form sensible and
unhappy beings? Why moral and natural evil? On whatever side I turn my
mind, everything appears dark and incomprehensible.

POSIDONIUS. It is a necessary consequence of the existence of this Supreme Being that His nature should be incomprehensible; for, if he exists,

there must be an infinite distance between Him and us. We ought to believe that He is, without endeavoring to know what He is, or how He operates. Are you not obliged to admit asymptotes in geometry, without comprehending how it is possible for the same lines to be always approaching, and yet never to meet? Are there not many things as incomprehensible as demonstrable, in the properties of the circle? Confess, therefore, that you ought to admit what is incomprehensible, when the existence of that incomprehensible reality has been proved.

LUCRETIUS. What! Must I renounce the dogmas of Epicurus?

POSIDONIUS. It is better to renounce Epicurus than to abandon the dictates of reason.

A Treatise on Toleration

This selection consists of the last seven sections of *The Treatise on Toleration*, which was written in 1762 but not published until 1764. Its point of departure was the judicial murder of Jean Calas, but it broadened out into a discussion of the general case against religious persecution. Joseph McCabe, the translator of the version reprinted here, remarked that it "did more than any other work ever published to discredit the savage intolerance of old days."

EXTREME TOLERANCE OF THE JEWS

Both under Moses, the judges, and the kings you find constant instances of toleration. Moses says several times (*Exodus* xx.) that "God punishes the fathers in the children, down to the fourth generation"; and it was necessary thus to threaten a people to whom God had not revealed the immortality of the soul, or the punishments and rewards of another life. These truths were not made known either in the Decalogue or any part of *Leviticus* or *Deuteronomy*. They were dogmas of the Persians, Babylonians, Egyptians, Greeks, and Cretans; but they by no means formed part of the Jewish religion. Moses does not say: "Honor thy father and thy mother if thou wouldst go to heaven"; but: "Honor thy father and thy mother, that thou mayst live long on the earth." He threatens the Jews only with bodily maladies and other material evils. Nowhere does he tell them that their immortal souls will be tortured after death or be rewarded. God, who himself led his people, punished or rewarded them at once for their good or bad actions. Everything was temporal. Those who ignorantly maintain that Moses taught the immortality of the soul strip the New Testament of one of its greatest advantages over the Old Testament. It is certain that the law of Moses spoke only of temporal chastisement, down to the fourth generation. However, in spite of the precise formulation of this law and the express declaration of God that he would punish down to the fourth generation, Ezekiel announces the very opposite to the Jews. He says (xviii. 20) that the son will not bear the iniquity of his father; and he even goes so far as to make God say that he had given them "statutes that were not good" (xx. 25).

The book of Ezekiel was nevertheless inserted in the canon of inspired writers. It is true that the synagogue did not allow anyone to read it until he was thirty years old, as St. Jerome tells us; but that was in order that young men might not make evil use of the too candid pictures of vice in chapters xvi. and xxiii. The book was always received, in spite of the fact that it expressly contradicted Moses.

When the immortality of the soul was at length admitted, which probably began about the time of the Babylonian captivity, the Sadducees continued to believe that there were no punishments and rewards after death, and that the power of feeling and thinking perished with us, like the power of walking and digesting. They denied the existence of angels. They differed from the other Jews much more than Protestants differ from Catholics, yet they remained in the communion of their brethren. Some of their sect even became high-priests.

The Pharisees believed in fatalism and metempsychosis. The Essenians thought that the souls of the just went to the Fortunate Islands, and those of the wicked into a kind of Tartarus. They offered no sacrifices, and met in a special synagogue. Thus, when we look closely into Judaism, we are astonished to find the greatest toleration in the midst of the most barbaric horrors. It is a contradiction, we must admit; nearly all nations have been ruled by contradictions. Happy the contradiction that brings gentler ways into a people with bloody laws.

WHETHER INTOLERANCE WAS TAUGHT BY CHRIST

Let us now see whether Jesus Christ set up sanguinary laws, enjoined intolerance, ordered the building of dungeons of the inquisition, or instituted bodies of executioners.

There are, if I am not mistaken, few passages in the gospels from which the persecuting spirit might deduce that intolerance and constraint are lawful. One is the parable in which the kingdom of heaven is compared to a king who invites his friends to the wedding-feast of his son (*Matthew* xxii.). The king says to them, by means of his servants: "My oxen and my fatlings are killed, and all things are ready. Come unto the marriage." Some go off to their country houses, without taking any notice of the invitation; others go about their business; others assault and slay the king's servants. The king sends his army against the murderers, and destroys their town. He then sends out on the high road to bring in to the feast all who can be found. One of these sits at table without a wedding dress, and is put in irons and cast into outer darkness.

It is clear that, as this allegory concerns only the kingdom of heaven, it certainly does not give a man the right to strangle or put in jail a neighbor who comes to sup with him not wearing a festive garment. I do not remember reading anywhere in history of a prince who had a courtier arrested on that ground. It is hardly more probable that, if an emperor sent his pages to tell the princes of his empire that he had killed his fatlings and invited them to supper, the princes would kill the pages. The invitation to the feast means the preaching of salvation; the murder of the king's envoys represents the persecution of those who preach wisdom and virtue.

The other parable (*Luke* xiv.) tells of a man who invites his friends to a grand supper. When he is ready to sit at table, he sends his servant to inform them. One pleads that he has bought an estate, and must go to visit it; as one does not usually go to see an estate during the night, the excuse does not hold. Another says that he has bought five pairs of oxen, and must try them; his excuse is as weak as the preceding—one does not try oxen during the night. A third replies that he has just married; and that, assuredly, is a good excuse. Then the holder of the banquet angrily summons the blind and the lame to the feast, and, seeing that there are still empty places, says to his valet: "Go out into the highways and hedges, and compel them to come in."

It is true that this parable is not expressly said to be a figure of the kingdom of heaven. There has, unhappily, been too much abuse of these words, "Compel them to come in"; but it is obvious that a single valet could not forcibly compel all the people he meets to come and sup with his master. Moreover, compulsory guests of this sort would not make the dinner very agreeable. According to the weightiest commentators, "Compel them to come in" merely means "Beg, entreat, and press them to come in." What, I ask you, have this entreaty and supper to do with persecution?

If you want to take things literally, will you say that a man must be blind and lame, and compelled by force, to be in the bosom of the Church? Jesus says in the same parable: "When thou makest a dinner or supper, call not thy friends, nor thy brethren, neither thy kinsmen, nor thy rich neighbors." Has anyone ever inferred from this that we must not dine with our kinsmen and friends when they have acquired a little money?

After the parable of the feast Christ says (*Luke* xiv. 26): "If any man come to me, and hate not his father, and mother, and wife, and children, and brethren, and sisters, yea, and his own life also, he cannot be my disciple. . . . For which of you, intending to build a tower, sitteth not down first and counteth the cost?" Is there anybody in the world so unnatural as to conclude that one must hate one's father and mother? Is it not clear that the meaning is: Do not hesitate between me and your dearest affections?

The passage in *Matthew* (xviii. 17) is quoted: "If he neglect to hear the Church, let him be unto thee as an heathen man and a publican." That does not absolutely say we must persecute pagans and the farmers of the king's taxes; they are cursed, it is true, but they are not handed over to the secular arm. Instead of the prerogatives of citizenship being taken from these farmers of taxes, they have received the greatest privileges. It is the only profession that is condemned in Scripture, and the one most in favor with governments. Why, then, should we not be as indulgent to our erring brethren as to the tax-gatherers?

The persecuting spirit further seeks a justification of itself in the driving of the merchants from the temple and the sending of a legion of demons from the body of a possessed man into the bodies of two thousand unclean animals. But who can fail to see that these are instances of the justice which God deigns to render to himself for the contravention of his law? It was a lack of respect for the house of the Lord to change its court into a merchant's shop. It was in vain that the Sanhedrim and the priests permitted this only for the sake of the sacrifices. The God to whom the sacrifices were made might assuredly destroy this profanation, though he was hidden in a human form; he might also punish those who introduced into the country such enormous herds of animals forbidden by a law which he deigned to observe himself. These cases have no relation whatever to persecution on account of dogma. The spirit of intolerance must be very poor in argument to appeal to such foolish pretexts.

Nearly all the rest of the words and actions of Christ breathe gentleness, patience, and indulgence. He does not even break out against Judas, who must betray him; he commands Peter never to use the sword; he reproaches the children of Zebedee, who, after the example of Elias, wanted to bring fire from heaven on a town that refused him shelter.

In the end Christ succumbed to the wicked. If one may venture to compare the sacred with the profane—God with a man—his death, humanly speaking, had some resemblance to the death of Socrates. The Greek philosopher was a victim to the hatred of the sophists, priests, and leaders of the people; the legislator of the Christians was destroyed by the Scribes, Pharisees, and priests. Socrates might have escaped death, and would not; Jesus Christ offered himself voluntarily. The Greek philosopher not only pardoned his calumniators and his wicked judges, but begged them to treat his children in the same way if they should ever be so fortunate as, like himself, to incur their hatred; the legislator of the Christians, infinitely superior, begged his father to forgive his enemies.

If it be objected that, while Socrates was calm, Jesus Christ seemed to fear death, and suffered such extreme anguish that he sweated blood—the strongest and rarest symptom of fear—this was because he deigned to stoop to all the weakness of the human body that he had put on. His body trembled—his soul was invincible. He taught us that true strength and grandeur consist in supporting the evils under which our nature succumbs. It is a splendid act of courage to meet death while you fear it.

Socrates had treated the sophists as ignorant men, and accused them of bad faith; Jesus, using his divine rights, treated the Scribes and Pharisees as hypocrites, fools, blind and wicked men, serpents, and vipers.

Need I now ask whether it is tolerance or intolerance that is of divine right? If you wish to follow Jesus Christ, be martyrs, not executioners.

THE ONLY CASES IN WHICH INTOLERANCE IS HUMANLY LAWFUL

For a government to have the right to punish the errors of men it is necessary that their errors must take the form of crime; they do not take the form of crime unless they disturb society; they disturb society when they engender fanaticism; hence men must avoid fanaticism in order to deserve toleration.

If a few young Jesuits, knowing that the Church has condemned the Jansenists, proceed to burn a house of the Oratorian priests because the Oratorian Quesnel was a Jansenist, it is clear that these Jesuits ought to be punished.

Again, if the Jesuits have acted upon improper maxims, and their institute is contrary to the laws of the kingdom, their society must be dissolved, and the Jesuits must be abolished and turned into citizens. The evil done to them is imaginary — the good is real. What hardship is there in wearing a short coat instead of a long black robe, and being free instead of being a slave?

If the Franciscan monks, carried away by a holy zeal for the Virgin Mary, go and destroy a Dominican convent, because the Dominicans believe that Mary was born in original sin, it will be necessary to treat the Franciscans in much the same way as the Jesuits.

We may say the same of the Lutherans and Calvinists. It is useless for them to say that they follow the promptings of their consciences, that it is better to obey God than men, or that they are in the true flock, and must exterminate the wolves. In such cases they are wolves themselves.

One of the most remarkable examples of fanaticism is found in a small Danish sect, whose principle was excellent. They desired to secure eternal salvation for their brethren; but the consequences of the principle were peculiar. They knew that all infants who die unbaptised are damned, and that those who are so fortunate as to die immediately after baptism enjoy eternal glory. They therefore proceeded to kill all the newly-baptised boys and girls that they could find. No doubt this was a way of securing for them the highest conceivable happiness and preserving them from the sin and misery of this life. But these charitable folk forgot that it is not lawful to do a little evil that a great good may follow; that they had no right to the lives of these children; that the majority of parents are carnal enough to prefer to keep their children rather than see them slain in order to enter paradise; and that the magistrate had to punish homicide, even when it is done with a good intention.

The Jews would seem to have a better right than any to rob and kill us. Though there are a hundred instances of toleration in the Old Testament, there are also some instances and laws of severity. God has at times commanded them to kill idolaters, and reserve only the marriageable girls.

Now they regard us as idolaters, and, although we tolerate them to-day, it is possible that, if they became masters, they would suffer only our girls to live.

They would, at least, be absolutely compelled to slay all the Turks, because the Turks occupy the lands of the Hittites, Jerbusites, Amorrhaeans, Jersensaeans, Hevaeans, Aracaeans, Cinaeans, Hamataeans, and Samaritans. All these peoples were anathematized, and their country, which was more than seventy-five miles long, was given to the Jews in several consecutive covenants. They ought to regain their possessions, which the Mohammedans have usurped for the last thousand years.

If the Jews were now to reason in this way, it is clear that the only reply we could make would be to put them in the galleys.

These are almost the only cases in which intolerance seems reasonable.

ACCOUNT OF A CONTROVERSIAL DISPUTE IN CHINA

In the early years of the reign of the great Emperor Kam-hi a mandarin of the city of Canton heard from his house a great noise, which proceeded from the next house. He inquired if anybody was being killed, and was told that the almoner of the Danish missionary society, a chaplain from Batavia, and a Jesuit were disputing. He had them brought to his house, put tea and sweets before them, and asked why they quarrelled.

The Jesuit replied that it was very painful for him, since he was always right, to have to do with men who were always wrong; that he had at first argued with the greatest restraint, but had at length lost patience.

The mandarin, with the utmost discretion, reminded them that politeness was needed in all discussion, told them that in China men never became angry, and asked the cause of the dispute.

The Jesuit answered: "My lord, I leave it to you to decide. These two gentlemen refuse to submit to the decrees of the Council of Trent."

"I am astonished," said the mandarin. Then, turning to the refractory pair, he said: "Gentlemen, you ought to respect the opinions of a large gathering. I do not know what the Council of Trent is, but a number of men are always better informed than a single one. No one ought to imagine that he is better than others, and has a monopoly of reason. So our great Confucius teaches; and, believe me, you will do well to submit to the Council of Trent."

The Dane then spoke. "My lord speaks with the greatest wisdom," he said; "we respect great councils, as is proper, and therefore we are in entire agreement with several that were held before the Council of Trent."

"Oh, if that is the case," said the mandarin, "I beg your pardon. You may be right. So you and this Dutchman are of the same opinion, against this poor Jesuit."

"Not a bit," said the Dutchman. "This fellow's opinions are almost as extravagant as those of the Jesuit yonder, who has been so very amiable to you. I can't bear them."

"I don't understand," said the mandarin. "Are you not all three Christians? Have you not all three come to teach Christianity in our empire? Ought you not, therefore, to hold the same dogmas?"

"It is this way, my lord," said the Jesuit; "these two are mortal enemies, and are both against me. Hence it is clear that they are both wrong, and I am right."

"That is not quite clear," said the mandarin; "strictly speaking, all three of you may be wrong. I should like to hear you all, one after the other."

The Jesuit then made a rather long speech, during which the Dane and the Dutchman shrugged their shoulders. The mandarin did not understand a word of it. Then the Dane spoke; the two opponents regarded him with pity, and the mandarin again failed to understand. The Dutchman had the same effect. In the end they all spoke together and abused each other roundly. The good mandarin secured silence with great difficulty, and said: "If you want us to tolerate your teaching here, begin by being yourselves neither intolerant nor intolerable."

When they went out the Jesuit met a Dominican friar, and told him that he had won, adding that truth always triumphed. The Dominican said: "Had I been there, you would not have won; I should have convicted you of lying and idolatry." The quarrel became warm, and the Jesuit and Dominican took to pulling each other's hair. The mandarin, on hearing of the scandal, sent them both to prison. A sub-mandarin said to the judge: "How long does your excellency wish them to be kept in prison?" "Until they agree," said the judge. "Then," said the sub-mandarin, "they are in prison for life." "In that case," said the judge, "until they forgive each other." "They will never forgive each other," said the other; "I know them." "Then," said the mandarin, "let them stop there until they pretend to forgive each other."

WHETHER IT IS USEFUL TO MAINTAIN THE PEOPLE IN SUPERSTITION

Such is the weakness, such the perversity, of the human race that it is better, no doubt, for it to be subject to all conceivable superstitions, provided they be not murderous, than to live without religion. Man has always needed a curb; and, although it was ridiculous to sacrifice to fauns or naiads, it was much more reasonable and useful to worship these fantastic images of the deity than to sink into atheism. A violent atheist would be as great a plague as a violent superstitious man.

When men have not sound ideas of the divinity, false ideas will take their place; just as, in ages of impoverishment, when there is not sound money, people use bad coin. The pagan feared to commit a crime lest he should be punished by his false gods; the Asiatic fears the chastisement of his pagoda. Religion is necessary wherever there is a settled society. The laws take care of known crimes; religion watches secret crime.

But once men have come to embrace a pure and holy religion, superstition becomes, not merely useless, but dangerous. We must not feed on acorns those to whom God offers bread.

Superstition is to religion what astrology is to astronomy — the mad daughter of a wise mother. These daughters have too long dominated the earth.

When, in our ages of barbarism, there were scarcely two feudal lords who had a New Testament in their homes, it might be pardonable to press fables on the vulgar; that is to say, on these feudal lords, their weak-minded wives, and their brutal vassals. They were led to believe that St. Christopher had carried the infant Jesus across a river; they were fed with stories of sorcery and diabolical possession; they readily believed that St. Genou healed gout, and St. Claire sore eyes. The children believed in the werewolf, and their parents in the girdle of St. Francis. The number of relics was incalculable.

The sediment of these superstitions remained among the people even when religion had been purified. We know that when M. de Noailles, Bishop of Chalons, removed and threw in the fire the pretended relic of the sacred navel of Jesus Christ the town of Chalons took proceedings against him. But his courage was equal to his piety, and he succeeded in convincing the people that they could worship Jesus Christ in spirit and truth without having his navel in their church.

The Jansenists contributed not a little gradually to root out from the mind of the nation the false ideas that dishonored the Christian religion. People ceased to believe that it sufficed to pray for thirty days to the Virgin to obtain all that they wished, and sin with impunity.

In the end the citizens began to suspect that it was not really St. Genevieve who gave or withheld rain, but God himself who disposed of the elements. The monks were astonished to see that their saints no longer worked miracles. If the writers of the life of St. Francis Xavier returned to this world, they would not dare to say that the saint raised nine people from the dead, that he was in two places at the same time, and that, when his crucifix fell into the sea, a crab restored it to him.

It is the same with excommunication. Historians tell us that when King Robert had been excommunicated by Pope Gregory V for marrying his godmother, the Princess Bertha, his servants threw out of the window the meat served up to the king, and Queen Bertha was delivered of a goose, in punishment of the incestuous marriage. I doubt if in our time the waiters of the king of France would, if he were excommunicated, throw his dinner out of the window, and whether the queen would give birth to a gosling.

There remains, it is true, a few bigoted fanatics in the suburbs; but the disease, like vermin, attacks only the lowest of the populace. Every day reason penetrates farther into France, into the shops of merchants as well as the mansions of lords. We must cultivate the fruits of reason, the more willingly since it is now impossible to prevent them from developing. France, enlightened by Pascal, Nicole, Arnaud, Bossuet, Descartes, Gassendi, Bayle, Fontenelle, and others, cannot be ruled as it was ruled in earlier times.

If the masters of error — the grand masters — so long paid and honored for brutalizing the human species, ordered us to-day to believe that the seed must die in order to germinate; that the earth stands motionless on its foundations — that it does not travel round the sun; that the tides are not a natural effect of gravitation; that the rainbow is not due to the refraction and reflection of light, etc., and based their decrees on ill-understood passages of Scripture, we know how they would be regarded by educated men. Would it be too much to call them fools? And if these masters employed force and persecution to secure the ascendancy of their insolent ignorance, would it be improper to speak of them as wild beasts?

The more the superstitions of the monks are despised, the more the bishops and priests are respected; while they do good, the monkish superstitions from Rome do nothing but evil. And of all these superstitions, is not the most dangerous that of hating one's neighbor on account of his opinions? And is it not evident that it would be even more reasonable to worship the sacred navel, the sacred foreskin, and the milk and dress of the Virgin Mary, than to detest and persecute one's brother?

VIRTUE BETTER THAN LEARNING

The less we have of dogma, the less dispute; the less we have of dispute, the less misery.

Religion was instituted to make us happy in this world and the next. What must we do to be happy in the next world? Be just. What must we do to be happy in this world, as far as the misery of our nature allows? Be indulgent.

It would be the height of folly to pretend to bring all men to have the same thoughts in metaphysics. It would be easier to subdue the whole universe by arms than to subdue all the minds in a single city.

Euclid easily persuaded all men of the truths of geometry. How? Because every single one of them is a corollary of the axiom, "Two and two makes four." It is not exactly the same in the mixture of metaphysics and theology.

When Bishop Alexander and the priest Arius began to dispute as to the way in which the Logos emanated from the Father, the Emperor Constantine at first wrote to them as follows (as we find in Eusebius and Socrates): "You are great fools to dispute about things you do not understand."

If the two parties had been wise enough to perceive that the emperor was right, the Christian world would not have been stained with blood for three hundred years.

What, indeed, can be more stupid and more horrible than to say to men: "My friends, it is not enough to be loyal subjects, submissive children, tender fathers, just neighbors, and to practice every virtue, cultivate friendship, avoid ingratitude, and worship Christ in peace; you must, in addition, know how one is engendered from all eternity, and how to distinguish the *homoousion* in the *hypostasis*, or we shall condemn you to be burned for ever, and will meantime put you to death?"

Had such a proposition been made to Archimedes, or Posidonius, or Varro, or Cato, or Cicero, what would he have said?

Constantine did not persevere in his resolution to impose silence on the contending parties. He might have invited the leaders of the pious frenzy to his palace and asked them what authority they had to disturb the world: "Have you the title-deeds of the divine family? What does it matter to you whether the Logos was made or engendered, provided men are loyal to him, preach a sound morality, and practice it as far as they can? I have done many wrong things in my time, and so have you. You are ambitious, so am I. The empire has cost me much knavery and cruelty; I have murdered nearly all my relatives. I repent, and would expiate my crimes by restoring peace to the Roman Empire. Do not prevent me from doing the only good that can efface my earlier barbarity. Help me to end my days in peace." Possibly he would have had no influence on the disputants; possibly he was flattered to find himself, in long red robe, his head covered with jewels, presiding at a council.

Yet this it was that opened the gate to all the plagues that came from Asia upon the West. From every disputed verse of Scripture there issued a fury armed with a sophism and a sword, that goaded men to madness and cruelty. The marauding Huns and Goths and Vandals did infinitely less harm; and the greatest harm they did was to join themselves in these fatal disputes.

OF UNIVERSAL TOLERATION

One does not need great art and skillful eloquence to prove that Christians ought to tolerate each other — nay, even to regard all men as brothers. Why, you say, is the Turk, the Chinese, or the Jew my brother? Assuredly; are we not all children of the same father, creatures of the same God?

But these people despise us and treat us as idolaters. Very well; I will tell them that they are quite wrong. It seems to me that I might astonish, at least, the stubborn pride of a Mohammedan or a Buddhist priest if I spoke to them somewhat as follows: —

This little globe, which is but a point, travels in space like many other globes; we are lost in the immensity. Man, about five feet high, is certainly a small thing in the universe. One of these imperceptible beings says to some of his neighbors, in Arabia or South Africa: "Listen to me, for the God of all these worlds has enlightened me. There are nine hundred million little ants like us on the earth, but my ant-hole alone is dear to God. All the others are eternally reprobated by him. Mine alone will be happy."

They would then interrupt me, and ask who was the fool that talked all this nonsense. I should be obliged to tell them that it was themselves. I would then try to appease them, which would be difficult.

I would next address myself to the Christians, and would venture to say to, for instance, a Dominican friar — an inquisitor of the faith: "Brother, you are aware that each province in Italy has its own dialect, and that people do not speak at Venice and Bergamo as they do at Florence. The Academy of La Crusca has fixed the language. Its dictionary is a rule that has to be followed, and the grammar of Matei is an infallible guide. But do you think that the consul of the Academy, or Matei in his absence, could in conscience cut out the tongues of all the Venetians and the Bergamese who persisted in speaking their own dialect?"

The inquisitor replies: "The two cases are very different. In our case it is a question of your eternal salvation. It is for your good that the heads of the inquisition direct that you shall be seized on the information of any one person, however infamous or criminal; that you shall have no advocate to defend you; that the name of your accuser shall not be made known to you; that the inquisitor shall promise you pardon and then condemn you; and that you shall then be subjected to five kinds of torture, and afterwards either flogged or sent to the galleys or ceremoniously burned. On this Father Ivonet, Doctor Cuchalon, Zanchinus, Campegius, Royas, Felinus, Gomarus, Diabarus, and Gemelinus are explicit, and this pious practice admits of no exception."

I would take the liberty of replying: "Brother, possibly you are right. I am convinced that you wish to do me good. But could I not be saved without all that?"

It is true that these absurd horrors do not stain the face of the earth every day; but they have often done so, and the record of them would make up a volume much longer than the gospels which condemn them. Not only is it cruel to persecute, in this brief life, those who differ from us, but I am not sure if it is not too bold to declare that they are damned eternally. It seems to me that it is not the place of the atoms of a moment, such as we are, thus to anticipate the decrees of the Creator. Far be it from me to question the principle, "Out of the Church there is no salvation." I respect it, and all that it teaches; but do we really know all the ways of God, and the full range of his mercies? May we not hope in him as much as fear him? Is it not enough to be loyal to the Church? Must each individual usurp the rights of the Deity, and decide, before he does, the eternal lot of all men?

When we wear mourning for a king of Sweden, Denmark, England, or Prussia, do we say that we wear mourning for one who burns eternally in hell? There are in Europe forty million people who are not of the Church of Rome. Shall we say to each of them: "Sir, seeing that you are infallibly damned, I will neither eat, nor deal, nor speak with you?"

What ambassador of France, presented in audience to the Sultan, would say in the depths of his heart: "His Highness will undoubtedly burn for all eternity because he has been circumcised?" If he really believed that the Sultan is the mortal enemy of God, the object of his vengeance, could he speak to him? Ought he to be sent to him? With whom could we trade? What duty of civil life could we ever fulfill if we were really convinced that we were dealing with damned souls?

Followers of a merciful God, if you were cruel of heart; if, in worshipping him whose whole law consisted in loving one's neighbor as oneself, you have burdened this pure and holy law with sophistry and unintelligible disputes; if you had lit the fires of discord for the sake of a new word or a single letter of the alphabet; if you had attached eternal torment to the omission of a few words or ceremonies that other peoples could not know, I should say to you: —

"Transport yourselves with me to the day on which all men will be judged, when God will deal with each according to his works. I see all the dead of former ages and of our own stand in his presence. Are you sure that our Creator and Father will say to the wise and virtuous Confucius, to the lawgiver Solon, to Pythagoras, to Zaleucus, to Socrates, to Plato, to the divine Antonines, to the good Trajan, to Titus, the delight of the human race, to Epictetus, and to so many other model men: 'Go, monsters, go and submit to a chastisement infinite in its intensity and duration; your torment

---

[1]All the men listed here were notorious criminals whose names would be familiar to Voltaire's French readers. Jean Chatel (1575–1594), a fanatic who made an unsuccessful attempt on the life of Henry IV, was tortured and executed. Voltaire was convinced that Chatel's act was inspired by the Jesuits, but this has never been proven. François Ravaillac (1578–1610) did assassinate Henry IV; he also was tortured and executed. He acted on purported orders from Heaven. Voltaire, who venerated Henry IV, always referred to Ravaillac with special loathing. Robert François Damiens (1715–1757), a religious fanatic who made an unsuccessful attempt on the life of Louis XV, was drawn and quartered by a crowd on the spot. Cartouche (meaning "cartridge") was a nickname of the brigand Louis Dominique Bourguignon (1693–1721), the chief of a band of highwaymen operating in and near Paris. He was captured in 1721 and broken on the wheel. His daring exploits have been celebrated in ballads, popular prints, plays, and films, and *cartouche* has become a French term for "highwayman." Unlike the three assassins, Cartouche was not mad and because of his exceptional boldness he has become something of a romantic figure in French history.

The doctrine that Voltaire denounces with such vehemence is sometimes known as "exclusive salvation," teaching that salvation is impossible "outside the Church." A Vatican Council in 1870 ruled that non-Catholics believing in God could be regarded as not being outside the Church, but that atheists and agnostics could not possibly be saved. This exclusion was removed by the Council of Vatican II, which declared that all men of good faith, seeking to do

shall be as eternal as I. And you, my beloved Jean Chatel, Ravaillac, Damiens, and Cartouche, who have died with the prescribed formulae, come and share my empire and felicity for ever.' "[1]

You shrink with horror from such sentiments; and, now that they have passed my lips, I have no more to say to you.

---

the will of God sincerely or the good as they know it, can be saved (see W. Abbott, ed., *Documents of Vatican II*, 1966). It is safe to say that liberal and humane Catholics never took this doctrine very seriously.

The men on the earlier of the two of Voltaire's lists are benefactors of the human race who were not Christians and who would be condemned to eternal damnation according to the doctrine of exclusive salvation in its older interpretation. Zaleicus, who lived in the seventh century B.C., was the first person to codify Greek law. Voltaire's "divine Antonine" is the Roman emperor and Stoic philosopher, Marcus Aurelius (121–180) who was noted for his concern for the poor, for lenient treatment of political criminals, and for attempting to make gladiatorial shows less brutal. The "good Trajan" is the Roman emperor Marcus Trajanus (53–117) who fostered literature and the arts and opposed persecution of the Christians. "Titus, the delight of the human race," is the Roman emperor Titus Flavius Vespasianus (39–81), the son of the Emperor Vespasian whom we met earlier as the reluctant worker of two not so miraculous cures (see p. 52 and p. 57). Titus stopped prosecutions for treason and was much loved because of the kind and considerate treatment of his subjects, especially those in distress. The sobriquet commonly applied to him was "amor et delicias generis humani" (love and delight of the human race).

The Philosophical Dictionary

The articles in this section are in the form in which they appeared in the last edition of the *Philosophical Dictionary* published in Voltaire's lifetime (1769). Expanded versions of several articles were published in the *Questions Concerning the Encyclopedia*. The additions to the articles on "Beauty," "Miracles," and "Resurrection" are found in the selections from the *Questions* (see pp. 186–202 below).

ALL IS GOOD

There was a fine clamor raised in the schools, and even among men who think, when Leibnitz, paraphrasing Plato, built his edifice of the best of all possible worlds and imagined that all was for the best in it. He asserted, in the north of Germany, that God could make but a single world. Plato at least had left him the liberty of making five, because there are only five solid regular bodies: the tetrahedron, or pyramid with three faces, with uniform base, the cube, the hexahedron, the dodecahedron, the icosahedron. But since our world is not shaped like any of Plato's five bodies, he had to allow God a sixth method.

Let us leave the divine Plato to one side. Leibniz, then, who was surely a better geometer than he, and a more profound metaphysician, did mankind the service of persuading us that we should be quite content, and that God could do no more for us, that indisputably, he necessarily chose, among all the possible choices, the best one.

"What will become of original sin?" they shouted at him. "Let it become what it may," said Leibnitz and his friend; but in public he wrote that original sin necessarily was a part of the best of worlds.

What! To be chased out of a place of delights, where we would have lived forever if we hadn't eaten an apple! What! To produce in misery miserable children, who suffer everything, who will make others suffer everything! What! To undergo all illnesses, feel all sorrows, die in pain, and for refreshment to be burned in the eternity of centuries! Is this really the best of available lots? It is not too *good* for us; in what way can it be good for God?

Leibnitz sensed that he had no reply to this: so he made fat books in which he disagreed with himself.

To deny there is evil — that can be done laughingly by a Lucullus who is in good health and who has a good dinner with his friends and his mistress in the salon of Apollo; but let him stick his head out the window, he will see unhappy people enough; let him catch a fever, he will be unhappy himself.

I don't like to quote; that's usually thorny work: you neglect what precedes and what follows the passage you quote, and expose yourself to a thousand quarrels. Nevertheless I must quote Lactantius, Church Father, who in chapter 13 of *The Wrath of God*[1] has Epicurus say this: "Either God wishes to expunge the evil from this world and cannot; or he can and does not wish to; or he neither can nor wishes to; or finally he wishes to and can. If he wishes to and cannot, that is impotence, which is contrary to the nature of God; if he can and does not wish to, that is wickedness, and that is no less contrary to his nature; if he neither wishes to nor can, that is wickedness and impotence at the same time; if he wishes to and can (which is the only one among these choices appropriates to God), where does the evil in this world come from?"

The argument is serious; and, indeed, Lactantius replies to it very feebly, by saying that God wishes evil, but has given us the wisdom with which to choose the good. It must be admitted that this reply is rather weak in comparison with the objection; for it supposes that God grants wisdom only through creating evil; and anyhow, our wisdom is a laughable one!

The origin of evil has always been an abyss whose bottom nobody has been able to see. It is that reduced so many ancient philosophers and legislators to supposing two principles, one good, and other bad. Among the Egyptians, Typhon was the bad principle; among the Persians, it was Arimane. It is well known that the Manicheans adopted this theology; but since these gentlemen never had conversation either with the good principle or the bad, we needn't believe every word they said.

Among the absurdities with which this world overflows, and which may be numbered among our evils, it is not a trifling one to have imagined two all-powerful beings fighting to see which of them would put more of himself into the world, and make a treaty like the two doctors in Molière: Pass me the emetic, and I'll pass you the bleeding cup.

Following the Platonists, Basilides[2] maintained, as early as the first century of the Church, that God has assigned the creation of our world to his lowest angels, and that these, lacking skill, made things as we see them now. This theological fable collapses before the powerful objection that it is not in the nature of an all-powerful and all-wise God to have a world built by architects who know nothing about their job.

Simon, who felt the force of this objection, attempted to forestall it by

---

[1] The original title of this work is *De Ira Dei*. The date of its publication is not known. Lactantius flourished c. 300.

[2] Alexandrian Gnostic flourished early in the second century.

saying that the angel who superintended the workshop was damned for botching his work; but burning the angel does not cure us.

Pandora's adventure among the Greeks does not answer the objection any better. The box holding all the evils, and at whose bottom hope remains, is admittedly a charming allegory; but this Pandora was made by Vulcan only to revenge himself on Prometheus, who had fashioned a man from mud.

The Indians did no better: after God created man, he gave him a drug which assured him everlasting health; man loaded his donkey with the drug; the donkey was thirsty; the serpent showed him a fountain, and while the donkey drank the serpent took the drug for himself.

The Syrians imagined that after man and woman had been created in the fourth sky, they took it into their heads to eat a pancake instead of the ambrosia which was their natural food. The ambrosia was exhaled through the pores; but after they had eaten the pancake, they had to go to the toilet. The man and woman asked an angel to show them where the bathroom was. "Do you see," the angel asked them, "that little planet, a mere nothing in size, which is some fifty million miles from here? There's the privy of the universe; go there as fast as you can." They went there; they were left there; and from that time on our world has been what it is.

We may still ask the Syrians why God permitted man to eat the pancake and why a host of such appalling evils should descend on us.

I move quickly from that fourth sky to Lord Bolingbroke, lest I grow bored. That man, who undoubtedly possessed great talent, provided the celebrated Pope with his plan for his *All is good*, which in fact we find word for word in Lord Bolingbroke's posthumous works, and which Lord Shaftesbury had earlier inserted into his *Characteristics*. Read in Shaftesbury the chapter on the moralists and there you will see these words:

"Much is alleged in answer to show why Nature errs, and how she came thus impotent and erring from an unerring hand. But I deny she errs. . . . 'Tis from this order of inferior and superior things that we admire the world's beauty, founded thus on contrarieties, whilst from such various and disagreeing principles a universal concord is established. . . . The vegetables by their death sustain the animals, and animal bodies dissolved enrich the earth, and raise again the vegetable world. . . . The central powers, which hold the lasting orbs in their just poise and movement, must not be controlled to save a fleeting form, and rescue from the precipice a puny animal, whose brittle frame, however protected, must of itself so soon dissolve."[3]

Bolingbroke, Shaftesbury, and Pope, their promoter, didn't resolve the question any better than the others: their *All is good* means nothing more than that everything is directed by immutable laws; who does not know

[3]*Characteristics, The Moralists* I, iii (1711).

that? You teach us nothing when you observe, with all the little children, that flies are born to be eaten by spiders, spiders by swallows, swallows by shrikes, shrikes by eagles, eagles to be killed by men, men to kill one another and to be eaten by worms and then — excepting one in a thousand — by devils.

Here's a clear and constant order among the animals of all species; here is order throughout. When a stone is formed in my bladder, it is by an admirable piece of machinery: gravely juices pass little by little into my blood, filter into the kidneys, pass through the urethras, deposit themselves in my bladder, assemble there by an excellent Newtonian attraction; the stone is formed, grows larger; I suffer evils a thousand times worse than death, by the most beautiful arrangement in the world; a surgeon, having perfected the art invented by Tubalcain,[4] comes to thrust a sharp and pointed iron into the perineum and seizes my stone with his pincers. It breaks under his efforts by a necessary mechanism; and, by the same mechanism, I die in horrible torments. *All this is good*, all this is the evident consequence of unchangeable physical principles; I agree, and I know it as well as you do.

If we were without feeling, there would be no objection to this natural philosophy. But that is not the issue; we ask you if there are not perceptible evils, and where they come from. "There are no evils," says Pope in his fourth epistle on the *All is good*; "or, if there are particular evils, they compose the general good."

Here's a strange general good, composed of the stone, the gout, all crimes, all sufferings, death, and damnation.

The fall of man is the ointment we put on all the specific maladies of body and soul, which you call the *general health*; but Shaftesbury and Bolingbroke jeered at original sin; Pope doesn't talk about it; it is clear that their system saps the Christian religion at its foundations, and explains nothing at all.

Nevertheless, this system has recently been approved by several theologians who are perfectly willing to put up with agreeable contradictions; we shouldn't begrudge anyone the consolation of reasoning as best he can about the deluge of evils that inundates us. It is right to let desperately sick men eat what they want. They have gone so far as to claim that this system is comforting.

"God, " says Pope,

> . . . *sees with equal eye, as God of all,*
> *A hero perish, or a sparrow fall,*
> *Atoms or systems into ruin hurled,*
> *And now a bubble burst, and now a world.*
> [*Essay on Man*, I, 87–90]

---

[4]Tubalcain in the Old Testament was "the forger of every cutting instrument of brass and iron" (*Genesis* iv, 22).

That's a pleasant consolation, I admit; don't you find a great relief in the ordinance of Lord Shaftesbury which says that God will not upset his eternal laws for the sake of an animal as puny as man? We must at least admit that this puny animal is right to cry out humbly and, crying out, to seek to understand why these eternal laws are not made for the well-being of every individual.

The system of *All is good* merely represents the author of nature as a powerful and malicious king, who does not care if it should cost the lives of four or five hundred thousand men, and if the others drag out their days in want and tears, provided that he accomplishes his work.

So then, far from consoling them, the notion of the best of possible worlds drives the philosophers who adopt it to despair. The question of good and evil remains an inexplicable chaos for those who search honestly; it is a witticism for those who argue: they are galley-slaves who jingle their chains. As for the unthinking, they closely resemble fish who have been brought from a river to a reservoir; they don't suspect that they are to be eaten during Lent. Similarly, on our own none of us knows a thing about the causes of our destiny.

Let us put at the end of almost all the chapters of metaphysics the two letters the Roman judges set down when they could not understand a cause: *N.L.*, *non liquet*, it is not clear.

BEAUTY

Ask a toad what beauty is, the supreme beauty, the *to kalon*.[5] He will tell you it is his lady toad with her two big round eyes coming out of her little head, her large flat snout, yellow belly, brown back. Interrogate a Negro from Guinea; for him beauty is a black, oily skin, sunken eyes, and flat nose.

Interrogate the Devil; he will tell you that the beautiful is a pair of horns, four claws, and a tail. Then consult the philosophers; they will answer you with jargon; they must have something conforming to the archetype of the beautiful in essence, to the *to kalon*.

I once attended a tragedy sitting next to a philosopher. "How beautiful it is!" he said. "What do you find beautiful in it?" I asked. He said, "The author has attained his goal." The next day he took medicine, which did him good. "It has attained its goal," I told him; "there's a beautiful medicine!" He understood that one can't say a medicine is beautiful, and that before we give anything the name *beautiful* it must make one feel admiration and pleasure. He admitted that the tragedy had inspired him with these two sentiments, and that the *to kalon*, the beautiful, lay there.

[5]"To kalon" is the Greek expression for "the beautiful." Voltaire evidently has Plato's teaching in mind according to which beauty is an objective characteristic.

We took a trip to England; the same piece was played there, perfectly translated; it made all the spectators yawn. "Oh, oh!" he said. "The *to kalon* is not the same for the English as for the French." He concluded after much reflection that the beautiful is often quite relative, so that what is decent in Japan is indecent in Rome, and what is fashionable in Paris is not so in Peking, and he thus saved himself the trouble of composing a long treatise on the beautiful.

BODY

Just as we don't know what a spirit is, so we are ignorant of what a body is: we see some of its properties; but what is the subject in which these properties reside? "There are only bodies," said Democritus and Epicurus; "There are no bodies," said the disciples of Zeno of Elea.

Bishop Berkeley of Cloyne is the last who claims, with a hundred sophisms, to have proved that bodies don't exist. They have, he says, neither color, nor odor, nor heat; these modalities are in your own sensations and not in the objects. He could have saved himself the trouble of proving this truth; it was known well enough. But from there he moves on to extension and solidity, which are the essence of a body; he thinks he can prove that there is no extension in a piece of green cloth, because the cloth is not really green; the sensation of green is in you alone, hence the sensation of extension also is in you alone. And, after he has thus destroyed extension, he concludes that solidity, which is attached to it, falls of its own weight — and thus there's nothing in the world but our ideas. So that, according to this scholar, ten thousand men killed by ten thousand cannon shots are fundamentally nothing but ten thousand apprehensions of our soul.

My lord, the bishop of Cloyne, had only himself to blame if he went to such ridiculous lengths. He believes he can show that there is no extension because a body seemed to him four times larger through his glasses than it was through his eyes, and four times smaller with the aid of another glass. From this he concludes that since a body cannot be at the same time four feet, sixteen feet, and a single foot in length, extension doesn't exist: hence there's nothing. All he needed to do was take a measure, and say: "Of whatever extension a body may appear to me, it is extended so many of these measures."

It would have been quite easy for him to see that extension and solidity are not like sounds, colors, tastes, odors, etc. Clearly, these are feelings excited in us by the configuration of parts; but extension is not a feeling. When this burning wood is extinguished, I am no longer warm; when the air no longer vibrates, I no longer hear anything; when this rose withers, I no longer smell it; but this wood, this air, and this rose have extension without any participation on my part. Berkeley's paradox isn't worth refuting.

It is useful to know how he was drawn into this paradox. A long time ago I had some conversations with him; he told me that he came to this opinion when he observed how men were unable to conceive what it is that receives extension. And in fact he triumphs in his book when he asks Hylas what that *substratum*, that substance, is. "It is the extended body," replies Hylas. Then the bishop (under the name of Philonous) laughs at him; and poor Hylas, seeing he has said that extension is subject to extension, and has therefore talked nonsense, is crestfallen, and admits that he doesn't understand it, that there is no body, the material world doesn't exist, there is nothing but a world of mind.

Hylas should merely have told Philonous: "We know nothing about the heart of this subject, this primal substance, extended, solid, divisible, mobile, shaped, etc.; I know it no better than I know the thinking, feeling, and willing subject; but still, that subject none the less exists, since it has essential properties of which it cannot be deprived."

We are all like most of the ladies of Paris: they live extremely well without knowing what goes into the stew; in the same way we enjoy bodies without knowing what they are composed of. What is the body made of? Of parts, and these parts resolve themselves into other parts. What are these last parts? Always bodies; you can go on dividing endlessly and never get any further.

Finally, a subtle philosopher,[6] observing that a picture is made of elements none of which is a picture, and a house of materials none of which is a house, fancied (in a little different fashion) that bodies are built from an infinity of little things which are not bodies; and these are called *monads*. This system nevertheless has its good side, and, were it a part of revealed religion, I would think it quite plausible; all these little beings would be mathematical points, a species of souls who only wait for clothes to get into.

CHINESE CATECHISM

Third Conversation

KOU. You are pressing me, Cu-su. In order for me to be rewarded or punished when I am gone, there must subsist something in me that goes on feeling and thinking after my death. Now, since nothing of me possessed

[6]Leibniz.

either feeling or thought before my birth, why should there be any such thing after my death? What could this incomprehensible part of me be? Will the buzzing of this bee remain when the bee is gone? Does the vegetation of this plant continue to exist after the plant has been uprooted? Is not vegetation a word that men use to signify the inexplicable manner in which the supreme Being has wished the plant to draw its sap from the ground? In the same way, soul is a word invented to express, feebly and obscurely, the springs of our life. All animals move; and that power of moving is called *active force*; but there is no distinct being that is this force. We have passions, memory, reason; they are not distinct things; they are not little persons who have a separate existence; they are generic words, invented to fix our ideas. Hence the soul, which signifies our memory, our reason, our passions, is itself only a word. Who makes movement in nature? it is God. Who makes all the plants vegetate? it is God. Who makes movement in the animals? it is God. Who makes the thought of man? it is God.

If the human soul[7] were a little person shut up in our body, directing its movements and ideas, wouldn't that be an unworthy contrivance for the eternal artisan of the world, and a sign of impotence in him? Was he, then, incapable of making automatons having the gift of movement and of thought in themselves? You taught me Greek, you made me read Homer; I find Vulcan a divine blacksmith when he makes tripods of gold that march to the council of the gods by themselves: but this Vulcan would seem a miserable charlatan to me if he had hidden one of his journeymen in the body of these tripods to make them move without our noticing it.

There are frigid dreamers who think that the planets revolve because of genii who push them ceaselessly; a beautiful intervention, but God was not reduced to this pitiful expedient: in a word, why postulate two springs for a mechanism when one will do? You dare not deny that God has the power to animate the little-known being we call *matter*; why then should he avail himself of another agent?

And much more: what would this soul be that you confer so generously on our body? Where would it come from? When would it come? Would the Creator of the universe need to lie continually in wait for men and women to couple, note the exact moment the seed leaves the body of the man and enters that of the woman, and then quickly dispatch a soul into that seed? And if that seed dies, what would become of the soul? It would then have been created unnecessarily, or would have to wait for another opportunity.

Here, let me say, is a strange occupation for the master of the world; and not only must he keep continual watch over the copulations of the human

[7]See the article "Soul" (note by Voltaire). The relevant parts of this article are reprinted below, pp. 152-154.

species, but he must do the same with all the animals; for they all have, like us, memory ideas, passions; and if a soul is required to form them, God must labor perpetually to forge souls for elephants and pigs, owls, fish, and bonzes.

What would you make of the architect of so many millions of worlds who would have to keep on mending his construction with invisible cement to keep it going!

These are only a few of the reasons that might make me doubt the existence of the soul.

CU-SU. You argue honestly, and this virtuous inclination would be agreeable to the supreme Being, even if it erred. You may deceive yourself, but you don't try to deceive yourself, and consequently you may be pardoned. But consider: you have only proposed doubts to me, and these doubts are sad ones. Admit more consoling probabilities: it is painful to be annihilated; hope to live. You know that a thought is not matter; why then is it so difficult for you to believe that God has endowed you with a divine principle which cannot be subject to death since it cannot be dissolved? Dare you say that it is impossible for you to have a soul? Certainly not, and if it is possible, isn't it highly probable that you have one? Could you reject so noble a system, so necessary to mankind? What are the difficulties that repel you?

KOU. I'd like to accept the system, but I'd like to have it proved first. I'm not at liberty to believe something I don't have the evidence for. I am forever struck with this great idea that God has made everything, that he is everywhere, that he pervades everything, that he gives movement and life to all; and if he is in all parts of my being, as he is in all parts of nature, I don't see what I need a soul for. What do I need that little subordinate being for, since I am animated by God himself? What good is that soul to me? We are not responsible for our own ideas, for we have them almost always in spite of ourselves; we have them when we are asleep; everything happens within us without our having a hand in it. In vain would the soul tell the blood and the animal spirits, "Flow, I beg you, in this fashion, to give me pleasure"; they will always circulate in the manner God prescribed for them. I prefer being the machine of a God who is demonstrated to me to being the machine of a soul about which I have doubts.

CU-SU. Well! If God himself animates you, never sully with crimes the God who is within you; and if he has given you a soul, let that soul never offend him. By either system you have a will; you are free; that is, you have the power to do what you will: avail yourself of that power to serve the God who gave it to you. It is good that you are a philosopher, but it is necessary that you be just. You will be so even more when you believe that you have an immortal soul.

Deign to answer me: isn't it true that God is sovereign justice?

KOU. Certainly; and if it were ever possible for him to cease to be (which is a blasphemy), I, for one, should still like to act justly.

CU-SU. Isn't it true that it will be your duty, when you are on the throne, to reward virtuous actions and to punish criminal ones? Would you want God not to do what you yourself are bound to do? You know that in this life there are and will always be instances of unrewarded virtue and unpunished crime; it is therefore necessary that good and evil should be judged in another life. It is this idea — so simple, so natural, so general — which has led to the establishment, in so many nations, of the belief in the immortality of our souls and in a divine justice that judges them when they have sloughed off their moral skin. Is there a system more reasonable, more agreeable to the Divinity, and more useful to mankind?

KOU. Why then have several nations not adopted this system? You know that we have in our province about two hundred families of the ancient Sinous,[8] who lived at one time in a part of Arabia Petraea: neither they nor their ancestors have ever believed in an immortal soul; they have their *five Books*, as we have our *five Kings*; I have read them in translation; their laws, inevitably similar to those of all other nations, command them to respect their parents, neither to steal nor lie, to be neither adulterers nor murderers; but these same laws say nothing about either rewards or punishments in another life.

CU-SU. If that idea hasn't yet developed in that poor nation, it will doubtless do so one day. But what do we care about one unfortunate little nation when the Babylonians, the Egyptians, the Indians, and all civilized nations have accepted this salutary dogma? If you were ill, would you reject a remedy approved by all the Chinese on the pretext that a few barbarians from the mountains did not wish to make use of it? God has given you reason; it tells you that the soul must be immortal; it is thus God himself who tells you so.

KOU. But how could I be rewarded or punished when I'll no longer be myself, when I'll no longer be anything of that which has constituted my person? It is only through my memory that I am always myself; I lose my memory in my last illness; would it therefore require a miracle to restore it to me after my death, to make me return the existence I have lost?

CU-SU. That is to say that if a prince butchers his family in order to reign, if he tyrannizes over his subjects, he can get off by saying to God: "That wasn't me, I lost my memory, you're mistaken, I'm no longer the same person." Do you think that God would be satisfied with such a sophism? . . .

---

[8]These are the Jews of the ten tribes who in their dispersion got as far as China; they are there called *Sinous* (note by Voltaire).

FANATICISM

Fanaticism is to superstition what delirium is to fever and rage to anger. The man visited by ecstasies and visions, who takes dreams for realities and his fancies for prophecies, is an enthusiast; the man who supports his madness with murder is a fanatic. Jean Diaz, in retreat at Nuremberg, was firmly convinced that the pope was the Antichrist of the Apocalypse, and that he bore the sign of the beast; he was merely an enthusiast; his brother, Bartholomew Diaz, who came from Rome to assassinate his brother out of piety, and who did in fact kill him for the love of God, was one of the most abominable fanatics ever raised up by superstition.[9]

Polyeucte, who goes to the temple on a solemn holiday to knock over and smash the statues and ornaments, is a less dreadful but no less ridiculous fanatic than Diaz. The assassins of the duke François de Guise, of William, prince of Orange, of king Henry III, of king Henry IV, and of so many others, were fanatics sick with the same mania as Diaz.[10]

The most detestable example of fanaticism was that of the burghers of Paris who on St. Bartholomew's Night went about assassinating and butch-

[9]The fratricide described by Voltaire occurred on March 27, 1546. The murderer's name was not Bartholomew but Alfonso Diaz. Otherwise Voltaire's account is quite accurate. He discussed the case at greater length in a letter to Frederick the Great, which Besterman has tentatively dated December 20, 1740. In this letter he gives as his source Antonio de Herrera (y Tordesillas), *Commentarios de los Heche de los Espanoles, Franceres y Venecianos y de otras Republicas* (Madrid 1624). Voltaire reports that Herrera saw nothing wrong in the murder of Jean Diaz but on the contrary praised Alfonso for his courageous deed. The letter to Frederick is available in English translation in B. R. Redmann (ed.), *The Portable Voltaire* (New York 1949).

[10]François de Lorraine, second Duke de Guise (1519–1563), together with his brother, the Cardinal de Lorraine (c. 1525–1574), effectively controlled the French government for several years after the accession of the youthful Francis II. The two brothers were noted for their arrogance and their opposition to toleration of the Huguenots. They were responsible for the massacre of Protestants at Vassy (1562), which led to the French Wars of Religion. François was assassinated while preparing to attack Orléans. William of Orange, also known as William the Silent (1533–1584), was the principal architect of Dutch independence. Born of Protestant parents, he was brought up as a Catholic. He seems to have been religiously indifferent but did his best to promote toleration and, more specifically, to protect the Protestants against the fury of the Counter-Reformation. In 1555 he became *stadtholder* (a position corresponding to governor) of Holland, Zeeland, and Utrecht. Holland was at that time under Spanish domination and William loyally served Phillip II as a diplomat, but he turned against the king when the latter encroached on the liberties of the Dutch and tried to introduce the Spanish Inquisition into Holland. Phillip denounced William as a traitor and put a high price on his head. He was assassinated by a Catholic fanatic while the struggle with Spain was still in progress. In his letter of December 20, 1740, to Frederick, Voltaire called William "the creator of the liberty and grandeur of the Dutch." It seems strange that Voltaire should list the assassination of de Guise along with those of William of Orange and Henry IV, both great friends of toleration and the common people. He seems to have held that regicide and assassination in general are always wrong. He does not seem to have considered what is implied by this totally indefensible proposition. One is tempted to link this horror on his part with his fear in later years that the spread of atheism would lead to murder, rape, and all kinds of hideous crimes (*see* the Introduction, pp. 44–45).

ering all their fellow citizens who did not go to mass, throwing them out of windows, cutting them in pieces.[11]

There are cold-blooded fanatics: such as judges who condemn to death those who have committed no other crime than failing to think like them; and these judges are all the more guilty, all the more deserving of the execration of mankind, since, unlike Clément, Châtel, Ravaillac, Damiens,[12] they were not suffering from an attack of insanity; surely they should have been able to listen to reason.

Once fanaticism has corrupted a mind, the malady is almost incurable. I have seen convulsionaries who, speaking of the miracles of St. Pâris, gradually grew impassioned despite themselves: their eyes got inflamed, their limbs trembled, madness disfigured their faces, and they would have killed anyone who contradicted them.

The only remedy for this epidemic malady is the philosophical spirit which, spread gradually, at last tames men's habits and prevents the disease from starting; for, once the disease has made any progress, one must flee and wait for the air to clear itself. Laws and religion are not strong enough against the spiritual pest; religion, far from being healthy food for infected brains, turns to poison in them. These miserable men have forever in their minds the example of Ehud, who assassinated king Eglon; of Judith, who cut off Holofernes' head while she was sleeping with him; of Samuel, who chopped king Agag in pieces. They cannot see that these examples which were respectable in antiquity are abominable in the present; they borrow their frenzies from the very religion that condemns them.

Even the law is impotent against these attacks of rage; it is like reading a

---

[11]Voltaire again and again refers to the Massacre of St. Bartholomew's Eve (August 24, 1572). Two days before the massacre Catherine de Medici, the Queen Mother, had ordered an attack on the Huguenot leader, Admiral Coligny. When this failed, the Duke D'Anjou (later Henry III), the third Duke de Guise (son of François de Guise), and Catherine's weak son, Charles IX, decided on a general massacre. The opportunity was furnished by the presence of many of the Huguenot leaders in Paris for the wedding of Henry of Navarre (later Henry IV) to Catherine's daughter, Margaret of Valois. The massacre continued in Paris until September 17. From Paris it spread to the provinces. The king had sent instructions to provincial governors to kill all leading Huguenots, and in several provinces the massacre extended to all known Protestants. Many Catholics, to their great credit, denounced the slaughter and some took Huguenots into their homes to protect them from the murderous mobs. At Vienne the bishop took the Protestants under his personal protection, but in most cities the bishops helped to inflame the soldiers and the populace. Estimates of the total number killed range from 5,000 to 30,000. Pope Gregory XIII and his cardinals attended a Mass of Thanksgiving to God for "this signal favor shown to Christian people." He ordered a special medal of commemoration to be struck and commissioned the famous artist Giorgi Vasari to paint a picture of the massacre bearing the inscription *Pontifex Colignii necen probat* (The Pope approves the killing of Coligny.) Voltaire regarded the massacre as one of the darkest days in human history. In the *Treatise on Toleration*, he described it as "without precedent in the annals of crime."

[12]Jacques Clement (1567–1589) was a Dominican friar who, encouraged by extremists of the ultra-Catholic League, assassinated Henry III. For the other assassins on this list, see p. 121, note 1.

court decree to a raving maniac. These fellows are certain that the holy spirit with which they are filled is above the law, that their enthusiasm is the only law they must obey.

What can we say to a man who tells you that he would rather obey God than men, and that therefore he is sure to go to heaven for butchering you?

Ordinarily fanatics are guided by rascals, who put the dagger into their hands; these latter resemble that Old Man of the Mountain who is supposed to have made imbeciles taste the joys of paradise and who promised them an eternity of the pleasures of which he had given them a foretaste, on condition that they assassinated all those he would name to them. There is only one religion in the world that has never been sullied by fanaticism, that of the Chinese men of letters. The schools of philosophers were not only free from this pest, they were its remedy; for the effect of philosophy is to make the soul tranquil, and fanaticism is incompatible with tranquility. If our holy religion has so often been corrupted by this infernal delirium, it is the madness of men which is at fault.

FATE

Of all the books that have come down to us, the oldest is Homer; there we find the ways of profane antiquity, coarse heroes, coarse gods made in the image of man; but there, too, we find the seeds of philosophy, and above all the idea of fate, which is the master of the gods, as the gods are the masters of the world.

In vain does Jupiter wish to save Hector; he consults the fates; he weighs in a scale of fates of Hector and Achilles; he finds that the Trojan must absolutely be killed by the Greek; he can't do anything against it; and from that moment on Apollo, the guardian spirit of Hector, is obliged to give him up (*Iliad*, book 22). To be sure, in his poem Homer often throws out quite contrary ideas, following the privilege of antiquity; but still he is the first in whom the notion of fate is to be found. So, it must have been quite fashionable in his time.

Among the little Jewish people, the Pharisees adopted the idea of fate only several centuries later; for the Pharisees, who were the first Jews to be scholars, were new men themselves. In Alexandria they mixed a part of Stoic dogma with ancient Jewish ideas. St. Jerome even claims that their sect does not antedate our common era by very much.

The philosophers never needed either Homer or the Pharisees to convince themselves that everything happens according to immutable laws, that everything is arranged, that everything is a necessary effect.

Either the world subsists by its own nature, by its own physical laws, or a supreme Being has created it in accordance with his supreme law: in either case, these laws are immutable; in either case, everything is necessary;

heavy bodies tend toward the center of the earth, and cannot tend to rest in the air. Pear trees can never bear pineapples. The instinct of a spaniel cannot be the instinct of an ostrich. Everything is regulated, correlated and circumscribed.

Man can only have a certain number of teeth, hairs, and ideas; there comes a time when he must lose his teeth, his hair, and his ideas.

It is a contradiction to say that what existed yesterday didn't exist, that what exists today does not exist; it is equally a contradiction to say that what has to exist doesn't have to exist.

If you could unsettle the destiny of one fly, there would be no reason on earth why you couldn't fashion the fate of all the other flies, all the animals, mankind, and nature; finally you would find yourself more powerful than God.

Imbeciles say: "My doctor pulled my aunt through a mortal illness; he has made my aunt live ten years longer than she should have." Others, who know better, say: "The prudent man makes his own fate."

> *Nullum numen abest, si sit prudentia, sed te*
> *Nos facimus, fortuna, deam, caeloque locamus.*
> [*Had we but wisdom we would see that Fortune*
> *Is not divine: we make her so, place her in heaven.*
>   Juvenal, *Satires*, X, 365–366.]

But often the prudent man, far from making his own destiny, succumbs to it; prudent men are created by fate.

Profound statesmen argue that if Cromwell, Ludlow, Ireton,[13] and a dozen other parliamentary leaders had been assassinated a week before they cut off Charles I's head, this king could have gone on living and died in his bed: they are right; they might add that if all England had been engulfed in the sea, this monarch wouldn't have died on the scaffold at *Witehall*, or white hall; but things were arranged in such a way that Charles had to have his throat cut.

Cardinal d'Ossat[14] was doubtless more prudent than a lunatic in a madhouse; but isn't it obvious that the organs of the sage d'Ossat were fashioned differently from the organs of a harebrain, just as the fox's organs are different from a crane's or lark's?

Your doctor saved your aunt; but he certainly didn't negate the order of nature to do so: he followed it. It is clear that your aunt couldn't prevent herself from being born in a certain town, that she couldn't prevent herself from having a certain illness at a certain time, that the doctor could not be

---

[13]Edmund Ludlow (c. 1617–1692) was one of the judges who condemned Charles I to death in 1649. Henry Ireton (1611–1651), Cromwell's son-in-law, held various commands in the parliamentary army and signed the death warrant of Charles I. In 1650 he was appointed lord deputy of Ireland where he sternly carried out Cromwell's policy of dispossessing the Irish and settling Englishmen.

[14]Arnaud d'Ossat (1536–1604), French cardinal and diplomat who brought about a reconciliation between Henry IV and the papacy.

anywhere but in the town where he was, that your aunt had to call him, that he had to prescribe the drugs that cured her.

A peasant believes that hail fell on his field by chance; but the philosopher knows there is no chance, and that, given the way this world is constituted, it couldn't possibly not have hailed on that day and in that place.

There are people who, afraid of this truth, grant only half of it, like debtors who offer their creditors half and demand remission for the rest. There are necessary events, they say, and others which are not necessary. If would be amusing indeed if one part of this world were ordered, and the other not; if part of what happens has to happen, and another part of what happens does not have to happen. If we examine this closely, we see that the anti-fatalistic doctrine is absurd; but there are many people fated to think badly, others not to think at all, and others to persecute those who think.

There are people who tell you: "Don't believe in fatalism; for then everything will seem inevitable to you, you won't work at anything, you will stagnate in indifference, you will love neither riches, honors, nor praises; you won't want to acquire anything, you will think of yourself as without capacities and without power; you will cultivate no talent; everything will perish in apathy."

Gentlemen, fear not, we shall always have passions and prejudices, since it is our destiny to be subjected to prejudices and passions; we know perfectly well that having great capacities and great talents no more depends on us than having beautiful hair or well-shaped hands; we are convinced that we ought not to be vain about anything, and yet we are always vain.

I necessarily have the passion to write this; and you — you have the passion to condemn me; both of us are equally foolish, equally the plaything of destiny. Your nature is to do evil, mine is to love the truth and to publish it in spite of you.

The owl which feeds on mice in his ruin, said to the nightingale: "Stop singing in your beautiful shade, come into my hole so I can eat you"; and the nightingale replied: "I was born to sing here and to laugh at you."

You ask me what will become of liberty. I don't understand you. I don't know what this liberty is that you speak of; you have been arguing about its nature for so long that it is certain you know nothing about it. If you would like to know, or rather if you could peacefully examine with me what it is, then turn to the letter L.

FINAL CAUSES

A man, it seems, must be mad to deny that stomachs were made to digest, eyes to see, ears to hear.

On the other hand, a man must have a strange love of final causes to assert that rocks were created to build houses, and that silkworms are born in China so that we might have satin in Europe.

But, you say, if God evidently did one thing by design, then he did all things by design. It is ridiculous to admit Providence in one case and deny it in others. Everything that was done was foreseen, was arranged. No arrangement without object, no effect without cause; hence everything is equally the result, the product, of a final cause; hence it is as true to say that noses were made to wear glasses, and fingers to be decorated with diamonds, as it is to say that ears were shaped to hear sounds and eyes to receive light.

I think this difficulty can be cleared up easily. When the effects are invariably the same at all times and in all places, when these uniform effects are independent of the beings to which they belong, then there is evidently a final cause.

All animals have eyes, and they see; all have ears, and they hear; all a mouth, with which they eat; a stomach, or something approximately like it, with which they digest; all an opening through which they void excrement, all an instrument of generation: and these gifts of nature work in them without human skill taking a hand. Here are final causes clearly established, and it is to pervert our thinking faculty to deny so universal a truth.

But rocks do not make buildings at all times and in all places; all noses do not wear glasses; all fingers do not have a ring; all legs are not covered with silk stockings. Hence a silkworm is not made to cover my legs as your mouth is made to eat and your behind to sit on the toilet. Hence there are effects produced by final causes, and a very large number of effects which cannot be so named.

But the former and the latter take part equally in the plan of general Providence; surely nothing happens despite it, nor even without it. All that belongs to nature is uniform, immutable, the immediate work of the Master; it is he who created the laws by which the moon is three-quarters responsible for the ebb and flow of the ocean, and the sun one-quarter; it is he who gave a rotating movement to the sun, by which this star sends light rays into the eyes of men, crocodiles, and cats, in five and a half minutes.

But if after many centuries we hit on the idea of inventing shears and spits, to clip the wool of sheep with the first, and to roast them with the second in order to eat them, what may we infer from this but that God made us so that some day we might necessarily become skillful and carnivorous?

To be sure, sheep were not made expressly to be roasted and eaten, since several nations abstain from this enormity; men were not essentially created to massacre one another, for the Brahmins and the Quakers kill no one; yet the clay from which we are kneaded often produces massacres, as it produces slanders, futilities, persecutions, and impertinences. It is not that the creation of man is the final cause of our madness and our idiocies: for a final cause is universal and invariable at all times and in all places; yet the horrors and absurdities of the human species are no less in the eternal order of things. When we thresh our wheat, the flail is the final cause of the separation of the grains. But if that flail, threshing my grain, crushes a thousand insects, that doesn't happen by my settled will—not does it happen by chance: these insects found themselves under my flail at this time, and they had to find themselves there.

It is a consequence of the nature of things that a man should be ambitious, that he should sometimes enlist other men, that he should be victor or vanquished; but we can never say: Man was created by God to be killed in war.

The instruments nature has given us cannot always be final causes in action, with an unfailing effect. Eyes made to see are not always open; every sense has its time of rest. There are even senses which we never use. For example, a miserable imbecile, shut up in a cloister at fourteen, forever shuts the door through which a new generation might emerge; but the final cause exists in her no less: it will operate as soon as she is free.

OF LIBERTY

A. Here's a battery of cannon discharged at our ears; do you have the liberty of hearing or not hearing it?

B. Doubtless I can't prevent myself from hearing it.

A. Do you want this cannon to carry off your head and the heads of your wife and daughter, who are walking with you?

B. What kind of suggestion is that? As long as I'm in my right mind, I can't want any such thing; that's impossible for me.

A. Good; you necessarily hear these cannon, and you and your family necessarily don't want to die from a cannon shot while you're walking; you neither have the power of not hearing it, nor the power of wanting to stay here.

B. That's clear.[15]

A. Accordingly you have taken about thirty steps to be out of the cannon's reach; you had the power of walking a few steps with me?

B. That's still quite clear.

A. And if you had been a paralytic, you couldn't have avoided being exposed to this battery; you wouldn't have had the power to be where you

---

[15]A dull-witted fellow objects in an honest, polite, and above all well-argued little book, that if the prince ordered B. to remain exposed to the cannon, he would stay there. Yes, surely, if he has more courage, or rather, more fear of shame than love of life, which often happens. First, the case here is quite different. Second, when the instinct of the fear of shame wins out over the instincts of self-preservation, this man is as much compelled to remain exposed to the cannon as he would be compelled to flee were he not ashamed to flee. The dull-witted author was compelled to offer ridiculous objections and hurl insults; and the philosophers feel compelled to make a little fun of him, and to forgive him (note added by Voltaire).

are: you would necessarily have heard and got a cannon shot, and you would necessarily have died.

B. Nothing is truer than that.

A. Then what does your liberty consist of, if not of the power your self has exercised, of doing what your will has exacted from absolute necessity?

B. You puzzle me; liberty, then, is nothing but the power of doing what I want to do?

A. Think about it, and see if liberty can be understood in any other way.

B. In that case, my hunting dog is as free as I am; he necessarily has the will to run when he sees a hare, and the power to run if his legs are all right. I have nothing on my dog, then: you reduce me to the condition of animals.

A. Those are the poor sophisms of the poor sophists who taught you. It makes you sick to be free like your dog! Well! Don't you resemble your dog in a thousand things? Don't you resemble your dog in a thousand things? Don't you have hunger, thirst, wakefulness, sleepiness, your five senses, in common with him? Would you like to smell other than through his nose? Why do you want to have a liberty different from his?

B. But I have a soul which thinks a great deal, and my dog hardly thinks at all. He has but simple ideas, and I have a thousand metaphysical ideas.

A. All right! you are a thousand times freer than he is: that is, you have a thousand times more power of thinking than he has; but you are not free in a different manner from him.

B. What! Am I not free to want what I want?

A. What do you mean by that?

B. I mean by that what everybody means. Don't people say daily: "Wills are free"?

A. A proverb is not a reason; explain yourself better.

B. I mean that I am free to want as I please.

A. With your permission, that makes no sense; don't you see that it's ridiculous to say: "I want to want"? You necessarily want, in consequence of ideas that present themselves to you. Do you want to get married, yes or no?

B. But if I told you that I want neither one nor the other?

A. You would be replying like the man who said: "Some think that cardinal Mazarin is dead, others think that he is alive, and I don't think either one or the other."

B. All right! I want to get married.

A. Ah! Now that's giving an answer! Why do you want to get married?

B. Because I'm in love with a young lady who is pretty, sweet, well educated, quite well off, sings well, has very decent parents; and I flatter myself that I am loved in return and welcome in her family.

A. There's a reason. You see that you cannot want without reasons. I declare to you that you are free to get married; that is; you have the power of signing the contract.

B. Indeed! I cannot want without reasons? Well! What will become of this other proverb: *Sit pro ratione voluntas:* my will is my reason, I will because I will?

A. That's absurd, my good friend: there would be an effect without a cause in you.

B. What! When I play at odd or even I have a reason for choosing even over odd?

A. Yes, of course.

B. And what is that reason, please?

A. It's that the idea of even has come to your mind rather than the opposite idea. It would be amusing if there were cases in which you will because there is a cause for willing, and some cases in which you will without cause. When you want to get married, you obviously feel the reason why; you don't feel it when you play at odd or even, and yet there must be one.

B. But once again, I'm not free then?

A. Your will is not free, but your actions are. You are free to act when you have the power to act.

B. But all those books I've read on the liberty of indifference. . . .

A. Are nonsense: there is no liberty of indifference; that is a term without sense, invented by people who had hardly any themselves.

MATTER

Sages who are asked, "What is the soul?" reply that they have no idea. If they are asked, "What is matter?" they give the same reply. It is true that professors, and above all school-boys, know it all perfectly; and when they have repeated that matter is extended and divisible, they think they have said everything; but when they are asked to say what this extended thing is, they find themselves puzzled. "It is composed of parts," they say. And what are these parts composed of? Are the elements of these parts divisible? Then they either are silent or else they talk a lot — which is equally suspicious. Is this almost unknown entity, called matter, eternal? All antiquity thought so. Does it have its own active force? Several philosophers have thought so. Are those who deny it right to deny it? You can't imagine that matter should be anything in itself. But how can you assert that in itself it does not have all the properties it needs? You don't know what its nature is, and yet you deny it modes which are in its nature; for, after all, once it exists, it must be of a certain kind, it must have shape; and, if it necessarily has shape, could not other modes enter into its configuration? Matter exists; you know that only by your sensations. Alas! What good have all these intellectual subtleties been since men began to think? Geometry teaches us a great many truths, metaphysics very few. We weigh matter, we measure it, we decompose it; and if we want to make one step beyond these crude operations, we find impotence within us and an abyss before us.

Kindly forgive the whole universe for mistakenly believing in self-exist-
measure it, we decompose it; and if we want to take one step beyond these
crude operations, we find impotence within us, and an abyss before us.
ing matter. Could it do anything else? How could men imagine that that
which is without succession has not always been? If it was not necessary for
matter to exist, why does it exist? And, if it had to be, why has it not always
been? No axiom has ever been more universally accepted than this: *Nothing
is made from nothing.* In fact, the contrary is incomprehensible. In all
nations, chaos has preceded the arrangement of the world made by a divine
hand. The eternity of matter has not injured the cult of the Divinity in any
nation. Religion has never been disquieted that an eternal God should be
recognized as the master of an eternal matter. Today we are lucky enough
to know by faith that God drew matter from nothingness; but no nation was
educated in this doctrine; even the Jews didn't know it. The first verse of
Genesis says that the gods, *Elohim,* not *Eloi,* made heaven and earth; it does
not say heaven and earth were created out of nothing.

Philo, who lived in the only period in which the Jews had any erudition,
says in his chapter on creation: "God, being good by his nature, did not
envy substance, matter, which had nothing good in itself, which had nothing in its nature but inertia, confusion, disorder. Bad though it was, he
deigned to make it good."

The idea of a chaos unraveled by a God is found in all the ancient
theogonies. Hesiod repeated what the Orient thought, when he said in his
Theogony: "Chaos was the first thing that existed." Ovid was the spokesman
for the whole Roman empire when he said:

> *Sic ubi dispositam, quisquis fuit ille deorum*
> *Congeriem secuit . . .*
> [*Whoever the god that brought order to*
> *The chaotic mass . . .*
> [*Metamorphoses*, I, 32–33]

Matter, in the hands of God, was thus felt to be like clay on the potter's
wheel, if it is permissible to use such feeble images to express divine
power.

Matter, being eternal, must have eternal properties, like configuration,
force of inertia, movement, and divisibility. But this divisibility is only the
consequence of movement; for without movement nothing divides, sepa-
rates, or arranges itself. Movement was thus regarded as essential to
matter. Chaos had been a confused movement, and the ordering of the
universe a regular movement, impressed on all bodies by the master of the
world. But how does matter have movement of itself? As it has, according to
all the ancients, extension and impenetrability.

But it can't be conceived without extension, and it can be conceived
without movement. To this, one might reply: "It is impossible for matter
not to be permeable; now, since it is permeable, something must contin-

ually pass through its pores; what good are these passages if nothing passes through them?"

Piling reply on reply, we shall never be finished; the system of eternal matter has very great difficulties, like all systems. That of matter created from nothing is no less incomprehensible. We must admit it, and not flatter ourselves that we are explaining it; philosophy does not explain everything. What incomprehensible things haven't we been obliged to accept as true, even in geometry? Can we conceive of two lines that approach one another forever, and still never touch?

To be sure, the geometers will tell us: "The properties of asymptotes are demonstrated; you cannot help but accept them as true; but creation is not demonstrated: why do you accept it as true? What difficulty do you find in believing, as all antiquity did, in eternal matter?" From another side you will be pushed by the theologian who will tell you: "If you believe in eternal matter, you then recognize two principles, God and matter; you fall into the error of Zoroaster, of the Manicheans."

We won't answer the geometers, because these fellows know only their lines and surfaces and solids. But we might say to the theologian: "In what am I a Manichean? Here are stones an architect has not made; he has raised an immense building with them; I don't accept two architects; brute stone obeyed power and genius."

MIRACLES

A miracle, according to the real meaning of the word, is something admirable. Then everything is a miracle. The marvelous order of nature, the rotation of a hundred million globes around a million suns, the activity of light, the life of animals — these are perpetual miracles.

According to accepted notions, we call *miracle* the violation of these divine and eternal laws. Let there be an eclipse of the sun during a full moon, let a dead man walk five miles carrying his head in his arms, and we'll call that a miracle.

Some natural scientists maintain that there are no miracles in this sense of the word; and here are their arguments.

A miracle is the violation of mathematical, divine, immutable, eternal laws. By this very statement, a miracle is a contradiction in terms. A law cannot be immutable and violable at the same time. But, they may be asked, can't a law be suspended by its author, since it was established by God himself? They have the insolence to answer, No, that it is impossible for the infinitely wise Being to make laws in order to violate them. They say that he might unsettle his machine, but only to make it go better; however, it is clear that, being God, he made this immense machine as best he could: if he had seen some imperfections resulting from the nature of the material, he would have attended to that in the beginning; so he will never change anything in it.

Moreover, God cannot do anything without reason; now that reason could make him temporarily disfigure his own work?

For the sake of men, they will be told. Then, they reply, it would be at least for the sake of all men; for it is impossible to conceive Divine Nature working for some men in particular, and not for the whole human race; and even the human race is quite unimportant: it is much less than a small anthill in comparison with all the beings that fill infinity. Now isn't it the most absurd piece of folly to imagine that the infinite Being would reverse the eternal working of the immense activity which makes the whole universe move, all for the sake of three or four hundred ants on this little mud pile?

But let's suppose that God had wanted to single out a small number of men by special favors: would he need to change what he had established for all times and places? Surely he has no need for this change, this inconstancy, to favor his creatures: his favors are in his very laws. He has foreseen everything, arranged everything, for them; all obey irrevocably the force that he has impressed on nature forever.

Why should God perform a miracle? To realize a certain plan concerning a few living beings! He would then be saying: "I could not complete a certain plan, with the universe ordered as it now is according to my divine decrees, my eternal laws; I am going to change my eternal ideas, my immutable laws, to try to execute what I could not do with them." This would be an admission of his weakness, not his power. It would seem to be the most inconceivable contradiction in him. Therefore, to dare palm off miracles on God is really to insult him (if men can insult God); it's to tell him: "You are a weak and inconsistent being." It is therefore absurd to believe in miracles—in one way or another it dishonors Divinity.

These philosophers are pressed hard; they are told: "In vain do you exalt the immutability of the supreme Being, the eternity of his laws, the regularity of his infinite worlds: our little mud heap proliferates with miracles; the histories are as full of prodigies as of natural events. The daughters of the high priest Anius changed everything they wanted to into wheat, wine, or oil; Athalide, Mercury's daughter, came back to life several times; Aesculapius revived Hippolytus; Hercules tore Alcestis from the grasp of death; Er came back to the world after spending two weeks in hell; Romulus and Remus were the children of a god and a vestal virgin; the Palladium fell from heaven in the city of Troy; Berenice's hair became a constellation; the hut of Baucis and Philemon was changed into a superb temple; Orpheus' head spoke oracles after his death; the walls of Thebes built themselves at the sound of the flute, in the presence of the Greeks; the cures performed in the temple of Aesculapius were innumerable, and we still have documents containing the names of eye-witnesses of Aesculapius' miracles."

Give me the name of a nation where incredible prodigies have not been performed, above all in times when they could hardly read and write.

The philosophers reply to these objections merely by laughing and shrugging their shoulders; but Christian philosophers say: "We believe in the miracles performed in our holy religion; we believe them with faith, and not with our reason, which we take care not to listen to; for, as everybody knows, when faith speaks, reason must hold its tongue. We believe in the miracles of Jesus Christ and his apostles firmly and absolutely, but allow us to doubt a little those of some others; for example, permit us to suspend our judgment on the things reported by a simple man to whom the title 'great' has been given. He maintains that a little monk was so accustomed to perform miracles that finally the prior prohibited him from exercising his talent. The little monk obeyed; but, when he saw a poor tiler falling from the top of a roof, he hesitated between the desire to save his life and holy obedience. He merely ordered the tiler to stay in the air until he had fresh instructions, and he ran quickly to inform his prior about the matter. The prior absolved him of the sin he had committed in starting a miracle without permission, and permitted him to finish it, provided he remained content with it and did nothing further. We will grant the philosophers that they may distrust this story a little."

But how dare you deny, the philosophers are further asked, that St. Gervasius and St. Protasius appeared to St. Ambrose in a dream, informing him of the place where their relics could be found? That St. Ambrose had them dug up, and that they cured a blind man? St. Augustine was then in Milan; it is he who reports this miracle: *Immenso populo teste*, he writes in his *City of God*, book XXII. This is one of the best-confirmed of miracles. The philosophers reply that they don't believe a word of it; that Gervasius and Protasius appeared to nobody; that it matters precious little to mankind whether it know where the remains of their carcasses are; that they have no more faith in this blind man than in Vespasian's[16] that it is a useless miracle; that God does nothing useless; and they hold firmly to their principles. My respect for St. Gervasius and St. Protasius doesn't permit me to share the opinion of these philosophers: I merely report on their incredulity. They make much of the passage in Lucian,[17] which is in *The Death of Peregrinus*: "When an adroit juggler turns Christian, he is sure to make his fortune." But, since Lucian is a secular author, he should have no influence over us.

[16]*See* pp. 52 and 57 of the Introduction on Vespasian's supposedly miraculous cures during his visit to Alexandria.

[17]Lucian of Samosata (c. 120–180), Greek satirist, who frequently made fun of religious beliefs. *The Death of Peregrinus* is the story of Peregrinus Poteus who spends his life trying to find the true religion. Disregarding logic he accepts them all and ends his life by walking into a pyre.

These philosophers cannot bring themselves to believe the miracles performed in the second century. In vain have eyewitnesses written that when St. Polycarp, bishop of Smyrna, was condemned to be burned and thrown into the flames, they heard a voice from heaven which exclaimed: "Courage, Polycarp! Be strong, show yourself a man!" that then the flames of the stake turned aside from his body and formed a pavilion of fire around his head, and a dove flew out of the midst of the stake; finally, they had to cut off Polycarp's head. "What is this miracle good for?" ask the unbelievers. "Why did the flames lose their power, and why didn't the executioner's ax lose its power? How is it that so many martyrs emerge safe and sound from burning oil, and they cannot resist the edge of the sword?" The reply is that it was the will of God. But the philosophers want to see all this with their own eyes before they believe it.

Those who fortify their arguments with science will tell you that the Fathers of the Church themselves often admitted that no more miracles were being performed in their time. St. Chrysostom expressly says: "The extraordinary gifts of the spirit were given even to the unworthy, because then the Church had need of miracles; but today they are not even given to the worthy, because the Church no longer needs them" Later he admits that there is no longer anybody who resurrects the dead, nor even anybody who cures the sick.

Despite the miracle of St. Gervasius and of Protasius, St. Augustine himself says in his *City of God: Cur, inquiunt, nunc illa miracula quae praedicatis facta esse non funt?* — "Why, they ask, are the miracles which, you boast, used to be performed no longer performed today?" And he gives the same reason for it: *Possem quidem dicere necessaria prius fuisse quam crederet mundus, ad hoc ut crederet mundus.* — "Indeed, I might say that miracles were necessary before the world believed, so that it might believe."

It is objected against the philosophers that in spite of this admission, St. Augustine still mentions an old cobbler of Hippo who went to pray in the chapel of the twenty martyrs after he had lost his clothes; when he came home he found a fish with a gold ring in its body, and the cook who cooked the fish said to the cobbler: "Here's what the twenty martyrs have given you."

To this the philosophers reply that there is nothing in the story that contradicts the laws of nature, that physical laws are in no way violated by a fish swallowing a gold ring and a cook giving this ring to a cobbler; there is no miracle here.

If one reminds these philosophers that according to St. Jerome, in his *Life of the Hermit Paul*, this hermit had several conversations with satyrs and fauns, that a raven brought him half a loaf for dinner for thirty years, and a whole loaf on the day St. Anthony came to see him, they would still reply that all this is not entirely against the laws of nature, that satyrs and fauns might have existed, and that in any case, if a tale is a piece of childishness, it has nothing in common with the true miracles of the Savior and his apostles. Several good Christians have objected to the history of St. Simeon Stylites, written by Theodoret. Many miracles the Greek Church accepts as authentic have been called in question by several Latins, just as Latin miracles have been suspect to the Greek Church; finally came the Protestants who have handled the miracles of both Churches very roughly.

A learned Jesuit,[18] who preached in India for many years, complains that neither he nor his brethren could ever perform a miracle. Xavier laments in several of his letters that he doesn't have the give of tongues; he says that among the Japanese he was like a mute statue. True, the Jesuits have written that he brought eight dead men back to life: that's a great deal; but we must also take into account that he brought them back to life fifteen thousand miles from here. Since then, there have been people who claim that the abolition of the Jesuits in France has been a much greater miracle than those of Xavier and Ignatius.

Be that as it may, all Christians agree that the miracles of Jesus Christ and his apostles are incontestably true, but that we may strongly doubt some miracles performed in recent times, which have not been fully authenticated.

For instance, it would be desirable that a miracle, for the sake of being fully verified, should be performed in the presence of the Academy of Sciences in Paris, or the Royal Society in London, and the Faculty of Medicine, assisted by a detachment of the regiment of Guards to keep back the crowd of the common people, whose impertinence might interfere with the performance of the miracle.

One day a philosopher was asked what he would say if he saw the sun stop; that is, if the movement of the earth around that star ceased, if all the dead came back to life, and if all the mountains threw themselves into the ocean together—all this to prove some important truth, like, say, versatile grace. "What would I say?" replied the philosopher. "I'd turn Manichean; I'd say that there is one principle that unmakes what the other principle has made."[19]

---

[18]Ospiniam, page 230 (note by Voltaire).

[19]The following information about the saints mentioned in this section may be of some interest. St. Gervasius and St. Protasius were martyrs. It is not known when they lived. Voltaire quite accurately reports that in the year 386 remains were found in Milan which purported to be those of the two martyrs and that their discovery was the result of a search ordered by St. Ambrose after their appearance in a dream.

St. Ambrose (c. 334–397) is usually regarded along with St. Augustine, St. Jerome, and Gregory the Great as one of the four great Latin doctors of the Church. He was Bishop of Milan from 374 until his death. One of his ruling principles was that "the emperor is within the Church and not above it." After the Emperor Theodosius had ordered a savage massacre in Salonika in 390 as a reprisal for the killing of the Roman governor, Ambrose forced Theodosius to do public penance.

St. Jerome (342–420), like Ambrose one of the leading Fathers of the early Church, revised the Latin version of the New Testament. He engaged in many heated controversies

RESURRECTION

We are told that the Egyptians built their pyramids only as tombs, and that their bodies, embalmed inside and out, waited to be revived by their souls at the end of a thousand years. But if their bodies were meant to come back to life, why was the embalmer's first care to pierce the skull with a small hook and draw out the brain? The idea of coming back to life without a brain leads us to suspect (if we may use this word) that the Egyptians hardly had one while they lived; but we must consider after all that most of the ancients thought the soul was seated in the chest. And why was the soul seated in the chest rather than elsewhere? Because in experiencing any emotions of the least violence we in fact feel a dilation or compression in the region of the heart, which led people to think that here was the soul's lodging place. This soul was an airy thing, a light shape that wandered where it could until it had found its body again.

The belief in resurrection is much older than historic times. Athalide, Mercury's daughter, was able to die and come back to life at will; Aescula-

---

—concerning celibacy, Pelagianism, and the teachings of Origen. His intemperateness and use of savage invective made him many enemies.

St. Polycarp (?–155), Bishop of Smyrna at a time when Christians were persecuted, was betrayed by a servant. He was taken before the proconsul in the stadium and asked to take an oath to the emperor and curse Jesus Christ. He refused and was ordered to be burned at the stake. When the flames did not seem to reach his body, the executioner was ordered to stab him. Voltaire seems to have been wrong in saying that Polycarp was beheaded.

St. John Chrysostom (347–407) joined the clergy at Antioch in 381. His sermons were noted for their eloquence and in 398 he was elected Archbishop of Constantinople. He could be tactless and abrasive and he incurred the hostility of many influential men including the emperor Theophilus. Eventually he was deprived of his position and banished, first to Cucusus in Armenia and then to Pithyios in Iberia. He died from exhaustion on the road to his second exile.

St. Antony (251–356) has been called the "classic representative" of the desert fathers who lived in remote places in caves, huts, and abandoned buildings. From 331 until his death he lived in a cave on Mt. Kolzin near the northwest corner of the Red Sea. Unlike some of the other desert fathers, he did not practice extreme forms of self-mortification. If the official dates are correct, he lived to the age of 105.

St. Simeon the Stylite (390–459) was the first and most famous of the "Pillar Ascetics." After subjecting himself to extreme austerities such as prolonged periods of fasting, he began to live on a pillar. At first the pillar was low, but eventually its height was raised to 60 feet. At the top was a platform that measured twelve square feet. Simeon spent the last 36 years of his life on the top of this pillar. He gave as reason for his strange mode of existence a desire to avoid the press of people who flocked to him for advice. Needless to say he achieved the opposite result and far more people came to view and talk to him. It is reported that he was full of kindliness and sympathy.

St. Francis Xavier (1506–1552) was strongly influenced by Ignatius of Loyola, his fellow student at the University of Paris, and he became one of the seven founding members of the Society of Jesus. He is remembered primarily for his extensive missionary work in Portuguese India and later in Japan. The miracles he supposedly worked may not stand up to criticism, but his successes in preaching and personal conversion were enormous. Xavier is the patron saint of Catholic missionaries in foreign countries.

pius brought Hippolytus back to life; Hercules, Alcestis, Pelops hacked into pieces by his father—all were resurrected by the gods. Plato relates that Er was resurrected for only two weeks.

Among the Jews, the doctrine of the resurrection was adopted by the Pharisees only long after Plato's time.

In the Acts of the Apostles there is a very odd occurrence, well worthy of attention. St. James and several of his companions advised St. Paul to go to the temple in Jerusalem and there observe all the ceremonies of the ancient law, Christian though he was: "Thus all will know that there is nothing in what they have been told about you but that you yourself live in observance of the law." This is to say quite clearly: "Go and lie, go and perjure yourself, go and publicly deny the religion you teach."

So St. Paul went to the temple for a week, but on the seventh day he was recognized and accused of coming there with foreigners and profaning it. Here is how he extricated himself from this affair:

"But when Paul perceived that one part were Sadducees and the other Pharisees, he cried out in the council, 'Brethren, I am a Pharisee, a son of Pharisees; with respect to the hope and the resurrection of the dead I am on trial.'"[20] The resurrection of the dead wasn't involved in the least in this whole business; Paul said it only to arouse the Pharisees and Sadducees against one another.

Verse 7. "And when he had said this, a dissension arose between the Pharisees and the Sadducees; and the assembly was divided."

Verse 8. "For the Sadducees say that there is no resurrection, nor angel, nor spirit; but the Pharisees acknowledge them all" etc.

It has been argued that Job, who goes back to very ancient times, knew the dogma of the resurrection. These words are cited: "For I know that my Redeemer lives, and at last he will stand upon the earth; or that I shall rise from the dead, that my skin shall return, and that I shall still see God in my flesh."

But several commentators understand by these words that Job hopes he will soon recover from his illness, and that he will not always remain stretched out on the ground, as he was then forced to be. What follows proves that this explanation is the right one, for the moment after he exclaims to his false and hardened friends: "When then do you say, Let us persecute him?" or rather: "For you shall say, Because we persecuted him." Doesn't this obviously mean: "You will repent of having offended me when you once again see me in my earlier condition of health and opulence." A sick man who says: "I shall get up again," does not say: "I shall come back to life." To place strained interpretations on clear passages is a sure way of never understanding them, or rather, of being regarded as a man of bad faith by honest men.

[20] Acts of the Apostles, chapter 23, verse 6 (note by Voltaire).

St. Jerome holds that the sect of the Pharisees arose only a short time before Jesus Christ. Rabbi Hillel is considered the founder of the Pharisaic sect, and Hillel was the contemporary of Gamaliel, who was St. Paul's master.

Some of the Pharisees believed that the Jews alone were resurrected, and that the rest of mankind weren't worth it. Others maintained that people would be resurrected only in Palestine, and that the bodies of those who had been buried elsewhere would be secretly transported to Jerusalem to rejoin their souls there. But St. Paul, writing to the inhabitants of Thessalonica, tells them that the second coming of Christ is for them and for him, that they will be his witnesses.

Verse 16. "For the Lord himself will descend from heaven with a cry of command, with the archangel's call, and with the sound of the trumpet of God. And the dead in Christ will rise first."

Verse 17. "Then we who are alive, who are left, shall be caught up together with them in the clouds to meet the Lord in the air; and so we shall always be with the Lord."[21]

Doesn't this important passage plainly prove that the first Christians counted on seeing the end of the world, as in fact it is predicted in St. Luke, even for the time in which St. Luke lived? If they failed to see the end of the world, if no one was resurrected at that time, what was deferred was not lost.

St. Augustine believed that children, and even children born dead, would be resurrected full grown. Origen, Jerome, Athanasius, Basil, didn't believe that women should be resurrected in their sex.

In a word, people have always disputed over what we were, what we are, and what we shall be.

Second Section

Father Malebranche proves the resurrection from caterpillars turning into butterflies. Of course, his proof is as slight as the wings of the insects from which he borrows it. Thinkers who can calculate offer arithmetical objections to the truth of resurrection, well proved though it is. They say that men and the other animals are really fed by, and get their growth from, the substance of their predecessors. The body of a man, reduced to ashes, scattered in the air and falling back to the surface of the earth, turns into a vegetable or wheat. Thus Cain ate a part of Adam; Enoch fed on Cain, Irad on Enoch, Mahalaleel on Irad; Methuselah on Mahalaleel; and thus there isn't one of us who hasn't swallowed a small portion of our first father. That is why it has been said that we are all of us cannibals. Nothing makes more sense after a battle; we don't only kill our brothers, but at the end of two or three years, when we have harvested on the battlefield, we have eaten

---

[21] Epistle to the Thessalonians, chapter 4 (note by Voltaire).

them all; undoubtedly we shall be eaten in turn. Now, when the time of resurrection comes, how shall we allot to each the body that belongs to him without losing a part of our own?

That is what men say who distrust resurrection; but the resurrectors have answered them very pertinently.

A rabbi named Samai proves the resurrection with this passage from Exodus: "I appeared to Abraham, Isaac, and Jacob; and I swore to give them the land of Canaan." Now, says this great rabbi, despite his oath, God did not give them that land; hence they will be resurrected to enjoy it, so that the oath may be fulfilled.

Dom Calmet,[22] that profound philosopher, finds a much more conclusive proof in vampires. He has seen vampires coming out of cemeteries to suck the blood of sleeping men; it is clear that these vampires could not suck the blood of the living if they were still dead; hence they were resurrected: that's final.

Another thing that's certain is that all the dead will creep under the surface of the earth on judgment day like moles, as the Talmud says, to emerge in the valley of Jehoshaphat, which lies between Jerusalem and the Mount of Olives. They will be rather crowded in the valley; but all that's necessary is to shrink the bodies proportionally, as was the case with Milton's devils in the hall of Pandemonium.

The resurrection will take place to the sound of the trumpet, according to St. Paul. There will have to be several trumpets, for thunder itself can hardly be heard more than seven or eight miles around. There is a question how many trumpets will be needed: the theologians haven't yet calculated the number; but they will.

The Jews say that queen Cleopatra, who doubtless believed in resurrection like all the ladies of her time, asked a Pharisee if people would be resurrected naked. The scholar replied that they would be fully clothed, because when sown wheat has died in the earth, it rises again in ear with a robe and tassels. This rabbi was an excellent theologian; he reasoned like Dom Calmet.

SELF-LOVE

A beggar of the suburbs of Madrid boldly asked alms. A passerby said to him, "Are you not ashamed to carry on this infamous trade, when you can work?" "Sir," replied the mendicant, "I ask you for money, and not for

[22]Antoine Augustin Calmet (1672–1757) was a learned Benedictine monk and prolific author of works on religious topics. He and Voltaire were on friendly terms, and in 1754 Voltaire spent several weeks working in the library of the abbey Senones presided over by Calmet. Poor Calmet was not the most critical of men. Thus in one of his works he tried to give the location of paradise. Voltaire lampooned him in several articles of the *Philosophical Dictionary*.

advice"; and turned his back on him with Castilian dignity. This gentleman was a haughty beggar: it took very little to wound his vanity. He asked alms for love of himself, and would not suffer the reprimand from a still greater love of himself.

A missionary, traveling in India, met a fakir loaded with chains, naked as a monkey, lying on his stomach, and lashing himself for the sins of his countrymen, the Indians, who gave him a few coins. "What a renunciation of self!" said one of the spectators. "Renunciation of myself!" said the fakir; "learn that I only lash myself in this world to serve you the same in the next, when you will be the horses and I the rider."

Those who said that love of ourselves is the basis of all our feelings and actions were right; and as no one has written to prove to men that they have a face, there is no need to prove to them that they possess self-love. This self-love is the instrument of our preservation; it is something like the instrument for the perpetuation of the race. It is necessary, it is dear to us, it gives us pleasure, and we must conceal it.

SOUL

. . . We call soul that which animates. Since our intelligence is limited, we know hardly anything more about the subject. Three-fourths of mankind go no further and don't worry about this thinking being; the other fourth look for it; no one has found it or will find it.

Poor pedant, you see a plant that vegetates, and you say *vegetation*, or even *vegetative soul*. You notice that bodies have and produce motion, and you said *force*; you see your hunting dog learn his craft from you, and you exclaim *instinct, sensitive soul*; you have complex ideas, and you said *spirit*.

But, please, what do you understand by these words? This flower vegetates, but is there any real being called *vegetation*? This body pushes another, but does it possess within itself a distinct being called *force*? This dog brings you a partridge, but is there a being called *instinct*? Wouldn't you laugh at a logician (had he been teacher to Alexander[23]) who told you: "All animals live, therefore there is in them a being, a substantial form, which is life"?

If a tulip could talk and were to tell you: "My vegetation and I are two beings evidently joined together," wouldn't you laugh at the tulip?

Let's see first of all what you know and what you are sure of: that you walk with your feet, that you digest with your stomach, that you feel with your whole body, and that you think with your head. Let's see if your reason could have given you enough insight by itself to conclude, without supernatural aid, that you have a soul.

---

[23]This teacher is, of course, Aristotle whose vitalistic theories Voltaire is ridiculing.

The first philosophers, whether Chaldaeans or Egyptians, said: "There must be something within us which produces our thoughts; that something must be very subtle; it is a breath, it is fire, it is ether, it is a quintessence, it is a faint image, it is an entelechy, it is a number, it is a harmony." Finally, according to the divine Plato, it is a compound of the *same* and the *other.* "It is atoms which think in us," said Epicurus, following Democritus. But, my friend, how does an atom think? Admit that you have no idea.

The opinion we should doubtless adopt is that the soul is an immaterial being; but certainly you can't imagine what that immaterial being is. "No," the scholars reply, "but we know that its nature is to think." And how do you know that? "We know it because it thinks." Oh, scholars! I'm afraid that you are as ignorant as Epicurus: the nature of the stone is to fall, because it falls; but I ask you what makes it fall.

"We know," they go on, "that a stone has no soul." Granted, I believe that too. "We know that a negation and an affirmation are not divisible, are not parts of matter." I am of your opinion. But matter, too, otherwise unknown to us, possesses qualities which are not material, which are not divisible; it has gravitation toward a center, which God has given it. Now, this gravitation has no parts; it is not divisible. The moving force of bodies is not a being composed of parts. Nor is the vegetation of organized bodies, their life, their instincts. These are not beings apart, divisible beings; you can no more cut in two the vegetation of a rose, the life of a horse, the instinct of a dog, than you can cut in two a sensation, a negation, an affirmation. Therefore your fine argument, drawn from the indivisibility of thought, proves nothing at all. . . .

The Greeks clearly perceived that thought often has nothing to do with the play of our organs; they held that these organs had an animal soul and that thoughts had a finer, subtler soul, a *nous.*

Here is this soul of thought, which has the ascendancy over the animal soul on a thousand occasions. The thinking soul commands its hands to take, and they take. But it does not tell its heart to beat, its blood to flow, its chyle to form; all this is done without it. Here are two souls deeply enmeshed, and hardly master in their own house.

Now, this animal soul certainly does not exist; it is nothing more than the movement of our organs. Take care, O man! Your feeble reason may have no more proof that the other soul exists. You cannot know it except through faith. You are born, you live, you act, you think, you wake, you sleep, without knowing how. God has given you the faculty of thinking, as he has given you all the rest; and if he had not come at the time appointed by his providence to teach you that you have an immaterial and immortal soul, you would have no proof of it whatever.

Let's look at the fine systems about souls your philosophy has fabricated.

One says that the soul of man is part of the substance of God himself; another, that it is part of the great whole; a third, that it is created from all eternity; a fourth, that it is made, and not created; others assert that God makes souls as they are needed, and that they arrive at the moment of copulation. "They are lodged in the seminal animalcules," exclaims one. "No," says another, "they inhabit the Fallopian tubes." "You are wrong," says a bystander; "the soul waits for six weeks, until the foetus is formed, and then it takes possession of the pineal gland; but if it finds a stunted embryo, it turns back and waits for a better opportunity." The latest opinion is that its dwelling is in the *corpus callosum*; this is the position assigned to it by La Peyronie; Still, the *corpus callosum* didn't make the same hit the surgeon did.

St. Thomas, in his question 75 and following, says that the soul is a form *subsistante per se*; that it is all in all; that its essence differs from its power; that there are three *vegetative* souls, namely, the *nutritive*, the *augmentative*, the *generative*; that the memory of spiritual things is spiritual and the memory of corporeal things is corporeal; that the rational soul is a form "immaterial as to operations and material as to being." St. Thomas wrote two thousand pages as forceful and clear as this; besides, he is the angel of the schoolmen.

Nor have there been fewer systems about the manner in which this soul will feel when it has left the body it feels with; how it will hear without ears, smell without a nose, and touch without hands; what body it will resume afterwards, the one it had at the age of two or of eighty; how the *I*, the identity of the same person, will subsist; how the soul of a man who went mad at the age of fifteen, and died mad at the age of seventy, will resume the thread of the ideas it had at the age of puberty; by what contrivance a soul, whose leg was cut off in Europe and which lost an arm in America, will recover this leg and this arm, which will have passed into the blood of some other animal after being transformed into vegetables. We should never be done if we tried to report all the extravagances this poor human soul has imagined about itself.

What is quite remarkable is that the laws of God's people don't say one word about the spirituality and immortality of the soul: nothing in the Decalogue, nothing in Leviticus, or in Deuteronomy.

It is quite certain, it is beyond doubt, that Moses nowhere offers the Jews rewards and punishments in another life, that he never speaks to them of the immortality of their souls, that he never gives them hopes of heaven, nor threatens them with hells: all is temporal.

SUPREME GOOD

Antiquity debated a good deal about the supreme good. It would have been just as well to ask, What is the supreme blue, or the supreme stew, the supreme walk, the supreme reading, etc.

Everyone finds his good where he can, and has as much of it as he can, in his own fashion.

> *Quid dem? quid non dem? renuis tu, quod iubet alter*
> [*What should I give, what not give? You refuse what another commands*
>   HORACE, *Epistles*, ii, ii, 63]
> *Castor gaudet equis; ovo prognatus eodem Pugnis*
> [*Castor delights in horses; he, born from the same egg, Likes fighting*
>   HORACE, *Satires*, ii, i, 25–26]

The greatest good is something that pleases you so strongly that you are completely unable to feel anything else, just as the greatest evil is something that deprives us of all feeling. These are the two extremes of human nature; and these two moments are short.

Neither extreme delight nor extreme torture can last a lifetime: the supreme good and the supreme evil are chimeras.

We have the beautiful fable of Crantor[24]: Wealth, Pleasure, Health, Virtue, compete at the Olympic games; each claims the apple. Wealth says: "I am the supreme good, for with me all goods are purchased." Pleasure says: "The apple belongs to me, for men desire wealth only to have me." Health asserts that without her there can be no pleasure, and wealth is useless. Finally, Virtue announces that she is superior to all three because with gold, pleasures, and health, a man may make himself quite miserable if he behaves badly. Virtue wins the apple.

The fable is quite ingenious, but it doesn't resolve the absurd question of the supreme good. Virtue is not a good, it is a duty; it is of a different nature, of a superior order. It has nothing to do with painful or agreeable sensations. The virtuous man with the stone and the gout, without help, without friends, destitute of necessities, persecuted, chained by a voluptuous tyrant who enjoys good health, is miserable; and his insolent persecutor, caressing a new mistress on his bed of purple, is happy. Say that the persecuted sage is preferable to his insolent persecutor; say that you like the one and detest the other; but confess that the sage in chains is beside himself with rage. If the sage will not admit this, he deceives you, he is a charlatan.

WAR

Famine, plague, and war are the three most precious ingredients of this vile world.

Under the classification of famine we may include all the unhealthy

---

[24]Greek moral philosopher (fl. fourth century, B.C.)

nourishment we are compelled to resort to in times of scarcity, abridging our life in the hope of sustaining it. In plague we include all the contagious illnesses, which number two or three thousand. These two gifts come to us from Providence.

But war, which unites all these gifts, comes to us from the imagination of three or four hundred people scattered over the surface of the globe under the name of princes or ministers; and it is perhaps for this reason that in dedications to some books they are called the living images of divinity.

The most determined courtier will easily agree that war always brings plague and famine in its train, if he has seen even a little of the hospitals of the German armies, and passed through some villages in which some great exploit of war had taken place.

Surely the art that desolates the countryside, destroys habitations, and, in an average year, leads to the death of forty thousand out of a hundred thousand men, is a very fine art. At first it was cultivated by nations who mobilized for their common good; for instance, the Diet of the Greeks declared to the Diet of Phrygia and neighboring nations that it intended to arrive on a thousand fishing boats in order to exterminate them if it could. The Roman people in assembly decided that it was to its interest to fight before harvest time against the people of Veii, or the Volscians. And some years later all the Romans, angry at all the Carthaginians, fought them for a long time on land and on sea. It's not this way today.

A genealogist proves to a prince that he is the direct descendant of a count whose parents had made a family compact, three or four hundred years ago, with a house that has disappeared even from memory. This house had farfetched claims to a province whose last proprietor died of apoplexy: the prince and his council conclude without difficulty that the province belongs to him by divine right. The province, which is several hundred miles away, protests in vain that it does not know him, that it has no desire to be governed by him, that one must at least have a people's consent before one gives it laws: these speeches don't even reach the ears of the prince, whose right is incontestable. At once he assembles a large number of men who have nothing to lose; he dresses them in coarse blue cloth at a hundred and ten sous the ell, edges their hats with coarse white yarn, makes them turn right and left, and marches to glory.

The other princes who hear of this escapade take part in it, each according to his strength, and cover a small space of land with more mercenary murderers than Genghis Khan, Tamerlane, or Bajazet ever had in their train.

Distant nations hear that there is going to be some fighting, and that they can make five or six sous a day if they want to join in: right away they divide themselves into two groups, like reapers, and sell their services to anyone ready to employ them.

These multitudes become infuriated with each other, not only without having any business in the proceedings, but even without knowing what is at stake.

At once there are five or six belligerent powers, sometimes three against three, sometimes two against four, sometimes one against five, all detesting one another equally, uniting and fighting with each other in turn; all in agreement on a single point, to do as much harm as possible.

The marvelous part of this infernal enterprise is that every murderer's chief has his flags blessed, and solemnly invokes the Lord before he goes out to exterminate his neighbors. If a chief has had the good fortune to butcher only two or three thousand men, he does not thank God for it; but when he has had ten thousand exterminated by fire and sword, and when, his grace abounding, some town has been destroyed from top to bottom, then they sing a long song in four parts, composed in a language unknown to all who did the fighting, and which besides is crammed with solecisms. The same song serves for marriages and births, as well as for murders: which is unforgivable, above all in the nation best known for new songs.

A thousand times natural religion has prevented citizens from committing crimes. A well-disposed soul is unwilling to commit them; a tender soul is afraid of them — a just and avenging God appears before it. But artificial religion encourages all the cruelties which are committed in company — conspiracies, seditions, pillagings, ambushes, taking towns by surprise, plundering, murders. Everyone marches gaily off to crime under the banner of his saint.

Everywhere a certain number of orators are paid to celebrate these murderous days; some are dressed in a long black jerkin, encumbered by a cropped cloak; others have a shirt over a gown; some wear two pendants of motley cloth over their shirt. All talk for a long time; they point to what was done of old in Palestine, applying it to a battle in Veteravia.

The rest of the year, these fellows declaim against vices. They prove in three propositions and by antitheses that ladies who spread a little rouge on their blooming cheeks will be the eternal objects of the eternal vengeance of the Eternal; that *Polyeucte*[25] and *Athalie*[26] are works of the Devil; that a man who has two hundred écus worth of fresh-water fish served at his table during Lent will infallibly be saved, while a poor man who eats two and a half sous worth of mutton will forever go to all the devils.

Of five or six thousand declamations of this kind, there are at most three or four, composed by a Gaul named Massillon,[27] which an honest man can read without disgust; but among all these speeches you will hardly find two in which the orator dares to stand up against war, this scourge and crime

---

[25] Play by Corneille (1640) dealing with an Armenian martyr, decapitated for his conversion to Christianity.

[26] Tragedy by Racine (1691).

[27] Jean-Baptiste Massillon (1663–1742), Oratorian priest noted for the eloquence of his sermons. Voltaire knew and liked him, describing him as "philosophical and tolerant."

which includes all other scourges and crimes. These miserable orators ceaselessly speak against love, which is the sole consolation of mankind and the sole means of restoring it; they say nothing about our abominable efforts to destroy mankind.

O Bourdaloue,[28] you have delivered a very poor sermon on impurity! But not one on these murders, so widely varied, on these rapes, these pillagings, this universal mania which desolates the world. All the vices of all ages and all places put together can never equal the evils produced by a single campaign.

Miserable physicians of souls, you shout for an hour and a quarter about some pin pricks, and you say nothing about the malady that tears us in a thousand pieces! Moral philosophers, burn all your books. As long as thousands of our brothers are honestly butchered for the caprice of some men, the part of mankind consecrated to heroism will be the most horrible thing in all nature.

What becomes of humanity, modesty, temperance, gentleness, wisdom, piety; and what do I care about them, while half a pound of lead, shot from six hundred feet away, shatters my body, and while I die at the age of twenty in inexpressible torments in the midst of five or six thousand dying men; while my eyes, opening for the last time, see the town in which I was born destroyed by iron and fire, and while the last sounds in my ears are the cries of women and children expiring under the ruins — all for the alleged interest of a man whom we don't know.

What is worse is that war is an inevitable scourge. If we look at it closely, we see that all men have worshipped the god Mars: Sabaoth, among the Jews, signifies the god of arms; but Minerva, in Homer, calls Mars a savage, insane, infernal god.

---

[28]Louis Bourdaloue (1632–1704), Jesuit priest famous for his oratorical powers.

The Ignorant Philosopher

The passages reprinted in this section are from *The Ignorant Philosopher*, first published in 1766. Voltaire referred to it as his "second *Traité*" and he discussed in it most of the same issues. Unlike the *Traité* it was written for immediate publication, and hence Voltaire did not directly criticize belief in life after death. He had drastically changed his views on the problem of evil and on free will, but he is even more fervent in his defense of the design argument and the claim that on basic moral questions all human beings agree. As the title suggests, Voltaire emphasizes the inability of human beings to answer many of the fundamental questions of philosophy. At one stage he thought of commissioning a frontispiece that would show three blind men groping after a fleeing donkey. This, he wrote in a letter, is a symbol of all philosophers who seek the truth.

AM I FREE?

Let us not yet quit the circle of our existence; let us examine ourselves as far as we are able. I remember one day a reasoner wanted to make me reason. He asked me if I was free? I replied that I was not in prison, that I had the key to my chamber, that I was perfectly free. "That is not what I asked you," he replied; "do you believe your will is at liberty to dispose or not to dispose you to throw yourself out of the window? Do you think, with the scholastic angel, that the free agent is an appetitive power, and the free agent is lost by sin?" I fixed my eyes upon the questioner to see his if he was not out of his mind; and I answered that I did not understand the least of his gibberish.

Nevertheless, this question as to the freedom of man greatly interested me; I read scholastics, and, like them, I was in the dark; I read Locke, and I discovered some rays of light; I read Collins's treatise,[1] which appeared to

---

[1] *A Philosophical Inquiry Concerning Human Liberty* (1715), which is a thoroughgoing defense of determinism, or "the doctrine of necessity" as it was then called. Anthony Collins (1676–1729) was a leading deist and free-thinker. His *Discourse on the Grounds and Reasons of the Christian Religion* (1734) was later described by Bishop Warburton as one of the most powerful books ever written against Christianity. Voltaire went one step further in calling Collins "one of the most terrible enemies of the Christian religion," adding that "unhappily" his anti-Christian works remained victorious.

159

me an improvement upon Locke; and I have never read anything since that has given me additional instruction. This is what my weak reason has conceived, with the assistance of these two great men, the only two who have, in my opinion, understood themselves in writing upon this subject, and the only two who have made themselves understood to others.

There is nothing without a cause. Every time that I will, this can only be in consequence of my judgment, good or bad; this judgment is necessary; consequently, so is my will. In effect, it would be very singular that all nature, all the planets, should obey eternal laws, and that there should be a little animal five feet high, who, in contempt of these laws, could act as he pleased, solely according to his caprice. He would act by chance; and we know that chance is nothing. We have invented this word to express the known effect of all unknown causes.

My ideas necessarily enter into my brain; how then can my will, which depends upon them, be free? I feel upon various occasions that this will is not free; thus when I am overwhelmed with illness, when I am transported with passion, when my judgment cannot comprehend objects that present themselves to me, etc. I should think, therefore, that the laws of nature, being always the same, my will is not more free in things that appear to me the most indifferent, than in those in which I find myself impelled by an invincible force.

To be really free is to have power. My liberty consists in doing what I choose; but I must necessarily choose what I will; otherwise it would be without reason, without cause, which is impossible. My liberty consists in walking when I have a mind to walk, and I do not have the gout.

My liberty consists in not doing a bad action when my mind necessarily represents it as a bad action; in subduing a passion, when my mind points out to me the danger of it, and the horror of the act powerfully combats my desire. We may suppress our passions — as I have already said — but then we are not freer in suppressing our desires than by letting ourselves be carried away by our inclinations; for in both cases we irresistibly pursue our last idea; and this last idea is necessary; wherefore I necessarily perform what this dictates to me. It is strange that men should not be content with this measure of liberty; that is to say, the power which they have received from nature of doing what they choose; the planets have it not; we possess it, and our pride makes us sometimes believe that we possess still more. We figure to ourselves that we have the incomprehensible and absurd gift of election, without reason, without any other motive than that of free-will.

No, I cannot forgive Dr. Clarke[2] for having sophistically opposed these truths, the force of which he felt, but which did not well agree with his systems. No, it is not allowed to such a philosopher as him to attack Collins

---

[2]The reference is to Clarke's *Remarks Upon a Book Entitled a Philosophical Inquiry Concerning Human Liberty* (1717).

as a sophist, by changing the state of the question, and reproaching Collins with calling man "a necessary agent." Agent or patient, what does it signify? An agent when he voluntarily moves; a patient when he receives ideas. What does the name to the thing? Man is in everything a dependent being, as nature is throughout dependent, and he cannot be excepted from other beings.

The preacher in Samuel Clarke stifles the philosopher; he distinguishes physical from the moral necessity. And what is a moral necessity? It appears probable to you that a queen of England, whose coronation ceremony is performed in a church, will not cast off her regal robes to throw herself quite naked upon the altar, though a similar adventure is related of a queen of Congo. You call this a moral necessity in a queen of our climate; but it is at the bottom a physical and eternal necessity, blended with the constitution of things. It is as certain this queen will not be guilty of such a folly as that she will one day die. Moral necessity is but a phrase; all that is done is absolutely necessary. There is no middle ground between necessity and chance; and you know there is no chance; wherefore all that happens is necessary.

To embarrass the thing still more, efforts have been made to distinguish again between necessity and constraint; but constraint, in fact, is nothing but necessity that is perceived, and necessity is a constraint that is unperceived. Archimedes is equally necessitated to remain in his chamber when shut in, as when he is deeply engaged with a problem, and the idea of going out does not occur to him.

Ducunt volentem fata, nolentem trahunt.[3]

The ignoramus who thinks in this manner, did not always think the same; but he is at length compelled to yield.

IS EVERYTHING ETERNAL?

Subject to eternal laws like every sphere that replenishes space, as the elements, animals, and plants, I view with astonishment everything that surrounds me; I search for my author, and the author of that immense machine of which I am scarcely a perceptible wheel.

I am not derived from nothing; for the substance of my father and mother, who bore me nine months in her womb, is something. It is evident to me that the sperm which produced me could not be produced from nothing; for how can nothing produce existence? I find myself subdued by this maxim of all antiquity: "Nothing arises from nothing, nothing can return to nothing." This axiom carries with it such dreadful power that it

[3]"The fates lead the willing man, they drag the unwilling one."

bears down all my understanding, without my being able to contend with it. No philosopher has ever lost sight of it. No legislator whatsoever has contested it. The *Cahut* of the Phoenicians, the *Chaos* of the Greeks, the *Tohu-bohu* of the Chaldaeans and the Hebrews, all show that the eternity of matter has ever been believed. My reason, perhaps deceived by so ancient and general an idea, tells me that matter must necessarily be eternal, because it exists; if it was in being yesterday, it was before. I cannot perceive any probability of its having begun to be, any cause why it had not been, any cause wherefore it received existence at one time more than at another. I therefore yield to this conviction, whether well or ill founded, and I list myself under the banner of the whole world, till such time as, having made some progress in my researches, I discover a luminary superior to the judgment of all mankind, which compels me to retract against my will.

But if, according to the opinion of so many philosophers of antiquity, the Eternal Being has always acted, what becomes of the *Cahut* and *Erebus of the Phoenicians, the Tohu-bohu* of the Chaldaeans, the *Chaos* of Hesiod? They will remain fables. Chaos is an impossibility in the eyes of reason; for it is impossible that, intelligence being eternal, there should ever have been anything contrary to the laws of that intelligence; but chaos is precisely contrary to all the laws of nature. Enter into the most horrid caverns of the Alps, under those ruins of rocks, ice, sand, water, unfashioned crystals, and minerals; they all submit to gravitation. Chaos never existed anywhere but in our heads, and has only served to assist Hesiod and Ovid in composing some elegant verses.

If our Holy Scripture says *Chaos* did exist, if it had adopted the *Tohu-bohu*, we would doubtless believe it, and with the most ready faith. We are, in this place, speaking only of the deceitful lights of our reason. We have confined ourselves, as we have said, to what we may discover by ourselves. We are children, who endeavor to go a few steps without leading-strings.

INTELLIGENCE

But in perceiving the order, the prodigious skill, and the mechanical and geometrical laws that reign in the universe, their causes and the innumerable ends of all things, I am seized with admiration and respect. I immediately judge that if the works of man, even my own, compel me to acknowledge an intelligence within us, I should acknowledge one far more superior actuating the multitude of so many works. I admit of this supreme intelligence, without fearing that I shall be obliged to change my opinion. Nothing staggers me with respect to this axiom, every work demonstrates a workman.

ETERNITY

Is this intelligence eternal? Doubtless, for whether I admit or reject the eternity of matter, I cannot reject the eternal existence of its supreme artisan; and it is evident that if it exists at present, it has always existed.

INCOMPREHENSIBILITY

I have as yet advanced only two or three steps in this vast undertaking; I want to know if this divine intelligence is something absolutely distinct from the universe, as the sculptor is distinguished from the statue; or whether this soul of the world is united to the world, and still penetrates it in the same manner as what I call my soul is united to me, and according to that of antiquity so well expressed in Virgil and Lucan:

> *Mens agitat molem et magno se corpore miscet, Jupiter est quodcumque vides quocumque moveris.*[4]

I find myself suddenly interrupted in the prospect of my vain curiosity. Miserable mortal, if I cannot fathom my own intelligence; if I cannot know by what I am animated, how can I have any acquaintance with that ineffable intelligence which visibly presides over matter entirely? There is one, as everything demonstrates, but where is the compass that will direct me toward its secret and eternal abode?

INFINITY

Is this intelligence infinite in power and immensity, as it is incontestably infinite in duration? I can know nothing of this by myself. It does exist, wherefore it has ever existed; that is clear. But what idea can I have of an infinite power? How can I conceive an infinity actually existing? How can I suppose that the supreme intelligence is in the vacuum? An infinity of extent is not the same as an infinity of duration. An infinity of duration has elapsed the instant that I am speaking of it; it is certain that I can add nothing to past duration, but I can always add to that space which I conceive, in the same manner that I can add to the numbers that I conceive. Infinity in numbers and extent is beyond the sphere of my understanding. Nothing that can be said can give me insight into this abyss. I happily feel that my difficulties and my ignorance can in no way be pernicious to morality; we may very well be incapable of perceiving either immensity of

---

[4]"Mind drives mass and mixes itself with great body (i.e., the whole universe); Jupiter is whatever you see wherever you move."

space replenished, or infinite power, which has created everything, and which may nevertheless be still able to perform; this will only serve to prove still more the weakness of our understanding; and this weakness will render us only still more submissive to that eternal Being whose work we are.

MY DEPENDENCE

We are His work. This is an important truth for us to know; for to know philosophically at what time He made man, what He did before, if He exists materially, or in a vacuum, if He is at one point, if He constantly acts or not, if He acts everywhere, if He acts without or within Himself; these are questions which strengthen the conviction of my profound ignorance.

I even see that there have been scarcely a dozen men in Europe who have written upon these abstract things with any kind of method; and if I could suppose that they had spoken in an intelligible manner, what would be the consequence? We have already found that things which so few persons can flatter themselves with understanding are useless to the rest of mankind. We certainly are the work of God, this is useful for me to know; and the proof is also clear. All things in my body are causes and effects; that is, spring, pulley, moving power, hydraulic machine, equilibrium of fluids, and chemical laboratory. It is therefore arranged by an intelligence (No. XV.). I am not indebted for this arrangement to the intelligence of my parents, for they certainly did not know what they did when they produced me; they were only the blind instruments of this eternal manufacturer, who animates the worm of the earth and makes the sun turn upon its own axis.

ETERNITY AGAIN

Born from seed, produced by other seed, has there been a continual succession, an unfolding without end of these seeds, and has all nature ever existed by a necessary succession from that Supreme Being who existed of Himself? If I were to believe only my feeble understanding, I should say it seems to me that nature has always been animated. I cannot conceive that the cause which continually and visibly actuates her, being at all times able to act, has not always acted. An eternity of idleness in the active and necessary being appears to me incompatible. I am inclined to believe that the world has ever issued from that primitive and necessary cause, as light emanates from the sun. By what concatenation of ideas do I find myself led to believe the works of the Eternal Being eternal? My conception, feeble as it is, has strength enough to rise to a being necessarily existing by Himself, but has not the strength to conceive *nothing*. The existence of a single atom proves to me the eternity of existence, but nothing proves to me a mere void. What, is that space filled that was once a vacuum? This appears absurd and contradictory. I cannot allow of this *nothing*, this *void*, unless revelation assists me in fixing my ideas, which carry me beyond time.

I am aware that an infinite succession of beings without origin is equally absurd; this is the opinion of Samuel Clarke,[5] but he does not undertake to affirm that God has not held this chain from all eternity; he dare not say that it was impossible for a being eternally active so long to display his works. It is evident that he could, and if he could, who will be bold enough to tell me that he did not? Once more I say that nothing but revelation can teach me the contrary. But we have not yet attained that revelation which destroys all philosophy, that light before which all other lights are eclipsed.

A NEW QUESTION

Convinced by my small share of reason that there is a necessary Eternal Being from whom I receive my ideas, without being able to divine how or wherefore, I ask what is this being? Has it the form of those intelligent and active species superior to ours in other worlds. I have already said I knew nothing of the matter. Nevertheless, I cannot affirm it to be impossible; for I perceive planets very superior to ours in extent, surrounded with more satellites than the earth. It is not improbable that they may be peopled with intelligences far superior to me, with bodies more robust, more active, and more durable. But their existence having no connection with mine, I shall leave it to the poets of antiquity to make Venus descend from her imaginary third heaven, and Mars from the fifth. My inquiries should be confined to the action of the Being necessarily presiding over myself.

A SOLE SUPREME ARTIST

A great part of mankind, observing the physical and moral evil diffused through this globe, imagined there were two powerful beings, one of which produced all the good, and the other all the evil. If they existed they were necessary; they therefore necessarily existed in the same place; there is no reason that what exists by its own nature should be excluded any place; they therefore penetrated each other — this is absurd. The idea of these two powerful enemies can drive its origin only from examples that strike us upon earth; we there observe gentle and ferocious men, useful and obnoxious animals, good masters and tyrants. There were two opposite powers devised, who presided over nature; this is only an Asiatic romance. There is

---

[5] *A Discourse Concerning the Being and Attributes of God*, in Volume 2 of Clarke's *Works* (1738), pp. 521–541.

throughout nature a manifest unity of design; the laws of motion and gravity are invariable; it is impossible that two supreme artists, in opposition to each other, could have followed the same laws. This alone has, in my opinion, overturned the Manichaean system, and voluminous writings are superfluous to explode it.

There is then a sole Eternal Power, to whom everything is united, on whom all depends; but whose nature is to me incomprehensible. St. Thomas tells us: "God is a pure act, a form that has neither gender nor predicament; He is nature, and the agent; He exists essentially, participatively, and noncupatively." When the Dominicans were masters of the Inquisition, they would have burned a man who would have denied these fine things—I should not have denied them, but I should not have understood them.

I am told that God is simple; I acknowledge that I do not understand any more the value of this word. It is true, that I should not attribute to him gross parts that I could separate; but I cannot conceive that the principal and master of all that is extended should not itself be extended. Simplicity, strictly speaking, appears to me to resemble too much a nonentity. The extreme weakness of my understanding has no instrument nice enough to lay hold of its simplicity. I shall be told that the mathematical point is simple, but the mathematical point does not really exist.

It is again said that an idea is simple, but I do not understand this a whit better. I perceive a horse; I have the idea of it, but I see in him only an assemblage of things. I see a color; I have the idea of color, but this color is extended. I pronounce the abstract names of color in general; of vice, virtue, truth, in general; but the reason is that I have had a knowledge of things colored, of things that have appeared to me virtuous or vicious, true or false. I express all this by a word; but I have no clear knowledge of simplicity. I know no more of it than I do of an infinity in numbers actually existing.

I am already convinced that not knowing what I am, I cannot know what is my author. I am every instant overwhelmed with my ignorance, and I console myself by incessantly reflecting that it is of no consequence to me to know whether my Master is or is not extended, provided I do nothing against that conscience He has given me. Of all the systems which men have invented about the Divinity, which, then, shall I embrace? Not one, unless it be that of adoring Him.

SPINOZA

After being immersed with Thales in the water, of which his first principle consisted; after glowing before Empedocles's fire; after running in a straight line in the vacuum, with Epicurus's atoms; after having calculated numbers with Pythagoras and heard his music; after having paid my respects to the Androgynes of Plato,[6] and having passed through all the regions of metaphysics and madness; I was at length desirous of being acquainted with the system of Spinoza.

He is not new; he has imitated some ancient Greek philosophers, and even some Jews; but Spinoza has done what no Greek philosopher, and much less a Jew, ever did. He has used an imposing geometrical method to calculate the net result of his ideas. Let us see if he has not methodically wandered with the trail that leads him.

He at first establishes a clear and incontestable fact. There is something, consequently there has eternally existed a necessary being. This principle is so true that the profound Samuel Clarke has availed himself of it to prove the existence of God.

This being must be found in all places where there is existence; for who can limit it?

This necessary being is then everything that exists; wherefore there is only one substance in the universe.

This substance cannot create another; for as it fills everything, where can a new substance be placed, and how can something be created from nothing? . . .

There are in the world thought and matter; that necessary substance which we call God is therefore thought and matter. All thought and all matter are then comprehended in the immensity of God; there can be nothing out of Him; they can only act within Him; He comprehends everything; He is everything.

Wherefore everything we call different substances is, in fact, nothing but the universality of the different attributes of the Supreme Being, who thinks in the brain of man, enlightens in the light, moves upon the winds, darts in the lightning, revolves in the planets, and exists in all nature.

He is not like a vile king of the earth, confined to his palace, separated from his subjects; He is intimately united with them; they are essential parts of Himself; if He were distinguished from them He would be no longer universal, He would not fill all space, He would be a being like another.

Though all the variable modifications in the universe are the effect of His attributes, nevertheless, according to Spinoza, He has no parts; "for," says he, "infinity has none, properly speaking." In conclusion, Spinoza pronounces that we must love this necessary, infinite, eternal God. These are his words:

"With regard to the love of God, this idea is so far from weakening it, that I think no other is so fit to increase it, since it teaches me that God is

---

[6]The reference is to the myth or fantasy attributed to Aristophanes in the *Symposium* (189c1–193e1) that men and women seek the other halves of the wholes they once were. These wholes are "androgynes," literally "men-women."

intimate with my being; that He gives me existence and all my properties; that He gives them to me liberally, without reproach, without interest, without subjecting me to anything but my own nature. It banishes fear, uneasiness, diffidence, and all the defects of a mean and sordid love. It teaches me that it is a possession I cannot lose, and which I the more advantageously possess, as I know and love it."

These ideas seduced many readers; there were even some, who having at first written against him, afterward embraced his opinion.

The learned Bayle is upbraided for having severely attacked Spinoza, without understanding him. Severely, I agree; but I do not think unjustly. He easily discovered the weak side of this enchanted castle; he saw that Spinoza, in fact, composed his God of parts, though he found himself compelled to retract, terrified at his own system. Bayle saw his frenzy in making God a star and a pumpkin, thought and smoke, beating and beaten. He saw that this fable is much beneath that of Proteus. Perhaps Bayle should have confined himself to the word "Modalities," and not parts, as Spinoza always makes use of the word "modalities." But, if I am not mistaken, it is immaterial whether the excrement of an animal is a modality or a part of the Supreme Being.

He did not indeed attack the reasons by which Spinoza maintains the impossibility of the creation; but the reason is that the creation, properly speaking, is an object of faith, and not of philosophy; because this opinion is no way peculiar to Spinoza, and all antiquity thought like him. He attacks only the absurd idea of a simple God, composed of parts, of a God that eats and digests himself, who loves and hates the same thing at the same time, etc. Spinoza constantly makes use of the word "God," and Bayle takes him according to his own expressions.

But at the bottom, Spinoza does not acknowledge any God; he has probably made use of this expression, he has said that we should serve and love God, only that he might not startle mankind. He appears to be an atheist, according to the full extent of the epithet; he is not such an atheist as Epicurus, who acknowledged useless and lazy gods; he is not like the greater part of the Greeks and Romans, who ridiculed the gods of the vulgar; he is such, because he acknowledges no Providence whatever, because he admits only of eternity, immensity, and the necessity of things; like Strato,[7] like Diagoras;[8] he does not doubt, like Pyrrho; he affirms, and

---

[7]Strato of Lampsacus (d. 269 B.C.) headed the Lyceum after Aristotle's successor Theophrastus. Among other things he revised Aristotle's physics, eliminating its teleological elements. He has frequently been taken to anticipate the view of naturalists and materialists that the universe is self-sustaining and hence in no need of a divine cause.

[8]Little is known with certainty about Diagoras. A number of historians accept the account that Democritus bought him as a slave and that Diagoras became an atheist as a result of his master's influence. He was prosecuted in Athens for making derogatory remarks about foreign rites and festivals and was forced to flee the city. He appealed to the injustice of the world as evidence for atheism.

what does he affirm? That there is only a single substance, that there cannot be two, that this substance is extended and thinking, and this is what none of the Greek or Asiatic philosophers ever said, who admitted of a universal soul.

He nowhere mentions in his book specific designs, which are manifested in all beings. He does not examine whether eyes were made to see, ears to hear, feet to walk, or wings to fly; he neither considers the laws of motion in animals and plants, nor their structure adapted to those laws, any more than the depth of mathematics, which governs the course of the stars; he is afraid to perceive that everything which exists attests a divine Providence; he does not rise from effects to their cause, but immediately placing himself at the head of the origin of things, he builds his romance in the same manner as Descartes constructed his — upon a supposition. He supposes, with Descartes, a plenum, though it has been strictly demonstrated that all motion is impossible in a plenum. This was his principal reason for looking upon the universe as one single substance. He was the dupe of his geometrical genius. How did it come to be that Spinoza, who could not doubt that spirit and matter existed, did not at least examine whether Providence had not arranged everything? How came it that he did not give a single glance toward those springs, those means, each of which has its design, and that he did not inquire whether they evinced a supreme artist? He must have been either a very ignorant *physician*, or a sophist swelled up with a foolish kind of pride, not to acknowledge a Providence every time he breathed and felt his heart beat; for this respiration and this motion of the heart are the effects of a machine so industriously complicated, and arranged with such powerful art, depending upon so many springs, all concurring to the same end, that it is impossible to be imitated, and impossible for a man of good sense not to admire it.

The modern Spinozists reply: "Do not worry about these consequences, which you inpute to us; we find, as you do, a succession of admirable effects in the organized bodies, and in all nature. The eternal cause is in the eternal intelligence which we admit, and which, with matter, constitutes the universality of things, which is God. There is but one single substance, which acts by the same modality of its thought upon the modality of matter, and which thus constitutes the universe, which forms but one whole inseparable entity."

To this we answer: How can you prove to us that the thought which gives motion to the stars, which animates man, which does everything, can be a modality, and that the excrements of a toad and a worm should be a modality of the same sovereign Being? Will you dare to say that so strange a principle is demonstrated to you? Do you not cloak your ignorance beneath words that you do not understand? Bayle has thoroughly unfolded the sophisms of your master in all the windings and all the obscurities of the style of a pretended and really much confused geometrician, which is that of this master. I refer you to him; philosophers should not exclaim against Bayle.

Be this as it may, I shall observe of Spinoza, that he very honestly deceived himself. It seems to me he did not suppress in his system those ideas which might be troublesome to him, only because he was too full of his own; he continued on his own road, without observing anything that might interrupt him, and this is what very often happens to us. Moreover, he inverted all the principles of morality, though he was himself a rigid moralist; so particularly sober that he scarcely drank a pint of wine in a month; so disinterested as to transfer to the heirs of the unfortunate Jan de Witt[9] a pension of two hundred florins, which this great man had granted him; so generous as to give away his fortune; ever patient in his illness and in his poverty; ever consistent in his conduct.

Bayle, who has so ill treated him, had nearly the same character. Each of them sought after truth all their lives by different roads. Spinoza frames a specious system in some respects, and very erroneous in the foundation. Bayle has combated all systems; what became of their writings? They have prevented the idleness of some readers, and this is the final result of all writing; and from Thales down to the professors of our universities, and the most chimerical reasoners, as well as their plagiarists, not one philosopher has influenced the conduct of the people around him. What is the reason? It is that men are led by custom and not by metaphysics. One eloquent man who is skillful and has some standing will be able to do more than other men; a hundred philosophers will be able to do nothing more if they are only philosophers.

THE BEST OF WORLDS

In my various peregrinations in search of instruction, I met with some disciples of Plato. "Come along with me," said one of them; "you are in the best of worlds; we have far surpassed our master, There were in his time only five possible worlds, because there are but five regular bodies; but now there are an infinity of possible universes; God has chosen the best; come, and you will be satisfied with it."

I humbly said that the worlds which God might create were either better, perfectly equal, or inferior. He could not choose the worst. Those which

---

[9]Jan (or Johan) DeWitt (1625–1672), leader of the Dutch Republic before the restoration of the house of Orange. At first highly popular, DeWitt fell into disfavor when Holland was devastated in its war with England and France. Among the many charges heard against him was one by Calvinist clergymen that he was secretly a free-thinker and a follower and friend of Spinoza. His brother Cornelis was falsely accused of plotting against the Prince of Orange. Both brothers were beaten to death and hung head downward on a lamppost by a crazed mob on August 20, 1672. It is not known whether DeWitt was really a free-thinker and follower of Spinoza, but he certainly admired and protected Spinoza who was grief-stricken when he heard about the death of the DeWitt brothers.

were equal, supposing such to be, could have no preference; they were ever completely the same; there could have been no choice among them; to fix upon one or the other was just the same. It was therefore impossible that he could avoid choosing the best. But how could the others be possible, when it is impossible they can exist?

He made some very curious distinctions, incessantly assuring me, without knowing what he said, that this world is the best of all really possible worlds. But being just then tortured with the kidney stone, which gave me an almost intolerable pain, the citizens of the best of worlds conducted me to the neighboring hospital. On the way two of these perfectly happy inhabitants were carried off by two creatures of their own likeness. They were loaded with irons, the one for debt, the other upon mere suspicion.

I do not know whether I was conducted into one of the best possible hospitals; but I was crowded among two or three thousand wretches like myself. Here were many defenders of their country, who informed me that they had been opened and dissected alive; that they had had arms and legs cut off; and that many thousands of their generous fellow-countrymen had been massacred in one of the thirty battles fought in the last war, which is about the hundred millionth war since wars began.

One might also meet in this house about a thousand persons of both sexes, who resembled hideous spectres, and who were rubbed with a certain metal, because they had followed the law of nature, and nature had, I know not how, taken the precaution of poisoning in them the source of life. I thanked my two guides.

After a very sharp iron had been thrust into my bladder, and some stones were extracted from this quarry—when I was cured, and I had no further complaints than a few disagreeable pains for the rest of my days—I made my representations to my guides. I took the liberty of telling them there was some good in this world, as the surgeons had extracted four flints from my torn entrails; but that I would much rather that bladders had been lanterns than quarries. I spoke to them of the innumerable calamities and crimes that were dispersed over this excellent world. The boldest of the two, who was a German and my countryman, told me that all this was a mere trifle.

Heaven was peculiarly propitious to man when Tarquin violated Lucretia and she stabbed herself, because the tyrants were thereupon driven out, and rapes, suicides, and war laid the foundation of a republic which conferred happiness upon those they vanquished. I had some difficulty in agreeing with this happiness. I did not immediately conceive the felicity of the Gauls and Spaniards, of whom it is said Caesar put three millions to the sword. Devastation and rape appeared to me things somewhat disagreeable, but the defender of optimism did not retract; he persevered in telling me, like Don Carlos' jailer: "Peace, peace, it is for your good." Having, however, at last put him on the defensive, he said that we should not consider this mere globule, where everything is jarring; but that in the star

Sirius, in Orion, Taurus, and elsewhere, everything is perfect. "Let us, then, go thither," said I.

A little theologian then took me by the arm. He told me, in confidence, that "those folks were mere dreamers; that it was not in the least necessary that there should be any evil upon earth; that it was expressly formed that there never should be anything but good; and in order to prove this, you must know that things formerly went on in this manner in Eden for ten or twelve days."

"Alas!" I replied to him, "it is a great pity, reverend father, that things did not continue so."

MONADS

The same German then laid hold of me again. He tutored me, and clearly taught me the nature of my soul.

"Everything in nature," said he, "consists of monads. Your soul is a monad, and as it is united with all the others, it necessarily has ideas of all that passes in them. These ideas are confused, which is very necessary; and your monad, as well as mine, is a concentric mirror of the universe.

"But believe not that you act in consequence of your thoughts. There is a pre-established harmony between the monad of your soul and the monads of your body, so that when your soul has an idea, your body has a motion, without the one being the result of the other. They are two pendulums that go together; or, if you will, the one resembles a man who preaches, while another makes gesticulations. You easily conceive that this must necessarily be so in the best of worlds; for — "

IS THERE ANY MORALITY?

The more I have observed men differ by climate, manners, languages, laws, doctrine, and the measure of their understanding, the more I have observed they have the same fund of morality. They have all a barbarous notion of justice and injustice, without knowing a word of theology. They have all acquired this notion at an age when reason begins to unfold itself; as they have naturally acquired the art of raising load with poles, and crossing a river on a piece of wood, without having learned mathematics.

It therefore appeared to me that this idea of justice and injustice was necessary for them, because they all agreed in this point, as soon as they could act and reason. The Supreme Intelligence which formed us has, then, been pleased that there should be justice upon earth, that we might live there for a certain time. It appears to me that, having neither instinct to nourish ourselves like animals nor natural arms like them, and vegetating for several years in the imbecility of infancy, exposed to every danger, the few men that would have escaped from the jaws of ferocious animals, from famine and misery, would have been employed in wrangling for a little nourishment and a few skins of animals; and they would have been destroyed like the children of the dragon of Cadmus,[10] as soon as they would have been able to have used any arms. At least, there would have been no society if men had not conceived the idea of some justice, which is the tie of all society.

How would the Egyptians, who raised pyramids and obelisks, and the wandering Scythians, who were even unacquainted with a cabin, have had the same fundamental notions of justice and injustice, if God had not given to each of them, from the beginning of time, that reason which, in unfolding itself, made them perceive the same necessary principles, in the same manner as he gave them affections and passions, which, having attained the degree of their development, necessarily perpetuate in the same manner the race of the Scythian and the Egyptian? I perceive a barbarous, ignorant, superstitious herd, a bloody and a furious people, who had not even a term in their jargon to signify geometry and astronomy. This people has, nevertheless, the same fundamental laws as the wise Chaldaean, who was acquainted with the course of the stars, and the Phoenician, still more learned, who availed himself of the knowledge of the stars to go and lay the foundation of colonies at the extremity of the hemisphere, where the ocean mingles with the Mediterranean. All these people aver that they should respect their fathers and mothers; that perjury, calumny, and homicide are abominable crimes; they therefore derive the same consequences from the same principles of their unfolded reason.

REAL UTILITY—THE NOTION OF JUSTICE

The notion of something just appears to me so natural, so universally received by all men, that it is independent of all law, of all compact, of all religion. Let me ask a Turk, a Gueber, or a Malabarian, for the money I lent him, to enable him to eat and clothe himself, and he will never think of replying: "Wait till I learn if Mahomet, Zoroaster, or Brahma commands me to restore your money." He will acknowledge that it is just that he should pay me, and if he does not perform it, either his poverty or his avarice predominates over the justice which he acknowledges.

[10] In his search for his sister Europa, who had been abducted by Zeus, Cadmus and his servants were met by an evil dragon whose body was swollen with venom, who had three poisonous tongues, and whose eyes sent out flames. The dragon at once killed all of Cadmus's servants but Cadmus managed to slay the dragon by running his sword through the creature's neck. Pallas Athene now descended from heaven, commanding Cadmus to turn up the earth and to sow the dragon's teeth as the seed of a new race. No sooner had Cadmus fulfilled the instructions of the goddess than a number of fully armed warriors emerged from the earth. They at once started fighting each other furiously. Before long only five were left. With these five "earthborn" warriors, Cadmus founded the city of Thebes.

I assert it as a fact, that there are no people who maintain that it is either just, right, proper, or honest, to refuse nourishment to one's father or mother, when it is practicable to bestow it; that no community has ever considered calumny as a good action, not even a sect of bigoted fanatics.

The idea of justice appears to me so much a truth of the first order, to which the whole universe has given its assent, that the greatest crimes which afflict society are all committed under the false pretence of justice. The greatest of all crimes, at least that which is the most destructive, and consequently the most opposite to the design of nature, is war; but there never was an aggressor who did not gloss over his guilt with the pretext of justice.

The Roman looters had all their invasions declared just, by priests named "Fetiales." Every freebooter, who finds himself at the head of an army, begins his foray by a manifesto, and implores the god of armies.

Petty thieves themselves, when united in a society, take care not to say: "Let us go and rob, let us go and despoil the widow and the orphan of their scanty pittance," but they say, "let us be just, let us recover our fortune from the hands of the rich, who have deprived us of it."

They have even a dictionary among them, which has been printed since the sixteenth century, and in this vocabulary, which they call "Argot," the words "theft," "robbery," "rape," are not to be met with. They make use of terms such as "gaining," "reimbursing," etc.

The word "injustice" is never uttered in a council of state, where the most unjust murder is proposed. Even the most bloody conspirators have never said: "Let us commit a crime." They have ever said: "Avenge our country for the crimes of a tyrant; let us punish what appears to us unjust."

In a word, servile flatterers, barbarous ministers, odious conspirators, the most infamous robbers, all pay homage against their will, to that virtue they trample upon.

I have been greatly astonished that among the French, who are enlightened and polished, maxims have been repeated upon the stage which are as shocking as they are false.

> La justice et le droit font des vaines idées,
> Le droit des rois consiste à rien épargner.[11]
> "Justice and right are vain ideas,
> the right of kings consists in sparing nothing."[12]

[11]Voltaire here refers to *Le jargon, ou langage de l'argot réformé*. It is not known when this book was first published. The only known authentic edition does not give the name of any author, but it carries the inscription "widow of Carroy."

[12]The play from which Voltaire quotes here is Corneille's *Pompée* (1644). The two lines occur, not consecutively, in a speech by Photin to Ptolomée in Act I, Scene 1. It should be pointed out that Corneille himself did not at all approve of the sentiments expressed by Photin and would have endorsed Voltaire's criticism. They are, however, entirely appropriate to the speaker and the situation in the play. Voltaire's criticism seems therefore completely gratuitous.

And this abominable speech is put in the mouth of Phocian, minister to young Ptolemy. But it is precisely because he is a minister that he should say the contrary; he should represent the death of Pompey as a necessary and just misfortune.

I believe, then, that the ideas, just and unjust, are as clear and universal as the ideas of health and sickness, truth and falsehood, convenience and inconvenience.

The limits of justice and injustice are very difficult to fix; as the middle state between health and disease, between the convenience and inconvenience of things, between falsehood and truth, is difficult to specify. They are shades that are interwoven; but glaring colors strike every eye.

For example, all men agree that we should restore what we have borrowed; but if I know that the person to whom I am indebted two millions will make use of it to enslave my country, should I put such fatal arms into his hands? Here are sentiments that are divided; but in general I should observe my oath when no evil results from it. This is what no one ever doubted.

IS UNIVERSAL CONSENT A PROOF OF TRUTH?

It may be objected that the consent of men at all times, and in all countries, is not a proof of truth. All people believed in the Magi, in sorcery, demons, apparitions, planetary influence, and a hundred other such follies. Might it not be the same with respect to justice and injustice?

I don't believe that this is so. First, it is false that all men believed these chimeras. They were, in fact, nourishment to feed the imbecility of the vulgar; but a great number of sages constantly ridiculed them. These numerous wise men, on the contrary, always acknowledged justice and injustice, as much and even more than the people.

The belief in sorcerers, demons, and the rest, is far from being necessary to mankind; the belief in justice is absolutely necessary, because it is an unfolding of that reason given by God; and the idea of sorcerers, people possessed, and similar follies is, on the contrary, a perversion of this same reason.

AGAINST LOCKE

Locke, who instructs and teaches me to mistrust myself, does he not sometimes impose upon himself like many others? He wants to prove the falsity of innate ideas; but does he not add a very bad reason to several good ones? He acknowledges it is not just to boil one's neighbor in a cauldron and eat him. He nevertheless says there have been nations of cannibals; and that these thinking beings would not have eaten men, if they had possessed the ideas of justice and injustice, which I suppose is necessary for the preservation of the human species (see No. XXXVI.)

Without inquiring whether there were, in fact, any nations of cannibals without examining the relations of the traveler Dampier,[13] who traversed all America, and who never saw any, but who, on the contrary, was received among all the savages with the greatest humanity: I reply as follows:

Conquerors have eaten their slaves taken in war. They imagined they did a very just action. They imagined they had a right over their life and death; and, as they had but few good meats for their table, they thought they were allowed to feed upon the fruit of their victory.

They were in this more just than the Romans, who, without reaping any advantages, strangled the captive princes that were chained to their triumphal cars.

The Romans and the savages had a very false idea of justice, I allow; but they, however, both thought they acted justly. And this is so true that the same savages, when they had admitted these captives into their society, looked upon them as their children; and the same ancient Romans have given a thousand examples of admirable justice.

AGAINST LOCKE AGAIN

I agree with the sagacious Locke, that there is no innate idea — no innate principle of practice. This is such an incontrovertible truth, that it is evident that all children would have a clear notion of God if they were born with this idea, and all men would then agree with this same notion — an agreement that has never been known.

It is also evident that we are not born with innate principles of morality, as we do not see how a whole nation could reject a principle of morality which had been engraved on the heart of every individual of that nation.

I suppose that we are all born with the moral principle that one should not persecute anyone for his way of thinking. Then how is it that whole communities have become persecutors? I suppose that each person carries within him the evident law that he ought to be true to his oath. Then how is it that these people, united together, have decreed that no faith should be kept with heretics? I repeat again, that instead of these chimerical innate ideas, God has given us reason, which is strengthened with age, and which teaches us all, when we are attentive without prejudice, that there is a God,

[13]William Dampier (1652–1715), English pirate, navigator, and naval officer, was the first Englishman to set foot in Australia. He published three books — A New Voyage Around the World (1697), Voyages and Discoveries, and A Discourse on Winds (both published in 1699) — which established his reputation as an explorer and scientist. Voltaire owned a French translation of the first of these. The experiences of Alexander Selkirk, one of Dampier's associates, on one of the islands west of Santiago, Chile, inspired Defoe's Robinson Crusoe (1719).

and that we should be just. But I cannot grant Locke the consequences he draws therefrom. He seems to approach too near Hobbes's system, though, in fact, he is very distant from it.

These are his words in the first book of his "Essay upon the Human Understanding":

> View but an army at the sacking of a town, and see what sense of
> moral principles or what touch of consciousness they exhibit for all
> the outrages they do.

No; they have no remorse, and why? Because they believe they act justly. Not one among them imagines the cause of the prince for whom they are fighting to be unjust. They risk their life for their cause — they fulfill the bargain they have made. They might have been killed in the assault, they therefore think they have a right to kill; they might have been plundered, they therefore think they may plunder.

Add to this, that they are intoxicated with fury, which does not reason. And to convince you that they have not divested themselves of the idea of justice and honesty, propose to these same soldiers much more money than the plunder of the city, handsomer women than those they have violated, upon condition only that instead of murdering in their rage three or four thousand enemies, who still offer resistance, and who may kill them, they go and cut the throats of their king, his chancellor, his secretaries of state, and his high almoner, you will not find a single soldier who does not reject your proposal with horror; and yet you propose but six murders, instead of four thousand, and you present them with a very valuable recompense. Why do they refuse you? Because they think it is just to kill four thousand enemies; but the murder of their sovereign, to whom they are bound by a solemn oath, appears to them abominable.

Locke continues his argument, and to prove the better that no rule of conduct is innate, he speaks of the Mingrelians, who out of sport, he says, bury their children alive; and of the Caribbees, who fatten them, in order to eat them.

It has already been observed that this great man was too credulous in relating these fables. Lambert,[14] who alone imputes to the Mingrelians the interment of their children alive, through wantonness, is not an author of sufficient credit to be quoted. Chardin,[15] who passes for a traveler of veracity, and who was ransomed in Mingrelia, would have spoken of this horrible custom if it had existed; and his affirming it would not have been sufficient to give it credit. Twenty travelers of different nations and reli-

[14]French traveler and author of *Recueil d'observations curieuse sur les moeurs, les costumes, les arts et les sciences de différent peuples de l'Asie, de l'Afrique et de l'Amérique* (1749).
[15]Jean Chardin (1643–1713), a French traveler and author of *Voyages en Perse et autres lieux de l'orient*. Voltaire's library contains an edition of this book published in Amsterdam in 1711 in three volumes.

gions should agree to confirm such a strange custom, in order to obtain a historical certainty of it.

It is the same with the women of the Antilles Islands, who raised their children to eat them. This is not in the nature of a mother. The human heart is not at all framed like that. To castrate children is a very delicate and very dangerous operation, which far from fattening them up, emaciates them for at least a whole year, and often kills them. Among the wealthy and the great, who were perverted by the excesses of luxury and jealousy, the refinement was practiced of having eunuchs to wait upon and guard their wives and concubines. Eunuchs were also in demand in Italy, and were employed at the pope's chapel, in order to have voices finer than those of women. But it is difficult to accept that in the islands of the Antilles savages had created the refinement of castrating little boys in order to eat them. What would they then have done with their little girls?

Locke further asserts that the holy men of the Mohammedan religion piously copulate with their she-asses, in order not to be tempted to commit the least fornication with the women of the country.[16] One has to put these tales along with the one about the parrot who had such a lovely conversation in the Brazilian language with Prince Maurice, a conversation that Locke was silly enough to report, without questioning if the prince's interpreter had been trying to make fun of him.[17] In this manner the author

---

[16]W. F. Fleming, the translator of *The Ignorant Philosopher*, evidently did not wish to offend the sensibilities of his readers. He does not explicitly mention the coupling of Mohammedan saints with their female asses. In his bowdlerized version, Voltaire is made to say: "Locke's assertions regarding the saints of the Mahometan religion and their useful quadrupeds, should be placed with Prince Maurice's story of the parrot. . . . " The two passages mentioning the castration of boys in the Antilles are simply suppressed. It may be of interest to note that Locke himself was too prudish to give the traveler's account in English. "The saints," he writes, "who are canonized amongst the Turks, lead lives, which one cannot with modesty relate. A remarkable passage to this purpose, out of the voyage of Baumgarten, which is a book, not every day to be met with, I shall set down at large, in the language it is published in." He then offers a lengthy quotation in Latin. In his edition of Locke's *Essay*, P. H. Nidditch supplies the following English translation: "We saw there (namely, near Balbes in Egypt) a holy Saracen sitting among the sandhills as naked as he came forth from his mother's womb. It is the custom, as we learned, among the Mohammedans, that they venerate and hold sacred those who are insane and devoid of reason. They reckon moreover that those who in the end willingly choose penance and poverty after having long lived as iniquitously as possible are to be revered as sacred. This class of men have virtually unbridled liberty to enter any houses they please, and to eat, drink, and what is more have sexual intercourse; and if there are any offspring resulting from the latter, they too are regarded as sacred. . . . That particular holy man whom we saw in that place was said to be held in exceedingly high public regard as sacred, superhuman, and of an especial integrity in that he never had intercourse with women or boys but only with she-asses and mules." It will be noted that Voltaire's quotation is not entirely accurate.

[17]The Prince who supposedly held a conversation in Portuguese with a parrot was Maurice of Nassau (1567–1625), son of William I of Orange, who was stadholder of Holland and Zeeland from 1585 until his death. After the assassination of his father (see p. 133, note 10), he assumed the military leadership of the united provinces of the Netherlands. He turned the Dutch Army into the most advanced and efficient in Europe and succeeded in driving the Spanish forces out of the northern provinces (1588–98). Maurice became embroiled in a violent struggle for power with Jan van Oldenbarnevelt (1547–1619), the pensionary (chair-

of the "Spirit of Laws" amuses himself in quoting the imaginary laws of Tonquin, Bantam, Borneo, and Formosa, upon the report of some travelers, or romancers, or persons misinformed. Montesquieu and Locke are two great men, in whom such simplicity appears to me inexcusable.

NATURE EVERYWHERE THE SAME

In giving up Locke at this point, I say with the great Newton: *"Natura est semper sibi consona"* — "Nature everywhere resembles herself." The law of gravitation, which acts upon a star, acts upon all stars, upon all matter. Thus the fundamental law of morality equally acts upon all civilized nations. There are a thousand differences in the interpretation of this law in a thousand circumstances; but the basis ever remains the same, and this basis is the idea of justice and injustice. Innumerable acts of injustice are committed in the fury of passion, as reason is lost in drunkenness; but when the intoxication is over, reason returns; and this, in my opinion, is the only cause of human society subsisting — a cause subordinate to the wants of each other's assistance.

How then have we acquired the idea of justice? As we acquired that of prudence, of truth, of convenience — by sentiment and reason. It is impossible for us to avoid thinking it a very imprudent action for a man to throw himself into the fire, in order to be admired, and who should hope afterward to escape injury. It is impossible for us to avoid thinking a man very unjust for killing another in his passion. Society is founded entirely upon these notions, which can never be torn from the heart, and it is for this reason that all society subsists, whatever extravagant and horrible superstition it may be subject to.

At what age are we acquainted with what is just and unjust? At the age when we know that two and two make four.

ON HOBBES

You, a profound and extravagant philosopher, a good citizen, a bold spirit, an enemy of Descartes, you who are deceived as he was, you whose errors in physics are great but pardonable because you came before New-

---

man) of the Estates of Holland who had loyally served Maurice's father and who had been Maurice's ally in the struggle against the Spanish Army. Oldenbarnevelt had become a disciple of Jacobus Arminius (1560–1609), one of the leaders of the "libertines" or "remonstrants" who attempted to purge Calvinism of its harsher doctrines. Although Maurice was known to feel contempt for theological disputes, he sided, purely for reasons of political convenience, with the orthodox Calvinists. Oldenbarnevelt was accused of treason and executed in May 1619. It is of interest that the famous legal philosopher Hugo Grotius (1583–1645) was tried along with Oldenbarnevelt and sentenced to life imprisonment. Grotius managed to escape two years later and flee to Paris.

ton, you have told truths that do not compensate for your errors, you who were the first to expose the chimeras of innate ideas, you who were the forerunner of Locke in many things, as well as of Spinoza, in vain do you astonish your readers by almost succeeding in proving to them that there are no laws in the world but the laws of convention; that there is no justice other than what has been agreed upon as such in a particular country. If you had been alone with Cromwell on a desert island, and Cromwell had killed you for having been a supporter of your king in England, would not such an offense be as unjust on your new island as in England?

You say in your "Law of Nature": "Every one having a right to all things, each has a right over the life of his fellow-creatures.[18] Are you not confusing power with right? Do you think that, in fact, power confers right? And that a robust son has nothing to reproach himself with for having murdered his burdensome and decrepit father? Whoever studies morality should begin by repudiating your book in his heart; but your own heart refutes it still more, for you were as virtuous as Spinoza, you were only amiss in not teaching the true principles of virtue, which you practiced yourself and recommended to others.

UNIVERSAL MORALITY

Morality appears to me so universal, so calculated by the universal Being that formed us, so destined to serve as a counterpoise to our fatal passions, and to solace the inevitable troubles of this short life, that from Zoroaster down to Lord Shaftesbury, I find all philosophers teaching the same morality, though they have all different ideas upon the principles of things

We find that Hobbes, Spinoza, and Bayle himself, who either denied the first principles, or at least doubted of them, have, nevertheless, strongly recommended justice, and all the virtues.

Every nation had peculiar religious rites, and very often absurd and revolting opinions in metaphysics and theology. But the point in question is to know whether we should be just. In this the whole universe agrees, as we said in No. XXXVI., and this statement cannot be too often repeated.

---

[18]Voltaire is not quoting Hobbes accurately, but the statement is an accurate report of what Hobbes said in several places. Thus he writes in *Leviathan*, Chapter 14: "every man has a right to every thing; even to one another's body" and again in Part I, Chapter 15 of *The Elements of Law*, "divers men have right not only to all things else, but to one another's persons." Ira O. Wade and L. Thieleman have expressed some doubt as to whether Voltaire ever read Hobbes's own works. However, Voltaire is known to have read and expressed admiration for the article on Hobbes in Diderot's *Encyclopédie* from which the information in the present section seems to have been obtained.

A Commentary on Beccaria's
Of Crimes and Punishments

This selection consists of four sections of Voltaire's "Commentary" on Beccaria's famous book. Beccaria's book appeared in 1764, Voltaire's in 1766. As noted in the Introduction, the title is too modest since Voltaire really wrote an independent work. The general aims of abolishing cruel laws and improving the administration of justice are the same but Voltaire discusses several topics not touched on by Beccaria, and his eloquence and deep emotional involvement result in a more powerful plea for reform.

PUNISHMENTS

The misfortunes of the wretched in the face of the severity of the law have induced me to look at the criminal code of nations. The humane author of the essay, *Of Crimes and Punishments*, is only too right in complaining that punishment is much too often out of proportion to the crime, and sometimes detrimental to the nation it was intended to serve.

Ingenious punishments, in which the human mind seems to have exhausted itself in order to make death terrible, seem rather the inventions of tyranny than of justice.

The punishment of the wheel was first introduced in Germany in times of anarchy, when those who seized royal power wished to terrify, by the device of an unheard-of torture, whoever would dare to rise up against them. In England they used to rip open the belly of a man convicted of high treason, tear out his heart, slap his cheeks with it, and then throw it into the fire. And what, very frequently, was this crime of high treason? During the civil wars, it was to have been faithful to an unfortunate king, and sometimes had to be explained according to the doubtful rights of a conqueror. In time, manners became milder; it is true that they continue to tear out the heart, but it is always after the death of the criminal. The torture is terrible but the death is easy, if death can ever be easy.

ON WITCHES

In 1749 a woman was burned in the Bishopric of Wurtzburg convicted of being a witch. This is an extraordinary phenomenon in the age in which we live. Is it possible that people who boast of their reformation and of trampling superstition under foot, who indeed supposed that they had reached the perfection of reason, could nevertheless believe in witchcraft, and the more than a hundred years after the so-called reformation of their reason?

In 1652 a peasant woman named Michelle Chaudron, living in the little territory of Geneva, met the devil going out of the city. The devil gave her a kiss, received her homage, and imprinted on her upper lip and right breast the mark that he customarily bestows on all whom he recognizes as his favorites. This seal of the devil is a little mark which makes the skin insensitive, as all the demonographical jurists of those times affirm.

The devil ordered Michelle Chaudron to bewitch two girls. She obeyed her master punctually. The girls' parents accused her of witchcraft before the law. The girls were questioned and confronted with the accused. They declared that they felt a continual pricking in certain parts of their bodies and that they were possessed. Doctors were called, or at least, those who passed for doctors at that time. They examined the girls. They looked for the devil's seal on Michelle's body — what the statement of the case called *Satanic marks.* Into them they drove a long needle, already a painful torture. Blood flowed out, and Michelle made it known, by her cries, that satanic marks certainly do not make one insensitive. The judges, seeing no definite proof that Michelle Chaudron was a witch, proceeded to torture her, a method that infallibly produces the necessary proofs: this wretched woman, yielding to the violence of torture, at last confessed every thing they desired.

The doctors again looked for the satanic mark. They found a little black spot on one of her thighs. They drove in the needle. The torment of the torture had been so horrible that the poor creature hardly felt the needle; thus the crime was established. But as customs were becoming somewhat mild at that time, she was burned only after being hanged and strangled.

In those days every tribunal of Christian Europe resounded with similar arrests. The faggots were lit everywhere for witches, as for heretics. People reproached the Turks most for having neither witches nor demons among them. This absence of demons was considered an infallible proof of the falseness of a religion.

A zealous friend of public welfare, of humanity, of true religion, has stated in one of his writings on behalf of innocence, that Christian tribunals have condemned to death over a hundred thousand accused witches. If to these judicial murders are added the infinitely superior number of massacred heretics, that part of the world will seem to be nothing but a vast scaffold covered with torturers and victims, surrounded by judges, guards and spectators.

ON CAPITAL PUNISHMENT

It is an old saying that a man after he is hanged is good for nothing, and that the punishments invented for the welfare of society should be useful to that society. It is clear that twenty vigorous thieves, condemned to hard labor at public works for the rest of their life, serve the state by their punishment; and their death would serve only the executioner, who is paid for killing men in public. Only rarely are thieves punished by death in England; they are transported overseas to the colonies. The same is true in the vast Russian empire. Not a single criminal was executed during the reign of the autocratic Elizabeth. Catherine II who succeeded her, endowed with a very superior mind, followed the same policy. Crimes have not increased as a result of this humanity, and almost always, criminals banished to Siberia become good men. The same thing has been noticed in the English colonies. This happy change astonishes us, but nothing is more natural. These condemned men are forced to work constantly in order to live. Opportunities for vice are lacking; they marry and have children. Force men to work and you make them honest. It is well known that great crimes are not committed in the country, except, perhaps, when too many holidays bring on idleness and lead to debauchery.

A Roman citizen was condemned to death only for crimes affecting the welfare of the state. Our teachers, our first legislators, respected the blood of their fellow citizens; we lavish that of ours.

This dark and delicate question has been long discussed: whether judges may punish by death when the law does not expressly require this punishment. This question was solemnly debated before Emperor Henry IV. He judged, and decided that no magistrate could have this power.

There are some criminal cases that are so unusual or so complicated, or are accompanied by such strange circumstances, that the law itself has been forced in more than one country to leave these singular cases to the discretion of the judges. If there really should be one instance in which the law permits a criminal to be put to death who has not committed a capital offense, there will be a thousand instances in which humanity, which is stronger than the law, should spare the life of those whom the law has sentenced to death.

The sword of justice is in our hands; but we ought to blunt it more often than sharpen it. It is carried in its sheath before kings, to warn us that it should be rarely drawn.

There have been judges who loved to make blood flow; such was Jeffreys in England; such in France was a man who was called *coupe-tête*. Men like these were not born to be judges; nature made them to be executioners.

ON SUICIDE

The famous Duverger de Hauranne, abbé of St. Cyran, considered the founder of Port Royal, wrote around 1608 a treatise on suicide which has become one of the rarest books in Europe.[1]

The Decalogue, he says, orders us not to kill. The murder of one's self seems to be just as much included in this precept as the murder of some one else. Now, if there are situations in which it is right to kill some one else, there are also situations in which it is right to kill one's self; however, a man should attempt to take his own life only after first consulting his reason.

Public authority, which serves in place of God, may dispose of our life. Human reason may also serve in place of Divine reason: a ray of the eternal light.

St. Cyran extends this argument to great length, which could be taken as sheer sophistry; but when he comes to an explanation and to particulars, it is more difficult to answer him. One might, he states, kill himself for the good of his prince, his country, or his family.

It is indeed true that we cannot condemn such men as Codrus and Curtius. Surely no ruler would dare to punish the family of a man wholly dedicated to his prince; indeed, there is no sovereign who would dare not to reward such a man. St. Thomas said the same thing well before St. Cyran. But we do not need Thomas or Bonaventura or Hauranne to know that a man who dies for his country is worthy of our praise.

The abbé of St. Cyran concludes that it is permitted to do for one's self what it is worthy to do for another. It is generally well known what Plutarch, Seneca, Montaigne, and a hundred other philosophers allege in favor of suicide. It is a common subject and an exhausted one. I do not claim here to present a defense of an action condemned by the laws; but

---

[1] The work to which Voltaire refers, *Questions royalle et sa decision* (The Royal Question and Its Resolution), is so little known that it is not even mentioned in comprehensive histories of the writings on suicide such as H. R. Fedden's *Suicide—A Social and Historical Study* (London, 1938). It was written in response to Henry IV's question "in what extremity, chiefly in time of peace, can a subject be obliged to save the life of the prince at the expense of his own life?" St. Cyran distinguished thirty-four cases in which a person can kill himself "innocently." Jean Duvergier de Hauranne (1581–1643), generally known as St. Cyran, was one of the early leaders of the Jansenist movement. He strongly influenced Antoine Arnauld, Pascal, and also John Wesley who translated St. Cyran's *Lettres chrétiennes et spirituelles* into English. Voltaire had a copy of St. Cyran's book, or rather pamphlet (it numbered no more than 56 pages) in his library, and in 1778, the year of his death, a new edition was published very possibly because he had mentioned it in several of his works.

neither the Old Testament nor the New ever forbade a man to depart from life when he could no longer bear it. No Roman law condemned self-murder. On the contrary, here is the law of Emperor Marcus Aurelius, which was never revoked.

"If your father or your brother, convicted of no crime, kills himself either to remove himself from grief or through weariness of life, or in despair or in madness, his will is valid, or if he dies intestate, his heirs inherit according to law."

Despite this humane law of our ancient masters, we still rip apart and pierce with a stake the body of a man who dies voluntarily; we render his memory infamous; we dishonor his family to the extent that we can; we punish the son for having lost his father, and the widow for being deprived of her husband. We even confiscate the possessions of the deceased, which is tantamount to plundering the patrimony of the living to whom it belongs. This custom, like many others, is derived from our canon law, which deprives those who die a voluntary death of the rights of burial. The conclusion drawn from this fact a that no one can inherit on earth the property of a man who is deemed to have no inheritance in heaven. The canon law is the section, *De Poenitentia*, assures us that Judas committed a greater sin in hanging himself than in betraying our Lord Jesus Christ.

Questions Concerning the Encyclopedia

The *Questions sur l'Encyclopédie*, published between 1770 and 1772, was the second of Voltaire's collection of articles published in alphabetical order. As previously mentioned, he included in it expanded versions of several of the articles from the *Philosophical Dictionary*. The additions to three of these — "Beauty," "Miracles," and "Resurrection" — are reprinted in this section. The *Philosophical Dictionary* did not have an article on "Identity," but some of the questions covered in the article on this topic in the *Questions* reprinted below were briefly discussed in "The Chinese Catechism." What Voltaire says about identity is strikingly similar to some of Hume's arguments in the section on "Personal Identity" in the *Treatise of Human Nature*. Voltaire greatly admired Hume, and we know that he read the *Inquiry Concerning Human Understanding*, but there is no evidence that he even saw the *Treatise*.

BEAUTY

There are actions which the whole world considers admirable. A challenge passed between two of Caesar's officers, mortal enemies, not to shed each other's blood behind a bush by thirds and fourths, as among us, but to decide which of them would best defend the camp of the Romans, about to be attacked by the barbarians. One of the two, after having repulsed the enemy, was near falling; the other flew to his assistance, saved his life, and gained the victory.

A friend devotes himself to death for his friend, a son for his father. The Algonquin, the French, the Chinese, will mutually say that all this is very beautiful, that such actions give them pleasure, and that they admire them.

They will say the same of great moral maxims. . . . of that of Zoroaster: "If in doubt that an action be just, desist", of that of Confucius: "Forget injuries; never forget benefits."

The negro, with round eyes and flattened nose, who would not give the ladies of our court the name of beautiful, would give it without hesitation to these actions and these maxims. Even the wicked man recognizes the beauty of the virtues which he cannot imitate. The beautiful, which only strikes the senses, the imagination, and what is called the spirit, is then often uncertain; the beauty which strikes the heart is not. You will find a number of people who will tell you they have found nothing beautiful in three-fourths of the "Iliad"; but nobody will deny that the devotion of Codrus for his people was fine, supposing it was true.

Brother Attiret, a Jesuit, a native of Dijon, was employed as designer in the country house of the Emperor Camhi, at the distance of some leagues from Peking.

"This country house," says he, in one of his letters to M. Dassaur, "is larger than the town of Dijon. It is divided into a thousand habitations on one line; each one has its courts, its parterres, its gardens, and its waters; the front of each is ornamented with gold varnish and paintings. In the vast enclosures of the park, hills have been raised by hand from twenty to sixty feet high. The valleys are watered by an infinite number of canals, which run a considerable distance to join and form lakes and seas. We float on these seas in boats varnished and gilt, from twelve to thirteen fathoms long and four wide. These barks have magnificent saloons, and the borders of the canals are covered with houses, all in different tastes. Every house has its gardens and cascades. You go from one valley to another by alleys, alternately ornamented with pavilions and grottoes. No two valleys are alike; the largest of all is surrounded by a colonnade, behind which are gilded buildings. All the apartments of these houses correspond in magnificence with the outside. All the canals have bridges at stated distances; these bridges are bordered with balustrades of white marble sculptured in bas-relief.

"In the middle of the great sea is raised a rock, and on this rock is a square pavilion, in which are more than a hundred apartments. From this square pavilion there is a view of all the palaces, all the houses, and all the gardens of this immense enclosure, and there are more than four hundred of them.

"When the emperor gives a fête all these buildings are illuminated in an instant, and from every house there are fireworks.

"This is not all; at the end of what they call the sea is a great fair, held by the emperor's officers. Vessels come from the great sea to arrive at this fair. The courtiers disguise themselves as merchants and artificers of all sorts; one keeps a coffee house, another a tavern; one takes the profession of a thief, another that of the officer who pursues him. The emperor and all the ladies of the court come to buy stuffs, the false merchants cheat them as much as they can; they tell them that it is shameful to dispute so much about the price, and that they are poor customers. Their majesties reply that the merchants are knaves; the latter are angry and affect to depart;

they are appeased; the emperor buys all and makes lotteries of it for all his court. Farther on are spectacles of all sorts."

When brother Attiret came from China to Versailles he found it small and dull. The Germans, who were delighted to stroll about its groves, were astonished that brother Attiret was so difficult. This is another reason which determines me not to write a treatise on the beautiful.

IDENTITY

This scientific term signifies no more than "the same thing." It might be correctly translated by "sameness." This subject is of considerably more interest than may be imagined. All agree that the guilty person only ought to be punished — the individual perpetrator, and no other. But a man fifty years of age is not in reality the same individual as the man of twenty; he retains no longer any of the parts which then formed his body; and if he has lost the memory of past events, it is certain that there is nothing left to unite his actual existence to an existence which to him is lost.

I am the same person only by the consciousness of what I have been combined with that of what I am; I have no consciousness of my past being but through memory; memory alone, therefore, establishes the identity, the sameness of my person.

We may, in truth, be naturally and aptly compared to a river, all whose waters pass away in perpetual change and flow. It is the same river as to its bed, its banks, its source, its mouth, everything, in short, that it not itself; but changing every moment its waters, which constitute its very being, it has no identity; there is no sameness belonging to the river.

Were there another Xerxes like him who lashed the Hellespont for disobedience, and ordered for it a pair of handcuffs;[1] and were the son of this Xerxes to be drowned in the Euphrates, and the father desirous of punishing that river for the death of his son, the Euphrates might very

---

[1]The event to which Voltaire refers occurred during the attempted invasion of Greece by the Persian armies under King Xerxes I (519–465 B.C.). The invasion was prepared with enormous care and extraordinary architectural skill. A channel was dug across the Isthmus of Athos and two boat "bridges" were constructed to allow the huge army to cross the strait of the Dardanelles, then known as the Hellespont. According to Herodotus, Xerxes had an army of five million men, but more recent historians estimate it at 360,000. Right after the boat bridges were completed, a tremendous storm destroyed the Persian squadrons while the Greeks were safely in port. This was the occasion for Xerxes' whipping of the Hellespont. It took him no more than seven days to rebuild the bridges and he then successfully invaded Greece, occupying Attica and pillaging Athens. However, he lost a major naval battle at Salamis. From then on Xerxes lost all interest in the war. He left some troops behind and desultory fighting continued for many years, but he himself returned to Persia where his prime occupation was the building of monumental architectural structures. Xerxes was a tyrannical ruler and he was murdered by the captain of his body guard. In the Old Testament he appears as Ahasverus. Händel wrote an opera about him, which contains the celebrated *Largo*.

reasonably say in its vindication: "Blame the waves that were rolling on at the time your son was bathing; those waves belong not to me, and form no part of me; they have passed on to the Persian Gulf; a part is mixed with the salt water of that sea, and another part, exhaled in vapor, has been impelled by a south-east wind to Gaul, and been incorporated with endives and lettuces, which the Gauls have since used in their salads; seize the culprit where you can find him."

It is the same with a tree, a branch of which broken by the wind might have fractured the skull of your great grandfather. It is no longer the same tree; all its parts have given way to others. The branch which killed your great grandfather is no part of this tree; it exists no longer.

It has been asked, then, how a man, who has totally lost his memory before his death, and whose members have been changed into other substances, can be punished for his faults or rewarded for his virtues when he is no longer himself? I have read in a well-known book the following question and answer:

"Question. How can I be either rewarded or punished when I shall no longer exist; when there will be nothing remaining of that which constituted my person? It is only by means of memory that I am always myself; after my death, a miracle will be necessary to restore it to me — to enable me to re-enter upon my lost existence.

"Answer. That is just as much as to say that if a prince had put to death his whole family, in order to reign himself, and if he had tyrannized over his subjects with the most wanton cruelty, he would be exempted from punishment on pleading before God, 'I am not the offender; I have lost my memory; you are under a mistake; I am no longer the same person.' Do you think this sophism would pass with God?"

This answer is a highly commendable one; but it does not completely solve the difficulty.

It would be necessary for this purpose, in the first place, to know whether understanding and sensation are a faculty given by God to man, or a created substance; a question which philosophy is too weak and uncertain to decide.

It is necessary in the next place to know whether, if the soul be a substance and has lost all knowledge of the evil it has committed, and be, moreover, as perfect a stranger to what it has done with its own body, as to all the other bodies of our universe — whether, in these circumstances, it can or should, according to our manner of reasoning, answer in another universe for actions of which it has not the slightest knowledge; whether, in fact, a miracle would not be necessary to impart to this soul the recollection it no longer possesses, to render it consciously present to the crimes which have become obliterated and annihilated in its mind, and make it the same person that it was on earth; or whether God will judge it nearly in the same way in which the presidents of human tribunals proceed, condemning a criminal, although he may have completely forgotten the crimes he has actually committed. He remembers them no longer; but they are remembered for him; he is punished for the sake of the example. But God cannot punish a man after his death with a veiw to his being an example to the living. No living man knows whether the deceased is condemmed or absolved. God, therefore, can punish him only because he cherished and accomplished evil desires; but if, when after death he presents himself before the tribunal of God, he no longer entertains any such desire; if for a period of twenty years he has totally forgotten that he did entertain such; if he is no longer in any respect the same person; what is it that God will punish in him?

These are questions which appear beyond the compass of the human understanding, and there seems to exist a necessity, in these intricacies and labyrinths, of recurring to faith alone, which is always our last asylum.

Lucretius had partly felt these difficulties, when in his third book (verses 877–878) he describes a man trembling at the idea of what will happen to him when he will no longer be the same man:

> *Nec radicitus e vita se tollit et eicit Sed facit esse sui quiddam super inscius ipse.*[2]

But Lucretius is not the oracle to be addressed, in order to obtain any discoveries of the future.

The celebrated Toland, who wrote his own epitaph, concluded it with these words: *"Idem futurus Tolandus nunquam"* — "He will never again be the same Toland."[3]

However, it may be presumed that God would have well known how to find and restore him, had such been his good pleasure; and it is to be presumed, also, that the being who necessarily exists, is necessarily good.

---

[2]"Nor does he completely remove and throw himself out of life, but moreover he himself ignorantly supposes that something of himself exists."

[3]John Toland (1670–1722) was born in Ireland and raised as a Catholic, but spent most of his adult life in England and later also in Holland and Germany where he had many friendly discussions with Leibniz. His most famous book *Christianity Not Mysterious* (whose first edition was published in 1696) led to prosecutions in Ireland as well as in England. In Ireland the book was burned by the common hangman and an order for Toland's arrest was issued. In England the book was denounced in Parliament and in the pulpit, but Toland was never tried. In *Christianity Not Mysterious,* Toland writes as a deist, but in several of his later works he is full of praise of Giordano Bruno and Spinoza and he there seems to incline to pantheism and materialism. He seems to have been a most lovable man who always sided with the underdog. He was a friend of the Jews and advocated increased Jewish immigration and naturalization of the Jews at a time when they could not be citizens. His pamphlet *Reasons for Naturalizing the Jews in Great Britain and Ireland, on the same foot with all other nations; containing also a defense of the Jews against vulgar prejudices in all countries* (1714) is a most remarkable document. Toland died in extreme poverty. His last words were "I am going to sleep." Voltaire greatly admired him and quoted his dying words as an excellent expression of the kind of attitude he himself favored toward death.

OF THOSE WHO HAVE BEEN SO IMPIOUSLY RASH AS TO DENY THE MIRACLES OF JESUS CHRIST.

Among the moderns, Thomas Woolston, a learned member of the University of Cambridge, appears to me to have been the first who ventured to interpret the Gospels merely in a typical, allegorical, and spiritual sense, and boldy maintained that not one of the miracles of Jesus was actually performed. He wrote without method or art, and in a style confused and coarse, but not destitute of vigor. His six discourses against the miracles of Jesus Christ were publicly sold at London, in his own house. In the course of two years, from 1727 to 1729, he had three editions of them printed, of twenty thousand copies each, and yet it is now very difficult to procure one from the booksellers.

Never was Christianity so daringly assailed by any Christian. Few writers entertain less awe or respect for the public, and no priest ever declared himself more openly the enemy of priests. He even dared to justify this hatred by that of Jesus Christ against the Pharisees and Scribes; and he said that he should not, like Jesus Christ, become their victim, because he had come into the world in a more enlightened age.

He certainly hoped to justify his rashness by his adoption of the mystical sense; but he employs expressions so contemptuous and abusive that every Christian ear is shocked at them.

If we may believe him, when Jesus sent the devil into the herd of two thousand swine, He did neither more nor less than commit a robbery on their owners. If the story had been told of Mahomet, he would have been considered as "an abominable wizard, and a sworn slave to the devil." And if the proprietor of the swine, and the merchants who in the outer court of the temple sold beasts for sacrifices, and whom Jesus drove out with a scourge, came to demand justice when he was apprehended, it is clear that he was deservedly condemned, as there never was a jury in England that would not have found him guilty.

He tells her fortune to the woman of Samaria, just like a wandering Bohemian or Gypsy. This alone was sufficient to cause His banishment, which was the punishment inflicted upon fortune-tellers, or diviners, by Tiberius. "I am astonished," says he, "that the gypsies do not proclaim themselves the genuine disciples of Jesus, as their vocation is the same. However, I am glad to see that He did not extort money from the Samaritan woman, differing in this respect from our clergy, who take care to be well paid for their divinations."

I follow the order of the pages in his book. The author goes on to the entrance of Jesus Christ into Jerusalem. It is not clear, he says, whether He was mounted on a male or female ass, or upon the foal of an ass, or upon all three together.

He compares Jesus, when tempted by the devil, to St. Dunstan, who seized the devil by the nose; and he gives the preference to St. Dunstan.

At the article of the fig-tree, which was cursed with barrenness for not producing figs out of season for them, he describes Jesus as a mere vagabond, a mendicant friar, who before He turned field-preacher was "no better than a journeyman carpenter." It is surprising, he says, that the court of Rome has not among all its relics some little fancy-box or joint-stool of His workmanship. In a word, it is difficult to carry blasphemy further.

After diverting himself with the probationary fish-pool of Bethesda, the waters of which were troubled or stirred once in every year by an angel, he inquires how it could well be, that neither Flavius Josephus, nor Philo should ever mention this angel; why St. John should be the sole historian of this miracle; and by what other miracle it happened that no Roman ever saw this angel, or ever even heard his name mentioned?

The water changed into wine at the marriage of Cana, according to him, excites the laughter and contempt of all who are not victimized by superstition.

"What!" says he, "John expressly says that the guests were already intoxicated, '*methus tosi*'; and God comes down to earth and performs His first miracle to enable them to drink still more!"

God, made man, commences His mission by assisting at a village wedding. "Whether Jesus and His mother were drunk, as were others of the company, is not certain. The familiarity of the lady with a soldier leads to the presumption that she was fond of her bottle; that her Son, was somewhat affected by the wine, appears from His answering His mother so 'waspishly and snappishly' as He did, when He said, 'Woman, what have I to do with thee?' It may be inferred from these words that Mary was not a virgin, and that Jesus was not her son; had it been otherwise, He would not have thus insulted His father and mother in violation of one of the most sacred commandments of the law. However, He complied with His mother's request; He fills eighteen jars with water, and makes punch of it." These are the very words of Thomas Woolston, and must fill every Christian soul with indignation.

It is with regret, and even with trembling, that I quote these passages; but there have been sixty thousand copies of this work printed, all bearing the name of the author, and all publicly sold at his house.

It is to the dead raised again by Jesus Christ that he principally directs his attention. He contends that a dead man restored to life would have been an object of attention and astonishment to the universe; that all the Jewish magistracy, and more especially Pilate, would have made the most minute investigations and obtained the most authentic depositions; that Tiberius enjoined all proconsuls, praetors, and governors of provinces to inform him with exactness of every event that took place; that Lazarus, who had been dead four whole days, would have been most strictly interrogated; and that no little curiosity would have been excited to know what had become, during that time, of his soul.

With what eager interest would Tiberius and the whole Roman senate have questioned him, and not indeed only him, but the daughter of Jairus and the son of the widow of Nain? Three dead persons restored to life would have been three attestations to the divinity of Jesus, which almost in a single moment would have made the whole world Christian. But instead of all this, the whole world, for more than two hundred years, knew nothing about these resplendent and decisive evidences. It is not till a hundred years have rolled away from the date of the events that some obscure individuals show one another the writings that contain the relation of those miracles. Eighty-nine emperors reckoning those who had only the name of "tyrants," never hear the slightest mention of these resurrections, although they must inevitably have held all nature in amazement. Neither the Jewish historian Josephus, nor the learned Philo, nor any Greek or Roman historian at all notices these prodigies. In short, Woolston has the imprudence to say that the history of Lazarus is so brimful of absurdities that St. John, when he wrote it, had liv'd beyond his senses.[4]

Supposing, says Woolston, that God should in our own times send an ambassador to London to convert the hireling clergy, and that ambassador should raise the dead, what would the clergy say?

He blasphemes the incarnation, the resurrection, and the ascension of Jesus Christ, just upon the same system; and he calls these miracles: "The most manifest and the most barefaced imposture that ever was put upon the world!"[5]

What is perhaps more singular still is that each of his discourses is dedicated to a bishop. His dedications are certainly not exactly in the French style. He bestows no flattery nor compliments. He upbraids them with their pride and avarice, their ambition and faction, and smiles with triumph at the thought of their being now, like every other class of citizens, in complete subjection to the laws of the state.

At last these bishops, tired of being insulted by an undignified member of the University of Cambridge, determined upon a formal appeal to the laws. They instituted a prosecution against Woolston in the King's Bench, and he was tried before Chief Justice Raymond, in 1729, when he was imprisoned, condemned to pay a fine, and obliged to give security to the amount of a hundred and fifty pounds sterling. . . .[6] Some time before his death, a female zealot meeting him in the street was gross enough to spit in his face; he calmly wiped his face and bowed to her. His manners were mild

[4]Volume II, Discourse VI, page 38 (note by Voltaire).
[5]Volume II, page 27 (note by Voltaire).
[6]A few lines in which Voltaire offers an inaccurate account of developments after Woolston's trial have been omitted. Contrary to Voltaire's assertion, Woolston did die in prison (see the Introduction to this volume, pp. 54–55).

and pleasing. He was obstinately infatuated with the mystical meaning, and blasphemed the literal one; but let us hope that he repented on his death-bed, and that God has showed him mercy.

About the same period there appeared in France the *testament* of John Meslier.[7]

It was both a wonderful and a melancholy spectacle to see two priests at the same time writing against the Christian religion. Meslier is still more violent than Woolston. He ventures to treat the devil's carrying off our Lord to the top of a mountain, the marriage of Cana, and the loaves and fishes, as absurd tales, injurious to the Supreme Being, which for three hundred years were unknown to the whole Roman Empire, and at last advanced from the dregs of the community to the throne of the emperors, when policy compelled them to adopt the nonsense of the people, in order to keep them the better in subjection. The declamations of the English priest do not approach in vehemence those of the priest of Champagne. Woolston occasionally showed discretion. Meslier never has any; he is a man so sensitively sore to the crimes to which he has been witness that he renders the Christian religion responsible for them, forgetting that it condemns them. There is not a single miracle which is not with him an object of scorn or horror; no prophecy which he does not compare with the prophecies of Nostradamus. He even goes so far as to compare Jesus Christ to Don Quixote, and St. Peter to Sancho Panza; and what is most of all to be deplored is, that he wrote these blasphemies against Jesus Christ, when he might be said to be in the very arms of death — at a moment when the most deceitful are sincere, and the most intrepid tremble. Too strongly impressed by some injuries that had been done him by his superiors in authority; too deeply affected by the great difficulties which he met with in the Scripture, he became exasperated against it more than Acosta and all the Jews; more than Porphyry, Celsus, Iamblichus, Julian, Libanius, Maximus, Simmachus, or any other whatever of the partisans of human reason against the divine incomprehensibilities of our religion. Many abridgments of his work have been printed; but happily the persons in authority suppressed them as fast as they appeared.

A priest of Bonne-Nouvelle, near Paris, wrote also on the same subject; and it thus happened that at the very time the abbé Becheran and the rest of the Convulsionaries[8] were performing miracles, three priests were writing against the genuine Gospel miracles.

---

[7]For details about Voltaire's discovery and use of Meslier's *Testament, see* the Introduction, pp. 14–15.

[8]Convulsionaries were Jansenists suffering from assorted physical maladies who, after the death of their ascetic leader François de Pâris, made pilgrimages to his tomb in the cemetery of St. Médard. There they scorched themselves, groaned and wept, and prayed for cures. Several of them testified to dramatic and sensational cures. Some of the excited Jansenists fell into cataleptic fits and were therefore called "convulsionaries." After three years of these goings on, the cemetery was closed by the authorities. God, as Voltaire put it, was forbidden

The most clever work that has been written against the miracles and prophecies is that of my Lord Bolingbroke. But happily it is so voluminous, so destitute of method, so verbose, and so abounding in long and sometimes complicated sentences, that it requires a great deal of patience to read him.

There have been some minds so constituted that they have been enchanted by the miracles of Moses and Joshua, but have not entertained for those of Jesus Christ the respect to which they are entitled. Their imagination — raised by the grand spectacle of the sea opening a passage through its depths, and suspending its waves that a horde of Hebrews might safely go through; by the ten plagues of Egypt, and by the stars that stopped in their course over Gibeon and Ajalon, etc. — could not with ease and satisfaction be let down again, so as to admire the comparatively petty miracles of the water changed into wine, the withered fig-tree, and the swine drowned in the little lake of Gadara. Wagenseil[9] said that it was like hearing a rustic ditty after attending a grand concert.

The Talmud pretends that there have been many Christians who, after comparing the miracles of the Old Testament with those of the New Testament, embraced Judaism; they consider it impossible that the Sovereign Lord of Nature should have wrought such stupendous prodigies for a religion He intended to annihilate. What! they exclaim, can it possibly be, that for a series of ages He should have exhibited a train of astonishing and tremendous miracles in favor of a true religion that was to become a false one? What! Can it be that God Himself has recorded that this religion shall never perish, and that those who attempt to destroy it shall be stoned to death, and yet that He has nevertheless sent His own Son, Who is no other than Himself, to annihilate what He was employed so many ages in erecting?

---

by the order of the king to work any miracles there. In the *Philosophical Dictionary* Voltaire has a short article on "convulsionaries" in which he ridicules both the hysterical Jansenists and their Jesuit opponents who were upset because they could not produce equally resplendent miracles. The one thing they are united on, he remarks, is opposition to the ideas of Montesquieu and the other *philosophes*.

[9]Johann Christoph Wagenseil (1633–1705), a German historian of broad interests, produced in 1695 a collection of juvenile books, which has been described as the first encyclopedia for children. His main interest, however, was Jewish history. Voltaire owned one of his books, *Tela ignea Satanae*, which reproduces a collection of Jewish writings. It should be pointed out that Wagenseil's interest in the Jews was not inspired by compassion for a much persecuted people or by any desire for legal equality such as found in Locke and Toland. He was, rather, inspired by what Voltaire would have facetiously called the laudable intention to convert the Jews from their false to the true religion. In 1707 he published in Nuremberg a work in German whose title tells everything — "Hope for the Salvation of Israel or Clear Proof of the Impending and as it seems Universally Approaching Great Conversion of the Jews Including Reflections on How, Aside from Divine Assistance, This Development Can Be Hastened."

There is much more to be added to these remarks; this Son, they continue, this Eternal God, having made Himself a Jew, adheres to the Jewish religion during the whole of His life; He performs all the functions of it, He frequents the Jewish temple, He announces nothing contrary to the Jewish law, and all His disciples are Jews and observe the Jewish ceremonies. It most certainly is not He who established the Christian religion. It was established by the dissident Jews who united with the Platonists. There is not a single dogma of Christianity that was preached by Jesus Christ.

Such is the reasoning of these rash men, who, with minds at once hypocritical and audacious, dare to criticize the works of God, and admit the miracles of the Old Testament for the sole purpose of rejecting those of the New Testament.

Of this number was the unfortunate priest of Pont-à-Mousson in Lorraine, called Nicholas Anthony; he was known by no other name. After he had received what is called "the four minors" in Lorraine, the Calvinistic preacher Ferri, happening to go to Pont-à-Mousson, raised in his mind very serious scruples, and persuaded him that the four minors were the mark of the beast. Anthony, driven almost to distraction by the thought of carrying about him the mark of the beast, had it immediately effaced by Ferri, embraced the Protestant religion, and became a minister at Geneva about the year 1630.

With a head full of rabbinical learning, he thought that if the Protestants were right in reference to the Papists, the Jews were much more so in reference to all the different sects of Christianity whatever. From the village of Divonne, where he was pastor, he went to be received as a Jew at Venice, together with a young apprentice in theology whom he had persuaded to adopt his own principles, but who afterwards abandoned him, not experiencing any call to martyrdom.

At first the minister, Nicholas Anthony, abstained from uttering the name of Jesus Christ in his sermons and prayers; in a short time, however, becoming animated and emboldened by the example of the Jewish saints, who confidently professed Judaism before the princes of Tyre and Babylon, he travelled barefooted to Geneva, to confess before the judges and magistrates that there is only one religion upon earth, because there is only one God; that that religion is the Jewish; that it is absolutely necessary to become circumcised; and that it is a horrible crime to eat bacon and blood pudding. He pathetically exhorted all the people of Geneva, who crowded to hear him, no longer to continue to be children of Satan, but to become good Jews, in order to deserve the kingdom of heaven. He was apprehended, and put in chains.

The little Council of Geneva, which at that period did nothing without consulting the council of preachers, asked their advice in this emergency. The most sensible of them recommended that poor Anthony should be bled in the cephalic vein, use the bath, and be kept upon gruel and broths; after which he might perhaps gradually be induced to pronounce the name of Jesus Christ, or at least to hear it pronounced, without grinding his teeth, as had hitherto been his practice. They added, that the laws bore with Jews; that there were eight thousand of them even in Rome itself; that many merchants are true Jews, and therefore that as Rome admitted within its walls eight thousand children of the synagogue, Geneva might well tolerate one. At the sound of "toleration" the rest of the pastors, who were the majority, gnashing their teeth still more than Anthony did at the name of Jesus Christ, and also eager to find an opportunity to burn a man, which could not be done every day, called peremptorily for the burning. They resolved that nothing could serve more to establish genuine Christianity; that the Spaniards had obtained so much reputation in the world only by burning the Jews every year, and that after all, if the Old Testament must prevail over the New Testament, God would not fail to come and extinguish the flames of the pile, as he did at Babylon for Shadrach, Meshac, and Abednego; in which case all must go back again to the Old Testament; but that, in the meantime, it was indispensable to burn Nicholas Anthony. On the breaking up of the meeting, they concluded with the observation: "We must put the wicked out of the way" — the very words they used.

The long-faced magistrates, Sarasin and Godefroi, agreed that the reasoning of the highest Calvinist council was admirable, and by the right of the strongest party, condemned Nicholas Anthony, the weakest of men, to die the same death as Calanus[10] and the counsellor Dubourg.[11] This sentence was carried into execution on April 20, 1632, in a very beautiful lawn or meadow, called Plain-Palais, in the presence of twenty thousand persons, who blessed the new law, and the wonderful sense of the magistrates Sarasin and Godefroi.

The God of Abraham, Isaac, and Jacob did not renew the miracle of the furnace of Babylon in favor of poor Anthony.

Abauzit,[12] an author of great veracity, relates in his notes, that he died in the greatest constancy, and persisted in his opinions even at the stake on the pile; he broke out into no passionate invective against his judges when the executioner was tying him to the stake; he displayed neither pride nor pusillanimity; he neither wept nor sighed; he was resigned. Never did martyr consummate his sacrifice with a more lively faith; never did philoso-

---

[10]Calanus was one of the so-called gymnosophists (a group of ascetics) taken by Alexander the Great from India back to Persia. When Calanus became ill, rather than suffer a slow decline, he had himself burned alive in a public ceremony.

[11]Anne Dubourg (1521–1559) was a Huguenot Counsellor of the parlement of Paris who openly condemned persecution for heresy. He was hanged and his body subsequently burned during the tyrannical rule of the Guises (see note on p. 133 above).

[12]The reference is to Firmin Abauzit (1679–1767), a Swiss historian and theologian whose works were in Voltaire's library.

pher contemplate a death of horror with greater firmness. This clearly proves that his folly or madness was at all events attended with sincere conviction. Let us implore of the God of both the Old and the New Testaments that he will grant him mercy.

I would say as much for the Jesuit Malagrida,[13] who was still more infatuated and mad than Nicholas Anthony; as I would also for the ex-Jesuits Patouillet and Paulian,[14] should they ever be brought to the stake.

A great number of writers, whose misfortune it was to be philosophers rather than Christians, have been bold enough to deny the miracles of our Lord; but after the four priests already noticed, there is no necessity to enumerate other instances. Let us lament over these four unfortunate men, led astray by their own deceitful reason, and precipitated by the gloom of their feelings into an abyss so dreadful and so fatal.

[13]What happened to the "infatuated and mad Jesuit Malagrida" is gruesome and should be better known. Malagrida was not perhaps as sympathetic a character as the tolerant and easy-going Jean Calas, but his fate is just as horrible. Gabriel Malagrida was born in Italy in 1689 and became a Jesuit very early in life. He was sent to Portugal and subsequently to northern Brazil where he founded convents, seminaries, and retreat houses. In 1750 he returned to Portugal and after another sojourn in Brazil lasting about three years, he lived in Portugal until his death. He became confessor to Queen Mariana and spriritual guide to numerous members of the nobility. He was a flamboyant preacher and a zealous and credulous man who acquired the reputation of a saint. The year after the Lisbon earthquake, he published a book which attributed the disaster to God's punishment of the people of Lisbon for their sinful way of life. In the meantime a commoner named Sebastian José de Carvalho e Melo (1699–1782) had become prime minister, and he manipulated the weak and indolent King José as he pleased. Carvalho has come down in history as the Marquis de Pombal, a title the king conferred on him at his own behest. The two groups in the way of his absolute power were a number of aristocratic families who treated him as an upstart and the Jesuits. Pombal used an unsuccessful attempt on the life of the king in 1758 as a pretext for a frightful reign of terror in the course of which he eliminated both opposition groups. The aristocrats came first. Pombal staged a series of mock trials in which the accused, most of them entirely innocent, were tortured, condemned, and executed, often in a single day. It is most probable that the assasination attempt was the work of the Marquis of Tavora with whose wife the king was openly carrying on an affair. After disposing of the noble families, Pombal had all the leading Jesuits arrested, charging them with complicity. Voltaire did not hear about any of this until February of 1759, when he expressed grave doubts about the truth of Pombal's charges. "It is quite understandable," he wrote, "that they [the Jesuits] may have encouraged the assassination and that they may have prayed for the success of that holy action; but the fact that they were brought to prison in bundles of laundry seems to me suspicious and makes me tremble for the truth of what is being charged against them." Pombal tried to picture himself as an "enlightened" despot and flooded Europe with anti-Jesuit manifestos at a time when the Jesuits were very much on the defensive in several countries. Although the books of all the Enlightenment thinkers were banned in Portugal, Pombal also tried to win the support of the *philosophes*. Voltaire was not impressed and remarked that Pombal exhibited "a superfluity of the laughable with a superfluity of the horrible." Malagrida, who was an old man when he had been arrested, became quite insane during his imprisonment. In prison he wrote two books which are said to be mad—*Life of St. Anne—Mother of Mary* and *Kingdom of the AntiChrist*—and they supposedly contained numerous heresies. Pombal hit on the idea of having Malagrida tried not only for treason but also for heresies. To guarantee a guilty verdict, he installed his younger brother Paulo as Inquisitor-General. On January 12, 1761, Malagrida was found guilty of treason as well as of blasphemy, impiety, and false prophecy. Although 72 years old, he was burned at the stake in a public square in Lisbon on September 20, 1761.

RESURRECTION OF THE ANCIENTS AND THE MODERNS

Resurrection of the Ancients

It has been asserted that the dogma of resurrection was much in vogue with the Egyptians, and was the origin of their embalmings and their pyramids. This I myself formerly believed. Some said that the resurrection was to take place at the end of a thousand years; others at the end of three thousand. This difference in their theological opinions seems to prove that they were not very sure about the matter.

Besides, in the history of Egypt, we find no man raised again; but among the Greeks we find several. Among the latter, then, we must look for the invention of resurrection.

But the Greeks often burned their bodies, and the Egyptians embalmed them, so that when the soul, which was a small, aërial figure, returned to its

---

The *auto-da-fé* lasted all day with two hours reserved for the reading of Malagrida's sentence. The author of the very sober article on Malagrida in the *New Catholic Encyclopedia* calls his execution "one of the saddest episodes of the Portuguese Inquisition." For reasons that are not clear Voltaire eventually accepted the view that Malagrida was implicated in the attempt on José's life, but he repeatedly spoke out against the horrible cruelty of the sentence. It may be of interest to note that Pombal did come to a bad end, though not nearly as bad as he deserved. José died in 1777 to be succeeded by his weak and neurotic daughter Maria I. The hatred of Pombal throughout the country was tremendous and she had to dismiss him from office. He first went to his palace at Oeiras and then to his home in the village of Pombal. Because of his age and because of Maria's constant attacks of guilt, he was never tried. Eventually, however, by a decree of August 16, 1781, he was found "culpable and deserving of exemplary punishment which I do not order to be executed in view of his present grave illnesses and decrepid age. . . . and also because the Marquis has begged for pardon and execrated the temerarious excesses he has committed." Pombal died on May 8, 1782. His family, evidently not chastened by events, arranged for a splendid funeral.

[14]Louis Patouillet (1699–1770) and Aime Paulian were two minor scoundrels who greatly irritated Voltaire while he was writing the *Questions* and who definitely do not belong on this list. They were among the group of writers, totally undistinguished themselves, who tried to cash in on the tremendous fame of the *Philosophical Dictionary*. Most of them were ex-Jesuits and they came out with long books refuting the *Philosophical Dictionary*. Voltaire made the mistake of reading these books and was greatly upset by their spiteful distortions. Patouillet and a particularly obnoxious and ignorant ex-Jesuit, with the melodious name of Claude François Nonnotte, had gotten under his skin to such an extent that as late as 1776, when he was composing an autobiographical fragment, their misdeeds and Damilaville's reply to them are prominently mentioned. An interesting scholarly work could be written about the libels provoked by Voltaire; starting with the Abbé Desfontaines' *Voltairomania* and culminating in the paranoid fantasies in the Abbé Barruel's *Memoires Illustrating the History of Jacobinism* of 1795 (*see* p. 241 below). There was probably no heretic or reformer who provoked so much spiteful abuse. Voltaire on his part never mastered the art of ignoring scurrilous criticism. His anger is understandable, but his replies in print were a serious mistake. They showed his tormenters that they had succeeded in one of their aims and fueled ever more vicious assaults. Both his wit and his common sense deserted him on such occasions. Only once, when dealing with an attack by his ablest and most malicious detractor, the critic Elie Frèron, did he find the right tone. "A snake bit Frèron," he said, and "the snake died of poisoning."

habitation, it might find it quite ready. This had been good if its organs had also been ready; but the embalmer began by taking out the brain and clearing the entrails. How were men to rise again without intestines, and without the medullary part by means of which they think? Where were they to find again the blood, the lymph, and other fluids?

You might conclude that it was still more difficult to rise again among the Greeks, where there was not left of you more than a pound of ashes at the utmost — mingled, too, with the ashes of wood, stuffs and spices.

Your objection is forceful, and I hold with you, that resurrection is a very extraordinary thing; but the son of Mercury did not the less die and rise again several times. The gods restored Pelops to life, although he had been served up as a ragout, and Ceres had eaten one of his shoulders. You know that Aesculapius brought Hippolytus to life again. This was a verified fact, of which even the most incredulous had no doubt; the name of *"Virbius,"* given to Hippolytus, was a convincing proof. Hercules had resuscitated Alceste and Pirithous. Heres did, it is true — according to Plato — come to life again for fifteen days only. Still it was a resurection; the time does not alter the fact.

Many grave schoolmen clearly see purgatory and resurrection in Virgil. As for purgatory, I am obliged to acknowledge that it is expressly in the sixth book. This may displease the Protestants, but I have no alternative:

> *Non tamen omne malum miseris, nec funditus omnes*
> *Corporea excedunt pestes, . . .*[15]

But we have already quoted this passage in the article on "Purgatory," which doctrine is here expressed clearly enough; nor could the people of that day obtain from the pagan priests an indulgence to abridge their sufferings for ready money. The ancients were much more severe and less corrupt than we are notwithstanding that they imputed so many foolish actions to their gods. What would you expect? Their theology was made up of contradictions, as the malignant say is the case with our own.

When their purgation was finished, these souls went and drank of the waters of Lethe, and instantly asked that they might enter fresh bodies and again see daylight. But is this a resurrection? Not at all; it is taking an entirely new body, not resuming the old one; it is a metempsychosis, without any relation to the manner in which we of the true faith are to rise again.

The souls of the ancients did, I must acknowledge, make a very bad bargain in coming back to this world, for seventy years at most, to undergo once more all that we know is undergone in a life of seventy years, and then suffer another thousand years' discipline. In my humble opinion there is no

---

[15]"Nevertheless, for wretched men not every evil nor all bodily plagues depart completely [when they die]" . . . (*Aeneid* 6, 736–737).

soul that would not tire of this everlasting vicissitude of so short a life and so long a penance.

Resurrection of the Moderns

Our resurrection is quite different. Every man will appear with precisely the same body which he had before; and all these bodies will be burned for all eternity, except, at most, one in a hundred thousand. This is much worse than a purgatory of ten centuries, in order to live here again a few years.

When will the great day of this general resurrection arrive? This is not positively known; and the learned are much divided. Nor do they any more know how each one is to find his own body again. Hereupon they start many difficulties.

1. Our body, they say, is, during life, undergoing a continual change; at fifty years of age we have nothing of the body in which our soul was lodged at twenty.

2. A soldier from Brittany goes into Canada; there, by a very common chance, he finds himself short of food, and is forced to eat an Iroquois whom he killed the day before. This Iroquois had fed on Jesuits for two or three months; a great part of his body had become Jesuit. Here, then, the body of a soldier is composed of Iroquois, of Jesuits, and of all that he had eaten before. How is each to take again precisely what belongs to him? And which part belongs to each?

3. A child dies in its mother's womb, just at the moment that it has received a soul. Will it rise again foetus, or boy, or man? If foetus, to what good? If boy or man, where will the necessary material come from?

4. To rise again — to be the same person as you were — you must have your memory perfectly fresh and present; it is memory that makes your identity. If your memory is lost, how will you be the same man?[16]

5. There are only a certain number of earthly particles that can constitute an animal. Sand, stone, minerals, metals, contribute nothing. It is only the soils favorable to vegetation that are favorable to the animal species. When, after the lapse of many ages, every one is to rise again, where shall be found the earth adapted to the formation of all these bodies?

6. Imagine an island, the vegetative part of which will support a thousand men, and five or six thousand animals for the nourishment and service of those thousand men; at the end of a hundred thousand generations we shall have to raise again a thousand millions of men. It is clear that matter will be wanting: *"Materies opus est, ut crescunt postera saecla."*[17]

---

[16]*See* "Identity," pp. 188–190 above.
[17]"There is need of matter, as future generations grow" (Lucretius).

7. And lastly, when it is proved, or thought to be proved, that a miracle as great as the universal deluge, or the ten plagues of Egypt, will be necessary to work the resurrection of all mankind in the valley of Jehoshaphat, it is asked: What becomes of the souls of all these bodies while awaiting the moment of returning into their cases?

Fifty rather knotty questions might easily be put; but the theologians would easily find answers to them all.

We Must Take Sides

This selection is a translation of two sections of *Il faut prendre un parti ou le principe d'action*, which first appeared in 1772. *We Must Take Sides* is a concise restatement, with some slight modifications, of Voltaire's philosophical views as they had been expounded in *The Philosophical Dictionary* and *The Ignorant Philosopher*.

OF EVIL AND, IN THE FIRST PLACE, THE DESTRUCTION OF BEASTS

We have never had any idea of good and evil, save in relation to ourselves. The sufferings of an animal seem to us evils, because, being animals ourselves, we feel that we should excite compassion if the same were done to us. We should have the same feeling for a tree if we were told that it suffered torment when it was cut; and for a stone if we learned that it suffers when it is dressed. But we should pity the tree and the stone much less than the animal, because they are less like us. Indeed, we soon cease to be touched by the awful destiny of the beasts that are intended for our table. Children who weep at the death of the first chicken they see killed laugh at the death of the second.

It is only too sure that the disgusting carnage of our butcheries and kitchens does not seem to us an evil. On the contrary, we regard this horror, pestilential as it often is, as a blessing of the Lord; and we still have prayers in which we thank him for these murders. Yet what can be more abominable than to feed constantly on corpses?

Not only do we spend our lives in killing, and devouring what we have killed, but all the animals slaughter each other; they are impelled to do so by an invincible instinct. From the smallest insects to the rhinoceros and the elephant, the earth is but a vast battle-field, a world of carnage and destruction. There is no animal that has not its prey, and that, to capture it, does not employ some means equivalent to the ruse and rage with which the detestable spider entraps and devours the innocent fly. A flock of sheep devours in an hour, as it crops the grass, more insects than there are men on the earth.

What is still more cruel is that in this horrible scene of reiterated murder we perceive an evident design to perpetuate all species by means of the bloody corpses of their mutual enemies. The victims do not expire until nature has carefully provided for new representatives of the species. Everything is born again to be murdered.

Yet I observe no moralist among us, nor any of our fluent preachers or hypocrites, who has ever reflected in the least on this frightful habit, which has become part of our nature. We have to go back to the pious Porphyry and the sympathetic Pythagoreans to find those who would shame us for our bloody gluttony; or we must travel to the land of the Brahmans. Our monks, the caprice of whose founders has bade them renounce flesh, are murderers of soles and turbots, if not of partridges and quails. Neither among the monks, nor in the Council of Trent, nor in the assemblies of the clergy, nor in our academies, has this universal butchery ever been pronounced an evil. There has been no more thought given to it in the councils of the clergy than in our public-houses.

Hence the great being is innocent of these butcheries in our eyes; or, indeed, we are his accomplices.

OF EVIL IN THE ANIMAL CALLED MAN

So much for the beasts; let us come to man. If it be not an evil that the only being on earth that knows God by his thoughts should be unhappy in his thoughts; if it be not an evil that this worshipper of the Deity should be almost always unjust and suffering, should know virtue and commit crime, should so often deceive and be deceived, and be the victim and the executioner of his fellows, etc.; if all that be not a frightful evil, I know not where evil is to be found.

Beasts and men suffer almost without ceasing; men suffer the more because, not only is the gift of thought often a source of torture, but this faculty of thinking always makes them fear death, which the beast cannot foresee. Man is a very miserable being, having but a few hours of rest, a few moments of satisfaction, and a long series of days of sorrow in his short life. Everybody admits and says this; and it is true.

They who have protested that all is well are charlatans. Shaftesbury, who set the fashion in this, was a most unhappy man. I have seen Bolingbroke torn with grief and rage; and Pope, whom he induced to put this miserable joke into verse, was one of the most pitiable men I have ever known, misshapen in body, unbalanced in temperament, always ill and a burden to himself, harassed by a hundred enemies until his last moment. At least let us have happy beings saying that all is well.

If by all is well it is merely meant that a man's head is happily placed above his shoulders, so that his eyes are better situated beside the root of his nose than behind his ears, we may assent. All is well in that sense. The laws of physics and mathematics are very well observed in his structure. A man who saw the beautiful Anne Boleyn, or the still more beautiful Mary Stuart, in her youth, would have said that it was well; would he have said it on seeing them die by the hand of the executioner? Would he have said it on seeing the grandson of the beautiful Mary Stuart perish in the same way in the heart of his capital? Would he have said it on seeing the great-grand-son even more miserable, because he lived longer?

Glance over the human race, if it be but from the proscriptions of Sylla to the Irish massacres.

Behold these battle-fields, strewn by imbeciles with the corpses of other imbeciles, whom they have slain with a substance born of the experiments of a monk. See these arms, these legs, these bloody brains, and all these scattered limbs; it is the fruit of a quarrel between two ignorant ministers, neither of whom would dare to open his mouth in the presence of Newton, Locke, or Halley; or of some ridiculous quarrel between two forward women. Enter the neighboring hospital, where are gathered those who are not yet dead. Their life is taken from them by fresh torments, and men make a fortune out of them, keeping a register of the victims who are dissected alive, at so much a day, under the pretext of healing them.

See these other men, dressed like comedians, earning a little money by singing, in a foreign language, a very obscure and insipid song, to thank the author of nature for this horrible outrage done to nature; and then tell me calmly that all is well . . . Say it to-day, the 24th of August, 1772; a day on which the pen trembles in my fingers, the two-hundredth anniversary of the massacre of St. Bartholomew.[1] Pass from these innumerable theatres of carnage to the equally unnumbered retreats of sorrow that cover the earth, to that swarm of diseases which slowly devour so many poor wretches while they yet live; think of that frightful ravage of nature which poisons the human race in its course, and associates the most abominable of plagues with the most necessary of pleasures. See that despised king Henry III, and that mediocre leader, the Duke of Mayenne,[2] struck down with the pox while they are waging civil war; and that insolent descendant of a Floren-tine merchant, Gondi, Retz, the priest, archbishop of Paris, preaching with sword in hand and body diseased.[3] To complete this true and horrible

---

[1]On the massacre of St. Bartholomew, *see* the note on p. 134.

[2]Duke Charles de Mayenne (1554–1611), a member of the notorious de Guise family. After two of his brothers had been murdered at the behest of Henry III, Mayenne assumed the leadership of the Catholic "League," which played a prominent role in the French Wars of Religion of the sixteenth century. He led one of the armies, which, following the assassina-tion of Henry III, attempted to prevent the Huguenot Henry IV from taking up his position as king of France. Although his forces were outnumbered, Henry defeated Mayenne in two major battles. With characteristic generosity he did not exact any kind of revenge.

[3]Paul de Gondi, later Cardinal de Retz (1613–1679), one of the leaders of the "Fronde," a political movement in which the aristocrats and the parlements joined forces against the absolutist regime of Cardinal Mazarin. After five years of changing fortunes (1648–1653), the Fronde was defeated and Retz had to flee the country, unable to return until 1661. There are few figures in French history whom Voltaire disliked more intensely and historians have generally shared his distaste. André Maurois referred to Retz as a "demagogic prelate" while Albert Guerard called him a "born agitator," a "genius for intrigue constantly brewing mischief," and "indefatigably plotting" for a variety of purposes. After he had retired from his life as intriguer and demagogue, Retz wrote his *Mémoires*, a work that is highly regarded both as literature and as source material for the history of the years 1648–1655. Voltaire's library contains the *Mémoires* in an edition in seven volumes published in Amsterdam in 1738.

picture, fancy yourself amid the floods and volcanoes that have so often devastated so many parts of the world; amid the leprosy and the plague that have swept it. And do you who read this recall all that you have suffered, admit that evil exists, and do not add to so many miseries and horrors the wild absurdity of denying them.

Letters

ON THE TREATMENT OF SORROW

Beuchot, who reproduced the original letter in Volume 51 (pp. 182–185) of his edition of Voltaire's works, gives 1728 as the date. If this is correct, the letter must have been written from England. The name of the respondent is unknown.

————

1728(?)

The squaring of the circle and perpetual motion are simple discoveries in comparison to the secret of bringing peace to a soul distraught by passionate grief. It is only magicians who pretend to calm storms with words. If an injured man, with a deep, gaping wound, begs his surgeon to close that wound so that only a slight scar shall remain, the surgeon replies: "That must be done by a greater physician than I am: only Time can mend what has been torn in a moment. I can amputate, cut out, destroy; Time alone can repair."

So is it with the wounds of the soul: the would-be comforter inflames and excites them: or, attempting to comfort, moves to fresh tears: but Time cures at last.

If one gets well into one's head that finally nature obliterates our deepest impressions: that after a certain time we have neither the same blood in our veins nor the same fibres in the brain, and, consequently, not the same ideas—that, in a word, we are really and physically no longer the same person; if, I say, we thus reflect, we shall find great help in the thought and shall hasten our recovery.

We must say to ourselves, "I have proved that the death of my relatives and my friends, after having half broken my heart for a while, has eventually left me perfectly calm: I have felt that, after a few years, a new soul was born in me: that the heart of twenty-five does not feel as the heart of twenty did, nor that of twenty as that of fifteen." Let us try, then, to put ourselves now as much as possible in the situation in which we shall certainly be one day: let us get the start of time in thought.

This, of course, supposes freedom of action on our part. He who asks advice must consider himself free, for it would be absurd to ask advice if it were impossible to take it. In business we always act on the assumption that we are free: let us so act in our passions, which are our most important business. Nature never intended that our wounds should be closed in a moment—that we should pass in a second from sickness to health: but wise remedies will certainly accelerate our cure.

I know no more powerful remedy for the sorrows of the heart than deep and serious application of the mind to other objects.

This application changes the gloomy tenor of the spirits—sometimes even makes us insensible to bodily ills. Any one who devotes himself to music or to reading a good book, which appeals at once to the mind and to the imagination, finds speedy relief from the sufferings of an illness: he also finds that, little by little, the pangs of the heart lose their sharpness.

He is obliged to think of something quite other than that which he is trying to forget: and one has to think often—nay, constantly—of what one wishes to retain. The strongest chains are, in the long run, those of custom. It depends, I believe, on ourselves to break the links which bind us to our sorrows and to strengthen those which attach us to happier things.

Not, indeed, that we are absolute masters of our thoughts: that implies much: but neither are we absolute slaves: and, once again, I believe that the Supreme Being has given us a little of His *liberty*, as He has given us a little of His *power of thought*.

Let us make use, then, of such weapons as we have. We undoubtedly add, by reading and thinking, to our *power of thought*: why should we, then, not also add to what is called our *liberty*? There is no one of our senses or our powers which has not been helped by effort. Why should liberty be the only one of man's attributes which he cannot increase?

Suppose, for instance, we see round us trees hung with a delicious but poisoned fruit, which a raging hunger incites us to pick: if we feel ourselves too weak to abstain, let us go (and going depends on ourselves) to places where there are no such fruits.

These are counsels which, like so many others, are no doubt easier to give than to follow: but we are in the presence of a disease wherein the patient must minister to himself.

ON GOD, THE SOUL AND UNIVERSAL MORALITY— TO FREDERICK THE GREAT

Early in their correspondence Voltaire mentioned the *Traité de métaphysique* to Frederick and offered to send him a copy. Mme. du Châtelet, who regarded the work as dangerous, vigorously protested against such an indiscretion. In response to Frederick's repeated requests to see the *Traité*, Voltaire eventually sent him an "extract," which, as we now know, was the chapter on free will of the third version of the *Traité*. It is the only part of this version that has survived (see the editorial note on p. 65 above).

You bid me, sir, give you an account of my metaphysical doubts. I therefore take the liberty of sending you an extract from a paper *On Liberty* . . .

Perhaps humanity, the principle of all my thoughts, overpowered me in this work. Perhaps the idea I am always pursuing, that there is neither vice nor virtue: that neither punishment nor reward is necessary: that society would be (especially among philosophers) an interchange of wickedness and hypocrisy if man had not full and absolute liberty — perhaps, I say, this opinion has led me too far in this work. But if you find errors in my judgment, forgive them for the sake of the principle which gave them birth.

I always reduce, so far as I can, my metaphysics to morality. I have honestly sought, with all the attention of which I am capable, to gain some definite idea of the human soul, and I own that the result of all my researches is ignorance. I find a principle — thinking, free, active — almost like God himself: my reason tells me that God exists: but it also tells me that I cannot know what he is. Is it indeed likely that we should know what our soul is when we can form no idea of light if we have had the misfortune to be born blind? I see then, with regret, that all that has been written about the soul teaches us nothing at all.

After my vain groping to discover its nature, my chief aim has been to try at least to regulate it: it is the mainspring of our clock. All Descartes' fine ideas on its elasticity tell me nothing of the nature of the spring: I am ignorant even of the cause of that flexibility: however, I wind up my timepiece, and it goes passably well.

I examine man. We must see if, of whatsoever materials he is composed, there is vice and virtue in them. That is the important point with regard to him — I do not say merely with regard to a certain society living under certain laws: but for the whole human race; for you, sir, who will one day sit on a throne, for the wood-cutter in your forest, for the Chinese doctor, and for the savage of America. Locke, the wisest metaphysician I know, while he very rightly attacks the theory of innate ideas, seems to think that there is no universal moral principle. I venture to doubt, or rather, to elucidate the great man's theory on this point. I agree with him that there is really no such thing as innate thought: whence it obviously follows that there is no principle of morality innate in our souls: but because we are not born with beards, is it just to say that we are not born (we, the inhabitants of this continent) to have beards at a certain age? We are not born able to walk: but everyone, born with two feet, will walk one day. Thus, no one is born with the idea he must be just: but God has so made us that, at a certain age, we all agree to this truth.

It seems clear to me that God designed us to live in society — just as he has given the bees the instincts and the powers to make honey: and as our social system could not subsist without the sense of justice and injustice, he has given us the power to acquire that sense. It is true that varying customs make us attach the idea of justice to different things. What is a crime in Europe will be a virtue in Asia, just as German dishes do not please French palates: but God has so made Germans and French that they both like good living. All societies, then, will not have the same laws, but no society will be without laws. Therefore, the good of the greatest number is the immutable law of virtue, as established by all men from Peiping to Ireland: what is useful to society will be good for every country. This idea reconciles the contradictions which appear in morality. Robbery was permitted in Lacedaemonia: why? because all goods were held in common, and the man who stole from the greedy who kept for himself what the law gave to the public, was a social benefactor.

It is said that there are savages who eat men, and believe they do well. I say those savages have the same idea of right and wrong as ourselves. As we do, they make war from anger and passion: the same crimes are committed everywhere: to eat your enemies is but an extra ceremonial. The wrong does not consist in roasting, but in killing them: and I dare swear there is no cannibal who believes that he is doing right when he cuts his enemy's throat. I saw four savages from Louisiana who were brought to France in 1723. There was a woman among them of a very gentle disposition. I asked her, through an interpreter, if she had ever eaten the flesh of her enemies and if she liked it; she answered, Yes. I asked her if she would be willing to kill, or to have killed, any one of her fellow-countrymen in order to eat him: she answered, shuddering, visibly horrified by such a crime. I defy the most determined liar among travelers to dare to tell me that there is a community or a family where to break one's word is laudable. I am deeply rooted in the belief that, God having made certain animals to graze in common, others to meet occasionally two and two, rarely, and spiders to spin webs, each species has the tools necessary for the work it has to do. Man has received all he needs to live in society, just as he has received a stomach in order to digest, eyes in order to see, a soul in order to judge.

Put two men on the globe, and they will only call good, right, just, what will be good for them both. Put four, and they will only consider virtuous what suits them all: and if one of the four eats his neighbor's supper, or fights or kills him, he will certainly raise the others against him. And what is true of these four men is true of the universe. Here, my lord, you have the foundation on which I have written this moral *Metaphysics;* but as far as virtue is concerned, have I the right to speak of it before you?

ON THE BLIND—TO DENIS DIDEROT

The "profound and brilliant work" that Diderot had sent to Voltaire was his *Letter on the Blind for the Use of Those Who See* (1749). It is an extremely interesting short treatise devoted primarily to questions in the theory of vision. Diderot had himself carried out extensive observations on the behavior of blind people and he was also familiar with the work of the British surgeon William Cheselden and oculists in France and Prussia who had successfully operated on cataracts and thereby enabled formerly blind people to see. At one place in the *Letter*, the blind mathematician Saunderson defends atheism in a dying speech directed to a clergyman by the name of Gervaise Holmes who had been summoned to his side. Saunderson attacks the design argument and also exclaims that his own blindness is incompatible with the existence of a good God. "Look at me, Mr. Holmes," Saunderson exclaims. "I have no eyes. What have we done, you and I, to God, that one of us has this organ while the other one has not?" There was in fact a blind mathematician by the name of Nicholas Saunderson (1682–1739) who was professor of mathematics at Cambridge from 1711 until his death. There is no evidence, however, that the actual Saunderson was an atheist and the speech that Diderot puts into Saunderson's mouth is purely fictitious. It is a statement of Diderot's own view. The book Voltaire promised to send to Diderot was *The Elements of the Newtonian Philosophy.*

JUNE 1749

I thank you, sir, for the profound and brilliant work you have been so good as to send me. The book I send you is neither the one nor the other, but in it you will find the story of the man born blind set forth in greater detail than in the earlier editions. I am entirely of your opinion as to what you say respecting the judgment formed in such a case by ordinary men of average good sense, and that formed by philosophers. I am sorry that in the examples you quote you forgot the case of the man born blind who saw men as trees when he was given sight.

I have read your book with great pleasure. It says much, and explains more. I have long honored you as much as I despise the stupid barbarians who condemn what they do not understand, and the wicked who unite themselves with the fools to denounce those who are trying to enlighten them.

But I confess I am not at all of the opinion of Saunderson, who denies God because he was born blind. I am, perhaps, mistaken, but, in his place, I should recognize a great intelligence who had given me so many substitutes for sight, and perceiving, on reflection, the endless relations between all things, I should have suspected an infinitely able workman. If it is very presumptuous to pretend to know what he is, and why he has made everything that exists, so it seems to me also presumptuous to deny that he exists. I am exceedingly eager to meet and talk with you, whether you think yourself one of His works, or a suitably organized part of eternal and permanent matter. Whatever you are, you are a worthy part of that great whole which I do not understand. Before I leave for Luneville I very much wish that you would do me the honor to join a philosophers' feast at my table with a few other wise men. I am not one myself, but I have a great passion for those who are wise after your fashion. Rest assured, sir, that I appreciate your merits, and that to render them fuller justice I long to see you and assure you how greatly I have the honor to be, etc.

ON THE ADVANTAGES OF CIVILIZATION AND LITERATURE —TO JEAN-JACQUES ROUSSEAU

LES DELICES, AUGUST 30, 1755

I have received your new book[1] against the human race, and I thank you for it. You will please those to whom you reveal the truth, but you will not improve them. You paint in most faithful colors the horrors of human society, from which our ignorance and weakness lead us to expect so much consolation. Nobody has ever used so much intelligence in trying to make us stupid.

After reading your work one is tempted to walk on all fours. However, as it is now some sixty years since I gave up that practice, it is unfortunately impossible for me to resume it: I will leave this natural posture to those more fit for it than you or I. I cannot embark to go and live with the savages of Canada, in the first place because the illnesses with which I am afflicted require the attention of a European physician and secondly because war has been carried to that country, and the example given by our nations has made the savages almost as wicked as we are. I am content to be a peaceful savage in the solitude I have chosen near your native land where you yourself ought to be.

I agree with you that science and literature have sometimes done a great deal of harm.

Tasso's enemies made his life a series of misfortunes; Galileo's enemies kept him languishing in prison at the age of seventy for understanding the revolution of the earth; and, what is still more shameful, forced him to retract.

As soon as your friends had begun the *Encyclopedic Dictionary*, those who dared to be their rivals attacked them as deists, atheists, and even Jansenists. If I venture to include myself among those whose works have brought them persecution as their only reward, I could show you a collection of wretches determined to ruin me. From the day I produced my tragedy *Oedipe* a library of absurd calumnies has been written against me: an

---

[1] *Discours sur l'origine de l'inégalité.*

ex-Jesuit priest[2] whom I saved from the extreme penalty rewarded me by defamatory libels; a still more culpable man[3] printed my work on the *Century of Louis XIV* with notes in which the crassest ignorance retails the most impudent lies; yet another sells to a publisher in my name a universal history supposed to be by me and the publisher is so avaricious and foolish as to print this shapeless tissue of blunders, wrong dates as well as mutilated facts and names;[4] and there are men sufficiently base and wicked to attribute this concoction to me. I could show you a society poisoned by this new kind of men, unknown to the whole of antiquity, who, unable to find an honest occupation like that of a lackey or manual laborer and unfortunately able to read and write, become brokers of literature, steal, disfigure and sell our manuscripts. I could complain that a gay trifle, written more than thirty years ago on the same subject that Chapelain[5] was foolish enough to treat seriously, is now in general circulation because of the breach of faith and infamous greed of wretches who have disfigured it with as much foolishness as malice, and who after thirty years sell everywhere this work which is certainly no longer mine and which is really by now theirs. I could add that most recently they have searched the most respectable archives in order to steal a part of the notes I deposited there when I was historiographer of France and sold the fruits of my labor to a bookseller in Paris. I could show you ingratitude, imposture and outright plunder pursuing me to the foot of the Alps and even to the brink of my grave.

But, sir, acknowledge that these thorns attached to literature and to fame are flowers compared with the other evils that have always inundated the earth. Admit that neither Cicero nor Lucretius nor Virgil nor Horace were

---

[2] The "ex-Jesuit" was Pierre François Guyot d'Esfontaines (1684–1745) who was jailed for sodomy, then a capital offense, when Voltaire secured his release (1724). D'Esfontaines profusely thanked Voltaire for his generosity, but rewarded it with vituperative attacks culminating in *Voltairomanie* (1738), one of the most vicious attacks on Voltaire ever published.

[3] The "even more culpable man" was Laurent Anglivial La Beaumelle who brought out a pirated edition of *The Century of Louis XIV*, which was sold in competition with Voltaire's own authorized version. He inserted false and offensive material prompting Voltaire to write his *Supplement du siècle de Louis XIV.* La Beaumelle was an outright scoundrel and blackmailer who continued to pursue Voltaire with abusive and threatening letters. In 1767 the French government came to Voltaire's assistance and ordered La Beaumelle to stop his harassments.

[4] The pirated work was Voltaire's *Essai sur les moeurs* and the publisher's name Jean Néaulme.

[5] The "gay trifle" was *La Pucelle* ("The Maid"), Voltaire's ribald poem satirizing Joan of Arc. Mme. du Châtelet thought it so dangerous that she kept the manuscript under lock and key. By 1755 numerous pirated editions were in circulation and in 1762 Voltaire finally published an authorized version. Voltaire did not really regard *La Pucelle* as a "trifle" but as one of his best and funniest productions. Jean Chapelain (1595–1674) was an extremely conservative poet and critic whose long-winded epic on Joan was also called *La Pucelle* (1656). Chapelain was a founding member of the Académie Française and is chiefly remembered for writing an attack on Corneille's *Le Cid* on behalf of the Academy.

the authors of the proscriptions[6] of Marius, of Sylla, of the debauched Anthony, of the imbecile Lepidus, of Gaius Octavius, the cowardly tyrant, scandalously named Augustus.

Admit that the jests of Marot[7] did not produce the massacre of St. Bartholomew[8] and that the tragedy of the *Cid* did not cause the wars of the Fronde. Great crimes are always committed by celebrated ignoramuses. What makes, and what will always make, the world a vale of tears is the insatiable greed and the indominatable pride of men from Thomas Couli Can[9] who could not read to a customs officer who can only count. Literature nourishes, refines and comforts the soul; and it is your glory even when you denounce it. You are like Achilles who declaims against glory and like Father Malebranche whose brilliant imagination wrote against the imagination.

M. Chapuis tells me that your health is very poor. You should come here to restore it in your native air, enjoy its liberty, drink with me the milk of its cows, and browse on our grass. I am very philosophically, and with the fondest esteem, sir,

Your very humble and very obedient servant.

Rousseau seems to have been delighted that the great Voltaire whom he admired or professed to admire so much had taken the trouble to write to him about his book. He answered on September 7, 1755, in a most affable letter that was full of flowery compliments. In view of some of Rousseau's remarks in the *Confessions* (see p. 218) it is worth mentioning that he repeatedly stressed the great good fortune of the citizens of Geneva of having Voltaire in their midst. "Sensible of the

---

[6] In Ancient Rome a person who had been condemned to death and whose property was forfeited to the state was said to have been "proscribed". This word was used because his name was "posted" or published in a certain place. Gaius Marius (c. 157–86 B.C.) and Lucius Cornelius Sulla or Sylla (138–78 B.C.), two exceptionally bloodthirsty Roman generals and consuls, were notorious for the many proscriptions they issued.

[7] Clément Marot (1496?–1544), French court poet, author of celebrated epigrams and elegies. He enjoyed the patronage of Francis I and Margaret of Navarre, but his support of the Reformation led to his imprisonment and exile. His allegory *Enfer* (Hell) was written while imprisoned at Chartres.

[8] *See* above p. 134.

[9] Thomas (also Thamas) Couli Can or Tahmasp Kouli Khan, better known as Nadir Shah of Persia (1688–1747), was an extremely successful Persian general who overthrew Abbas, the last ruler of the Safavid dynasty, and made himself shah. His many victories greatly expanded the Persian Empire. In Chapter CLXII of the *Essay on Customs*, Voltaire devotes several pages to Kouli Khan's exploits and to the combination of cleverness and extreme ruthlessness that enabled him to become the absolute ruler of his country. When in 1736 Kouli Khan "caused himself to be declared king of Persia," Voltaire writes, "he did not forget the old custom of putting out the eyes of those who had any title to the throne, which piece of cruelty he practiced upon his own sovereign, Shah Thames (Abbas)." The last years of Kouli Khan's reign were characterized by tyranny, greed, and paranoid suspicions resulting among other things in the blinding of his own son. He was assassinated by his nephew.

honor which you do my country," he wrote, "I share the gratitude of my fellow-citizens; and I hope that it will be only augmented when they shall have profited by the instructions you can give them." You, he addressed Voltaire, "who know so well how to paint virtue and liberty, teach us to cherish them within our walls, as we do in your writings!"

It will not have escaped the reader that Voltaire did not allow himself to get involved in any detailed discussion of the theses of Rousseau's *Discourse*. Some of the opening banter of his letter make it clear that he was not particularly sympathetic, but we now know that he detested Rousseau's book. Maurice Cranston has called attention to the fact that the marginal notes on Voltaire's copy of the *Discourse* betrays an extreme antipathy. Of a total of forty-one marginal notes, forty are hostile.

ON THE LISBON EARTHQUAKE—TO JEAN ROBERT TRONCHIN

The Lisbon earthquake occurred on November 1, 1755. This letter is the first written comment by Voltaire, preceding both the *Poem on the Lisbon Earthquake* and *Candide*.

LES DÉLICES, 24 NOVEMBER 1755

This, sir, is indeed a cruel science. It would be very difficult to discover how the laws of motion bring about such frightful disasters in the *best of possible worlds*. A hundred thousand ants, our neighbors, crushed in one blow in our ant-heap, half of them perishing no doubt in horrendous agonies beneath debris from which it was impossible to extricate them; families ruined in all parts of Europe; the fortune of a hundred merchants of your country [Switzerland] swallowed up in the ruins of Lisbon. What a miserable game of chance human life is! What will the preachers say, especially if the palace of the Inquisition has been left intact? I flatter myself that the reverend fathers, the inquisitors, will have been crushed just like other people. That ought to teach men not to persecute men, for while some holy scoundrels burn some fanatics, the earth swallows up both.

. . . I believe that our mountains protect us from earthquakes. Goodbye, my dear correspondent, keep me informed about the sequels of this frightful adventure.

LETTRE

DE

J. J. ROUSSEAU

A

MONSIEUR

DE VOLTAIRE.

LE 18. AOUT 1756.

1759.

r. Lettre de Rousseau à Voltaire du 18 août 1756:
titre de la première édition connue.

Appendix: Rousseau's Letter to Voltaire on Providence

Few letters written in the eighteenth century have become as famous as the one reprinted here. Rousseau believed that Voltaire wrote *Candide* as answer to the letter. This has been questioned, but the letter was certainly one of the precipitating causes of *Candide* and it is of great interest in its own right. Like Voltaire, Rousseau rejected Christianity. His deism was, however, combined with a metaphysical optimism quite similar to that of Leibniz and Pope. Unlike Voltaire, he was also an ardent believer in life after death and, perhaps most important of all, he was altogether opposed to the rationalism of Voltaire and the Encyclopedists.

Voltaire had asked his friend Thieriot in June 1756 to send copies of the "Poem on the Lisbon Earthquake" to D'Alembert, Diderot, and Rousseau, evidently hoping for sympathetic responses. He had always regarded Rousseau as an eccentric and there is no suggestion that he was particularly irritated by Rousseau's letter. He courteously acknowledged it, calling the letter *tres belle*. However, he refused to be drawn into a discussion of the arguments. He explained that one of his nieces who was staying with him was seriously ill and needed constant attention. Addressing him as *mon cher philosophe*, he assured Rousseau of his esteem and repeated the invitation for a visit with which he had concluded his letter of August 30, 1755 (see 216 above). Rousseau was pleasantly surprised by Voltaire's friendliness. In a letter to a friend he spoke of Voltaire's generosity in glowing terms. "A man," he wrote, "who is able to take my letter as he did deserves to be called a philosopher," and Rousseau was now willing to "join esteem and friendship for Voltaire's person" to the admiration he had always felt for Voltaire's works.

Rousseau had clearly intended to publish his letter, but said he would not do so without Voltaire's permission, which was not forthcoming. In 1759, however, it was published in Germany without Rousseau's knowledge. Rousseau discovered this fact on June 13, 1760, in a letter from his friend, the Abbé Trublet. The letter had been published in a journal edited by Jean Henri Formey, the secretary of the Royal Society in Berlin who had found it in pamphlet form in a bookshop. Fearing Voltaire's anger, Rousseau lost no time in writing to him on June 17. He apologized at some length for the publication of the letter and assured Voltaire that he had nothing to do with it. He suggested that it might be best to publish an authorized version that could also contain a reply by Voltaire. This entirely rational portion of the letter was followed by a remarkable outburst, which R. A. Leigh, a highly sympathetic commentator, has described as a "regular declaration of war." "I do not like you sir," Rousseau wrote,

> You have done me injuries which could not be anything but
> extremely painful to me — to me, your disciple and
> admirer . . . You have ruined the city of Geneva. In gratitude for
> the praise I have lavished on you when among them, you have
> alienated my fellow-citizens from me. It is you who will cause me
> to die on foreign soil, and so little honored as to be thrown into
> the gutter . . . I hate you . . . "

There can be no doubt that Voltaire was shaken by this totally unprovoked outburst. He did not reply to Rousseau, but in letters to D'Alembert and Thieriot, both written on June 23, 1760, he complained that Rousseau had gone completely mad. It should be explained that Rousseau's charges were without any foundation. Voltaire did become Rousseau's implacable enemy and later he acted in ways that were far from admirable, but he had not ruined Geneva and he had not in any way alienated the Genevese from Rousseau. Rousseau reprinted the whole of his letter of June 13, 1760 in his *Confessions* and he there explained that several years earlier when he heard that Voltaire had settled in Geneva he had given up the city "as lost." He had also realized that it was senseless to return to Geneva. He knew himself to be timid and a bad speaker and he could not possibly compete with Voltaire, who was not only "arrogant and wealthy" but also "magnificently eloquent" and the idol of both the women and the young people. Competing with such a man would "uselessly expose himself to danger." This seems pure paranoia. What Rousseau never explained is why there would have been any need to compete with Voltaire or for what the two would have competed. He also conveniently forgot to mention that in 1755 he had described Voltaire's presence in Geneva as a great blessing (see pp. 215–216 above) or his enthusiastic remarks about Voltaire's character after receiving the friendly answer to his letter on the Lisbon earthquake.

AUGUST 18, 1756

Your last two poems, sir, reached me in my retreat, and although all my friends know how much I love your writings, I do not know from whom they could have been sent, if not from you.[1] I found in them pleasure with instruction and recognized the hand of the master; thus, I believe I must thank you for both the copies and the work itself. I will not tell you that everything seems to me equally good, but the things I do not like inspire in me all the more confidence for those that enrapture me; it is not without difficulty that I sometimes defend my reason against the charms of your poetry, but it is to render my admiration more worthy of your works that I endeavor not to admire everything.

I will do more; I will tell you straightforwardly not about the beauties that I perceived in these two Poems, a task that would frighten my laziness, nor even about the defects that perhaps more talented people than I will notice, but about the displeasures which trouble in this instance the taste that I acquired from your lessons, and I will tell you about them still moved by a first reading, when my heart listened avidly to yours, loving you as my brother, honoring you as my master, finally, flattering myself that you will recognize in my intentions the frankness of an upright soul and in my discourse the tone of a friend of truth who speaks to a philosopher. Besides, the more your second Poem enchants me, the more freely I take issue with the first, for if you are not afraid to oppose yourself, why should I fear to be of your opinion? I must believe that you do not really believe in the views you refute so well.

All of my grievances are against your *Poem on the Disaster of Lisbon* because I expected it to have impressions worthier of the humanity that seems to have been your inspiration. You reproach Pope and Leibniz for jeering at our troubles by maintaining that all is good, and you greatly exaggerate the picture of our miseries. Instead of the consolations that I hoped for, you do nothing but distress me. It would appear that you are afraid that I do not sufficiently realize how unhappy I am, and you think, it seems to me, that you could calm me by demonstrating to me that everything is evil.

Do not be mistaken, sir; the result is the contrary of what you propose. This optimism that you find so cruel consoles me in the same sorrows that you portray as intolerable. The poem of Pope eases my troubles and gives me patience; yours intensifies my troubles, incites me to muttering, and, depriving me of everything except a weakened hope, reduces me to despair. In this strange opposition between what you prove and what I experience, diminish my perplexity and tell me which is wrong: sentiment or reason.

[1] The volume which Voltaire had sent to Rousseau, with his friend Thieriot acting as intermediary, included the *Poèm sur la Loi naturelle* as well as the *Poème sur le désastre de Lisbonne*.

"Man, be patient," say Pope and Leibniz, "your troubles are actually a necessary effect of your nature and of the constitution of this universe. The eternal and beneficent Being who rules would have wanted to safeguard you from them: of all the possible economies, he chose that which united the least evil and the greatest good, or to say the same thing even more bluntly, if he did not do better, it is because he could not do better.

Now, what does your poem tell me? "Suffer forever, unhappy one. If there is a God who created you, undoubtedly he is all-powerful, he could prevent all your ills; never hope, therefore, that they will end; for one would not know why you exist, if it is not to suffer and die." I do not know what such a doctrine can have that is more consoling than Optimism and fatality itself: for me, I admit that it would seem even more cruel than Manicheism. If the difficulty of the origin of evil forced you to alter any one of the perfections of God, why do you want to justify his power at the expense of his goodness? If it is necessary to choose between two errors, I prefer the first.

You, sir, do not want your work to be regarded as a poem against providence, and I will take care not to give it this name, although you characterized as a book against mankind a work where I pleaded the cause of mankind against itself.[2] I know the distinction that has to be made between the intention of an author and the consequences that can be derived from his doctrine. The just defense of myself obliges me only to point out to you that in portraying human miseries, my purpose was excusable and even laudable, as far as I am concerned; for I showed men how they made their own misfortunes and, consequently, how they could avoid them.

I do not see how one can look for the source of moral evil elsewhere than in free, perfected, later corrupted man; as for physical evils, if sensitive and impassive matter is a contradiction, as it seems to me, they are inevitable in every system of which man is a part, and, thus, the question is not at all why man is not perfectly happy, but why he exists.[3] Moreover, I believe I have shown that with the exception of death, which is almost not an evil, other than through the preparations that precede it, most of our physical ills are still our work. Without leaving your subject of Lisbon, admit, for example, that nature had in no way assembled there twenty thousand houses of six to seven stories and that if the inhabitants of this large city had been dispersed more equally and lodged less densely, the damage would have been considerably less and perhaps nil. All of them would have fled at the first shock and they would have been seen the next day at twenty leagues from there,

---

[2]Rousseau here refers to Voltaire's letter of August 30, 1755, about the *Discours sur l'orgine de l'inégalité.* This letter is reprinted above, pp. 212–214.

[3]This seems to be an obscure formulation of the view that physical evils are due to the fact that matter is inherently inert.

as happy go lucky as if nothing had happened. But they remain and they insist on staying around the Mazures, to expose themselves to new tremors because what they abandon is worth more than what they can carry away. How many unfortunate ones perished in this disaster because one wanted his clothing, another his papers, another his money? Does one not know that the body of each man became the least part of himself, and that it almost is not worth the trouble of saving it when one has lost all the rest?

Would you have wanted the earthquake to have taken place in the depths of a desert rather than in Lisbon? Can one doubt that it also occurs in deserts? But we do not speak about them at all because they do no harm to the gentlemen of the cities, the only men we take into account. They do little harm even to animals and savages who live scattered in these remote places and who fear neither the caving in of roofs nor the burning of houses. But what would such a privilege signify? Should it be said, therefore, that the order of the world must change according to our caprices, that nature must be subject to our laws, and to prevent an earthquake anywhere we have only to build a city there?

There are events that strike us often more or less according to the aspects by which they are considered, and which lose much of the horror they inspire at first sight, when they are examined closely. I learned in *Zadig,* and nature confirms for me from day to day, that an accelerated death is not always a real evil and that it can sometimes pass for a relative good. Of so many men crushed under the ruins of Lisbon, several undoubtedly avoided even greater misfortunes, and although such a description may be moving and provide a subject for poetry, it is not certain that a single one of these unfortunate ones suffered more than if in the ordinary course of events he would have awaited, in great anguish, the death that surprised him. Is there an end more sad than that of a dying man whom one overwhelms with useless caring, whom a notary and prospective heirs do not allow to breathe, whom doctors assassinate in his bed at their ease, and whom barbarous priests torture by emphasising his impending death? As for me, I see everywhere that the ills to which nature subjects us are less cruel than those which we add.

But no matter how ingenious we may be in using beautiful institutions to foment our miseries, to date, we have not been able to perfect ourselves to the point of making life a burden and to prefer nothingness to our existence, without which discouragement and despair would soon take hold of the greatest number, and mankind could not exist for long. However, if it is better for us to be than not to be, that would suffice to justify our existence even though we would expect no compensation for the ills that we have to endure, and even though these ills would be as great as you depict them. But it is difficult to find, regarding this point, good faith on the part of men and good calculation on the part of philosophers, because the latter, in the comparison of good and ill always forget the sweet sentiment of existence, independent of any other sensation, and that the vanity of despising death engages others to calumniate life, almost like women who with a stained dress and scissors claim to prefer holes to stains.

Like Erasmus, you think that few people would want to be reborn to the same conditions in which they lived; but such a one holds his merchandise very high who would lower its price a great deal if he had some hope of concluding the sale. Besides, whom must I believe you to have consulted about that? The rich, perhaps; sated with false pleasures, but not knowing the true ones, always bored with life and always fearful of losing it. Perhaps men-of-letters, of all the orders of men, the most sedentary, the most unhealthy, the most reflective, and, consequently, the most unhappy? Do you want to find men of better composition, or at least generally more sincere, and who forming the greatest number must, at least for that reason, be given preference? Consult an honest bourgeois who will have spent an obscure and tranquil life, without projects and without ambition; a good artisan who lives comfortably from his profession; even a peasant, not from France, which claims that it is necessary to make them die of misery in order to be able to live, but, for example, from your country and, generally, from any free country. I dare state as a fact that there is not perhaps in the Upper Valais a single highlander unhappy with his almost monotonous life and who would not accept willingly, instead of the paradise he awaits and which is due him, the deal of being reborn unceasingly to vegetate in this way. These differences make me believe that it is often the abuse that we make of life that makes it a burden for us and that I have a much less good opinion of those who are angry to have lived than of one who can say with Cato: "Nec me vixisse poenitet, quoniam ita vixi, ut frustra me natum non existimem."[4] That does not prevent the sage from being able sometimes to move willingly, without complaint and without despair, when nature or fortune brings him very distinctly the order to depart. But according to the ordinary course of events, with whatever ills human life is sown, it is not on the whole a bad present, and if it is not always an evil to die, it is very rarely one to live.

Our different ways of thinking are the reason why I find several of your proofs not very convincing, for I am not unaware of the extent to which human reason adopts the form of our opinions rather than that of truth and that of two men who have opposite views one may think he has demonstrated what the other sees only as a sophism.

When you attack, for example, the chain of being, so well described by Pope, you say that it is not true that if one removed an atom from the world the world could not exist. You cite in that respect M. de Crousaz,[5] then you

---

[4] "And I am not sorry to have lived, since I have lived in such a way that I do not think that I was born in vain."

[5] In one of the notes to the poem on the Lisbon earthquake, Voltaire had quoted with approval a critical remark to this effect by the "scholarly geometrician" Jeanpierre de Crousaz' *"Commentaire sur la traduction en vers, de mr. l'abbé du Resnel, de l'Essay de m. Pope sur l'homme"* (Geneva, 1738). In 1737 Crousaz (1663–1748) had published in Lausanne *Examen de l'essai de m. Pope sur l'homme* which also attacked Pope's *Essay*.

add that nature is not submitted to any precise measure nor to any precise form, that no planet moves in an absolutely regular curve, that no known being is a precisely mathematical figure, that no precise quantity is required for any operation, that nature never acts rigorously, that thus one has no reason to be sure that one less atom on earth would be the cause of the destruction of the earth. I admit, sir, that regarding that, I am more struck by the force of the assertion than by that of the reasoning and that on this occasion I would yield with more confidence to your authority than to your proofs.

With respect to M. de Crousaz, I have not read any of his work against Pope and I am perhaps not in a position to understand him, but what is very certain is that I will not concede to him what I am disputing with you and that I have as little faith in his proofs as in his authority. Far from thinking that nature is not at all subjected to the precision of quantities and figures, I believe totally to the contrary that it alone follows this precision rigorously because it alone knows how to compare exactly the ends and means and to measure the force of resistance. As for these presumed irregularities, can one doubt that they all have their physical cause and can we deny that it exists just because we do not perceive it? These apparent irregularities come undoubtedly from some laws which we do not know and which nature follows just as faithfully as those which are known to us, from some agent which we do not perceive and whose obstacle or concourse has fixed measures in all its operations. Otherwise, it would be necessary to say flatly that there are actions without principles and effects without cause, which is repugnant to every philosophy.

Let us assume that there are two weights in equilibrium and yet unequal; that to the smallest is added the quantity by which they differ; either the two weights will still remain balanced and one will have a cause without effect or the balance will be broken and one will have an effect without cause; but if the weights were of iron and there were a speck of magnetic material hidden under one of the two, the precision of nature would then remove from it the appearance of precision, and by dint of exactness, it would seem to lack any. There is not a figure, an operation, a law in the physical world to which one cannot apply some similar example to the one I have just proposed with respect to weight.

You say that no human being is a precisely mathematical figure; I ask you, sir, if there is any figure that is not really regular, and if the most bizarre curve is not as regular in the eyes of nature as a perfect circle is to ours. I imagine, moreover, that if some body could have this apparent regularity, it would be only the universe itself, supposing it full and limited. For these mathematical figures, being only abstractions, have a relationship only to themselves, whereas all those of natural bodies are relative to other bodies and to movements which modify them; thus, that would still prove nothing against the precision of nature, even if we were in agreement about what you mean by this word "precision."

You distinguish events which have effects from those which have none; I doubt whether this distinction is solid. Every event seems to me to have necessarily some effect, either moral or physical or composed of both, but one which is not always perceptible, because the concatenation of events is still more difficult to follow than that of men. Since, in general, one need not look for effects more considerable than the events which produce them, the smallness of the causes often renders the examination ridiculous, although the effects are certain, and often also several almost imperceptible effects are united to produce a considerable event. Add that such an effect does not fail to occur although it acts outside of the body that produced it. Thus, the dust that a carriage raises cannot do anything to the pace of the carriage and affect the course of the world. But since there is nothing extraneous to the universe, everything that is made in it necessarily acts upon the universe itself.

Therefore, sir, your examples appear to me more ingenious than convincing. I see a thousand plausible reasons why it was not indifferent to Europe that on a certain day the heiress of Burgundy was well or badly coiffed, nor to the destiny of Rome that Caesar turned his eyes to right or left and spat from one or the other side, while going to the senate on the day that he was punished. In a word, recalling the grain of sand cited by Pascal,[6] in several respects I share the opinion of your Brahmin,[7] that if all events do not have perceptible effects, it appears to me incontestable that all have real ones of which the human mind easily loses the thread, but which are never confused by nature.

You say that it is demonstrated that celestial bodies make their revolution in nonresistant space; this was assuredly a beautiful thing to demonstrate; but following the practice of the ignorant, I have very little faith in demonstrations that go beyond my reach. I would imagine that to build the latter, one would have reasoned approximately in the following manner: such force acting according to such law must give to the stars such movement in a nonresistant milieu; now, the stars have exactly the calculated movement; hence, there is no resistance at all. But who can know if there are not, perhaps, a million other possible laws, without counting the true one, according to which the same movements would be explained by the latter better yet in a fluid than in the void? Has not the horror of the void explained for a long time most of the effects that one has since attributed to the action of air? Other experiments having subsequently destroyed the horror of the void, has not everything been found full? Has one not

[6]The reference is to the observation in Pascal's *Pensées* that a grain of sand in his urethra caused Cromwell's death and thus prevented the damage he would have done to Christianity had he gone on living.

[7]Rousseau here confuses two of Voltaire's stories, the *Good Brahmin* and *Zadig*. It was the hermit in *Zadig* who engaged in reflections similar to Rousseau's.

reestablished the void on new calculations? Who will maintain that an even more exact system will not destroy it again? Let us leave the difficulties that a physicist would perhaps raise regarding the nature of light and illuminated spaces; but do you believe in good faith that Bayle, whose wisdom and restraint in matters of opinion I admire as much as you do, would have found yours so well demonstrated? In general, it seems that the skeptics forget themselves a little as soon as they take a dogmatic tone and that they ought to use the term "demonstrate" more soberly than anyone else. One boasts of knowing nothing while affirming so many things!

Moreover, you have made a very pertinent correction to Pope's system, by observing that there is no proportional gradation between created beings and the Creator and that if the chain of created beings wind up with God, it is because he holds it and not because he terminates it.

On the good of the whole preferable to that of its part, you have man say: I must be as dear to my master, being that I am thinking and feeling, as the planets which probably do not feel anything. Undoubtedly, this material universe must not be more dear to its author than a single thinking and feeling being; but the system of this universe which produces, conserves and perpetuates all thinking and feeling beings must be more dear to him than a single one of these beings. He can, therefore, despite his goodness, or even through his goodness, sacrifice something of the happiness of individuals for the conservation of the whole. I believe to be, I hope to be, worth more in the eyes of God than the land of a planet, but if the planets are inhabited, as is probable, why should I be worth more in his eyes than all the inhabitants of Saturn? It is vain to ridicule these ideas; it is certain that all analogies favor the assumption of such a population and that only human pride is against it. Now, with this population assumed, the conservation of the universe seems to have for God himself a morality which is multiplied by the number of inhabited worlds.

That the cadaver of man may nourish worms, wolves or plants, is not, I acknowledge, an indemnification for the death of this man; but if in the system of this universe it is necessary to the conservation of mankind that there be a circulation of substance among men, animals and vegetables, then the particular ill of an individual contributes to the general good. I die, I am eaten by worms, but my children, my brothers will live as I have lived, my cadaver fertilizes the earth whose productions they will eat and I do by the order of nature and for all men what Codrus, Curtius, the Cesies, the Philenes, and a thousand others did for a small number of men.

To return, sir, to the system that you attack, I believe that one cannot examine it properly without distinguishing carefully the particular ill, whose existence no philosopher has ever denied, from general ill that the optimist denies. It is not a question of knowing if each one of us suffers or not, but if it was good that the universe exists, and if our ills were inevitable in its constitution. Thus, it seems that the addition of an article would render the proposition more exact, and instead of *everything is good,* it would perhaps be better to say, *the whole is good or everything is good for the whole.* Then it is very evident that no man would be able to give direct proofs either pro or con, for these proofs depend on a perfect knowledge of the constitution of the world and of the purpose of its author, and this knowledge is incontestably beyond human intelligence. The true principles of optimism can be derived neither from the properties of matter nor from the mechanics of the universe, but only by induction of the perfections of God who presides over everything: so that one does not prove the existence of God by the system of Pope, but the system of Pope by the existence of God, and it is undoubtedly from the question of providence that the question of the origin of evil is derived. If these two questions have not been treated better, one more than the other, it is that one has always reasoned so badly about providence that the absurdities one has said about it have greatly confused all the corollaries that one could derive from this great and consoling dogma.

The first who have damaged God's cause are the priests and the devout who cannot imagine that everything happens according to established laws, and so think divine justice is always involved in purely natural events; to be sure of this, they punish and chastise the wicked, reward the good regardless of whether the outcome is good or evil. I do not know if this is good theology, but I think it a bad method of reasoning to found the proofs of providence on what is both for and against it, and to attribute to providence what would in any case happen without it.

The philosophers in their turn do not appear to me more reasonable, when I see them find fault with heaven, cry out that all is lost when they have a toothache or that they are poor or that they are being robbed and hold God accountable, as Seneca says, for the protection of their valises. If some tragic accident had made Cartouche or Caesar[8] perish in their childhood, one would have said, "what crime had they committed?" These two brigands lived, and we say, "why were they allowed to live?" In contrast, one of the devout will say in the first instance, God wanted to punish the father by taking his child from him, and in the second, God was preserving the child for the punishment of the people. Thus, whatever position nature took, providence is always right according to the devout and always wrong according to the philosophers. Perhaps, in the order of human things it is neither wrong nor right because everything depends on universal law and there is no exception for anyone. It is to be believed that particular events are nothing in the eyes of the master of the universe, that his providence is only universal, that he is content to preserve the types and species and to preside over everything without worrying in what manner each individual

---

[8]On Cartouche *see* note 1, pp. 121–122 above. Rousseau regarded Julius Caesar as a major criminal on quite the same level as Cartouche.

spends this short life. Would a wise king who wanted everyone in his lands to be happy need to worry if the inns are good? A traveller might complain for a night when they are bad, and laugh the rest of his life over such misplaced irritation. *Commorandi enim natura diversorium nobis, non habitandi dedit.*[9]

To think correctly in this regard, it seems that things ought to be considered relatively in the physical order and absolutely in the moral order: the greatest idea that I can have about providence is that each material being is disposed in the best possible way with respect to the whole and each intelligent and sensitive being in the best possible way with respect to himself, which means in other words that for one who feels his existence, it is better to exist than not to exist. But you have to apply this rule to the total duration of each sensitive being and not to any particular instant of his duration such as human life. This shows how greatly in the case of human life the question of providence depends on that of the immortality of the soul which I have the good fortune to believe in, being fully aware that reason can doubt it, and on that of eternal damnation that neither you nor I nor anybody thinking properly about God will ever believe in.

If I bring back these diverse questions to their common principle, it seems to me that they all relate to that of the existence of God. If God exists, he is perfect; if he is perfect, he is wise, powerful, and just; if he is wise and powerful, all is well; if he is just and powerful, my soul is immortal; if my soul is immortal, thirty years of life are nothing for me and are perhaps necessary for the maintenance of the universe. If one grants me the first proposition, one will never destroy the following ones; if one denies it, it is not at all necessary to argue about its consequences.

Neither one of us is in this last case. At least, far from my being able to presume anything of the kind on your part, from reading the collection of your works, I gather from a large part the sweetest, the most consoling ideas about the divinity, and I much prefer a Christian of your persuasion to that of the Sorbonne.

As for me, I will admit naively that neither the affirmative nor the negative case can be demonstrated on this point by the light of reason and that if the theist founds his sentiment only on probabilities, the atheist, even less precise, seems to me to establish his only on contrary possibilities. Moreover, the objections on both sides are insoluble because they turn upon things about which men do not have any true idea. I agree about all that, and yet I believe in God just as strongly as I believe any other truth because to believe and not to believe are of all things what least depends on my will in all the world, that doubt is a state too violent for my soul, that when my reason fluctuates my faith cannot remain long in suspense and

---

[9]"Nature has given an inn to us for a brief stay, not for permanent habitation."

determines the outcome without the aid of reason and that, finally, a thousand ideas draw me to the most consoling side and join the weight of hope to the balance of reason.

That, then, is a truth from which we both set out, and with the support of which you will see how easily optimism can be defended and providence justified; and it is not to you that one needs repeat the worn but solid arguments that have so often been expounded on this subject. As for philosophers who do not accept this principle, one must not dispute with them over such matters because what is for us an intuitive proof cannot be for them a rational demonstration, and it is not a reasonable argument to say to a man "You must believe this because I believe it." They, on their part, also need not argue at all with us about these same matters because they are only the corollaries of the principal proposition that an honest adversary scarcely dares to oppose to them, and, in their turn, they would be wrong to demand that one prove to them the corollary independently of the proposition which serves as its basis. I think that they must not demand a proof from the believer yet for another reason, namely, that there is inhumanity in troubling tranquil souls and in distressing men wastefully when what one wants to teach them is neither certain nor useful. I think in a word that by your example one would not be able to attack too strongly superstition which troubles society nor respect too much religion that supports it.

But, like you, I am indignant that the faith of each is not in its most perfect liberty and that man dares to govern the interior of consciences where we would not be able to penetrate, as if it depended on us to believe or not to believe in matters where demonstration does not occur at all, and that one could ever subject reason to authority. Do the kings of this world have any insight into the other, and are they right to torment their subjects here below in order to force them to go to paradise? No, every human government is limited by its nature to civil duties, and whatever the sophist Hobbes may have been able to say, when a man serves the state well he owes no account of the manner in which he serves God.

I do not know whether one day this just Being will not punish every tyranny exercised in his name; at least, I am very sure that he will not share it and will not refuse eternal happiness to any nonbeliever who is virtuous and of good faith. Can I without offending his goodness and even his justice doubt that an upright heart may redeem an involuntary error and that irreproachable morals are worth a thousand bizarre cults ordained by men and rejected by reason? I will say more; if I could have the option to buy works at the expense of my faith and compensate for my supposed unbelief by the strength of my virtue, I would not hesitate an instant; and I would prefer to be able to say to God, "I have done the good that is agreeable to you without thinking about you and my heart followed your will without knowing it" than to say to him as it will be necessary that I do one day, "I loved you, and have not ceased to offend you; I knew you, and did nothing to please you."

There is, I admit, a kind of profession of faith that may be imposed by law, but apart from the principles of morality and natural law, it must be a purely negative creed; for there can exist religions that attack the basis of society, and one must start by exterminating those religions in order to ensure the tranquillity of the state. Among the dogmas to be proscribed intolerance is without question the most odious. But it must be rooted out at its source, because the most sanguinary fanatics change their language when their fortunes change, and they preach nothing but patience and sweetness when they are not themselves the strongest ones. Thus I call intolerant in principle any man who imagines that it is impossible to be good unless one believes what he believes and who damns mercilessly anyone who thinks differently from him. In fact, religious believers are seldom disposed to leave those they condemn in peace in this world, and a saint who believes he lives among the damned readily anticipates the work of the Devil. If there were intolerant nonbelievers who wanted to force people to believe nothing, I would banish them no less severely than those who want to force people to believe everything it pleases them to have believed.

I should like therefore to have in every State a moral code or a kind of declaration of civil faith that contains positively the social maxims that each one would be bound to reject, not as impious, but as seditious. Thus, every religion which could agree with the code would be admitted, every religion which would not agree with it would be proscribed, and each one would be free to have none other than the code itself. This work, done with care, would be, it seems to me, the most useful book that has ever been composed, and perhaps the only necessary one for men. Here is a subject for you, sir; I passionately hope that you will undertake this work and embellish it with your poetry so that each one who is able to learn it would easily carry in his heart from childhood on these sentiments of sweetness and of humanity that shine in your writings and which will always be lacking in religious fanatics. I urge you to meditate on this project which should please your soul. You have given us in your poem on natural religion the catechism of man; give to us now in what I propose to you the catechism of the citizen. It is a matter to be considered at length and perhaps to reserve for the last of your works in order to culminate by a good deed for mankind the most brilliant career that a man of letters has ever experienced.

In conclusion, sir, I cannot refrain from noting a rather singular difference between you and me on the subject of this letter. Covered with glory and disillusioned with empty splendor, you live freely in the midst of abundance; very sure of your immortality, you tranquilly philosophize on the nature of the soul, and if the body or the heart suffers, you have

Tronchin as a doctor and as a friend; yet, you find nothing but evil on the earth. And I, an obscure man, poor and tormented by an illness without remedy, I meditate with pleasure in my retreat and find that all is well. Whence come these apparent contradictions? You have explained it yourself; you enjoy, but I hope, and hope embellishes everything.

I have as much trouble leaving this boring letter as you will have finishing it. Pardon me, great man, for what may be an indiscrete zeal, but one which I would not display if I esteemed you less. God forbid if I want to offend the contemporary whose talents I honor the most and whose writings speak the best to my heart: but it is a question of the reality of providence from which I expect everything. After having drawn from your writings consolations and courage, I find it hard that now you remove all that in order to offer me only an uncertain and vague hope, rather as a current palliative than as a future compensation. No, I have suffered too much in this life not to expect another. All the subtleties of metaphysics will never make me doubt for a moment the immortality of the soul and a beneficent providence. I feel it, I believe it, I want it, I hope for it, I will defend it to my last breath, and, of all the disputes I have entered into, this will be the only one where my own personal interest will not be forgotten.

I am with respect, sir.

Annotated Bibliography

WORKS BY VOLTAIRE

The number of editions of Voltaire's works in French is vast. Writing in 1872, Lord Morley noted in the Preface to his biography of Voltaire that "the large number of complete and elaborate editions of Voltaire's works which were undertaken and executed in the years between the overthrow of the Empire (1815) and the overthrow of the Monarchy in 1830, is one of the most striking facts in the history of books." Among the editions somewhat inaccurately referred to as "complete," three stand out from the rest. The first is the so-called Kehl edition, published between 1784 and 1789 in 70 volumes and edited by Pierre de Beaumarchais, the Marquis de Condorcet, and Jacques Decroix. It is known as the Kehl edition because it was not safe to bring it out in France and it had to be printed in the German town of Kehl. Copies of this magnificently produced edition are in every good library and the text, after 200 years, is still easily legible. It contains numerous critical footnotes by Condorcet, the great idealistic reformer and radical, who ended as one of the victims of Robespierre. Condorcet had known Voltaire and greatly admired him, but he also thought him much too conservative on many issues. The second highly regarded edition, published between 1828 and 1840 and running to 72 volumes, was edited by A. J. Q. Beuchot. Basing himself on Beuchot's scholarship, Louis Moland produced an edition in 52 volumes between 1877 and 1885. This is now regarded as the standard edition, but a superior and truly definitive edition is gradually appearing. Published by the Voltaire Foundation of the Taylor Institution at Oxford, it is under the general editorship of W. H. Barber. Begun in 1968, 65 volumes have so far been published. When it is complete, it will run to 135 volumes not including indexes. Voltaire's vast correspondence has been collected by Theodore Besterman in 107 volumes (Geneva 1953–1965). A second edition appeared between 1968 and 1977 as volumes 85–135 of the *Complete Works,* now in the course of publication at Oxford.

Voltaire was perhaps the first writer with a large international public, and English translations of many of his books appeared shortly after their original publication. As noted in the Introduction to this book, the *Philosophical Letters* actually appeared in English a year before its French publication. In 1763 a 38-volume edition of the *Works of M. de Voltaire* was published in London, translated with notes by Tobias Smollett, T. Francklin, and others. Smollett was a Scottish novelist and physician who also had a distinguished career as publisher and translator. The Smollett edition came out when Voltaire was alive and when some of his most important works had not yet appeared. For this reason and also because several of his books had been published anonymously, the Smollett edition was far fom complete. It is interesting to note, however, that Smollett managed to include *Candide.* In 1901 an edition in 22 huge volumes (each volume really being the equivalent of two large books) appeared in New York bearing the following inscription on the title page:

"Notes by Tobias Smollett, revised and modernized with new translations by William F. Fleming." In actual fact the Smollett translations were used verbatim without any revision, but the "Fleming edition," as it came to be called, contains several of the important works such as the *Philosophical Dictionary* and the *Ignorant Philosopher* not included in Smollett. The translation of the *Philosophical Dictionary* is based on the text appearing in Kehl, which included material from the *Questions Concerning the Encyclopedia* and several other of Voltaire's writings such as his contributions to Diderot's *Encyclopedia*. The translation is identical with one published in six volumes by J. H. L. Hunt in London in 1824. The Hunt version appeared in several other shapes, some running to ten volumes. In most of these the translator's name is not given, but in one of them the name supplied is J. G. Gorton. Extensive research has not located any translator or editor by the name of William F. Fleming.

Many translations of individual volumes have been published during the twentieth century and several of these are still in print. Of the many translations of *Candide,* that by the British novelist Richard Aldington may be especially recommended. It is available in H. M. Block (ed.), *Candide and Other Writings* (New York 1956). This collection, which is in print, also contains Block's excellent translation of the major portions of the *Commentary on the Book "Of Crimes and Punishments."* The text of the *Philosophical Dictionary*, as it appeared in the last version brought out by Voltaire in 1769, is available in translations by Peter Gay (New York 1962) and T. Besterman (London 1970). Gay's translation is somewhat free, but it brilliantly succeeds in preserving the spirit of the original. It contains a preface by André Maurois and a valuable editorial introduction with a great deal of information about the composition of the *Philosophical Dictionary* which is not easily obtainable elsewhere. Unlike other admirers, Gay does not play down Voltaire's anti-Semitism. The entire text of the *Treatise on Toleration* is included in *Selected Works of Voltaire*, translated by Joseph McCabe and published in London in 1935 in "The Thinker's Library," a series that had enormous sales among free-thinkers in the 1930s and 1940s. This volume also contains the "Poem on the Lisbon Earthquake," the very late polemical work "We Must Take Sides," and such violently anti-Christian pieces as "Epistle to the Romans," the "Sermon of the 50," and "The Questions of Zapata." All the excellent translations in this book are by McCabe.

Two editions of the *Philosophical Letters* are currently in print. The one by Ernest Dillworth, from which there is a selection in the present volume, dates from 1951. A more recent translation by L. W. Tancock under the title *Letters from England* was published in London in 1980. An exact reproduction of the 1738 translation of *The Elements of the Newtonian Philosophy* was reprinted in 1967 in London. This is a text of the earlier of Voltaire's two books on Newton. As mentioned in the Introduction, these works were combined by Voltaire into one book in 1741. A translation of it is available in the Smollett edition.

All of Voltaire's histories are available in the 22-volume Fleming edition of 1901. Much livelier and at the same time more accurate translations of several of the histories are found in *The Age of Louis XIV and Other Selected Writings of Voltaire* (New York 1965). The editor and translator of this splendid book is J. H. Brumfitt whose introduction is extremely interesting and informative. This book is presently out of print and it would be a happy idea for a reprint house to bring it back. An amusing if rather slight anti-Christian work of 1767, *Les Lettres à s. a. mgr. le prince*, whose full title in English is "Letter to His Highness, the Prince of . . . On Rabelais and Other Writers Who Have Been Accused of Attacking the Christian Religion," was published in English translation in New York in 1920 as part of a volume of Voltaire's works entitled *Essays and Criticisms*. Voltaire here discusses, among others, Vanini, Swift, Spinoza, Uriel Acosta, Meslier, and several of the English deists including Collins and Toland.

Three one-volume editions of Voltaire's letters are available in English. S. G. Tallentyre (pseudonym for Evelyn B. Hall, ed.), *Voltaire in His Letters* (New York 1919) contains several letters discussing philosophical topics. More recent are T. Besterman (ed.), *Select Letters of Voltaire* (London 1963) and R. A. Brooks (ed.), *The Selected Letters of Voltaire* (New York 1973).

BOOKS AND ARTICLES ABOUT VOLTAIRE

The secondary literature on Voltaire is enormous. In the rest of this bibliography I list some outstanding critical and biographical studies as well as a number of contemporary works dealing with the issues discussed by Voltaire and treated in the Introduction. Except for a few items of very special interest, I have confined myself to books and articles available in English.

Among recent books about Voltaire, two works by Haydn Mason deserve special mention, *Voltaire* (London 1975) and *Voltaire — A Biography* (London and Baltimore 1981). To avoid confusion I refer to these as Mason I and Mason II. Mason II is an exceptionally valuable biographical study based on the most minute research on all major aspects of Voltaire's life and character. Unlike other biographers who admire Voltaire, there is no attempt here to play down his less appealing features. Mason I concentrates on Voltaire's theories and publications. It contains, among other things, informative and lucid accounts of his work as a historian and as a philosopher. A. J. Ayer's *Voltaire* (London and New York 1986) is excellent in its biographical chapters and also on Voltaire's work as a historian. It is surprisingly skimpy on Voltaire's technical philosophy, discussing his views on free will and ethics, but neglecting such major topics as Voltaire's critique of Cartesian dualism, the question of survival, miracles, and the design argument. Perhaps the best-known recent biography is Besterman's *Voltaire* (London 1969; 3rd ed. 1976). This large book is occasionally described as the standard biography. It would be a pity if such an opinion became generally accepted. The book does indeed contain a great deal of useful information, but it is exceedingly diffuse and it contains numerous misstatements, whose falsehood could be known only to an exceptionally well-informed reader. To give an illustration, Besterman asserts that Voltaire rejected the death penalty, when, as we saw in the Introduction, he wrestled with the question and in the end always concluded that capital punishment was necessary in certain cases. In general, Besterman writes more like an attorney for Voltaire than a detached biographer. It is regrettable to have to make these comments because there can be no question about Besterman's important contributions to Voltaire scholarship.

Among earlier biographies, those by John Morley (1872), Gustave Lanson (1906), Richard Aldington (1925), the great Danish literary historian, Georg

Brandes (1930), A. N. Brailsford (1935), and Alfred Noyes (1936) can be confidently recommended. Lanson's book, of which an English translation appeared in 1960, gives an excellent and carefully balanced account of Voltaire's life and also of his work in different areas, including philosophy. Alfred Noyes, the distinguished British poet, was a believing Catholic. His book is a remarkably sympathetic account of Voltaire's life and ideas and is particularly moving in its defense of Voltaire's moral integrity against his many detractors, Christian and otherwise. *The Spirit of Voltaire* (New York 1938) by Norman L. Torrey, one of the leading Voltaire scholars of an earlier generation, is a character study rather than a biography. Like all of Torrey's writings on Voltaire, it is highly informative. It may be noted that Torrey also wrote the article on Voltaire in the *Encyclopedia of Philosophy* (Vol. 8, pp. 262–270).

The first of five volumes constituting a new full-scale biography of Voltaire (in French) appeared in 1985. The editor of this project is the distinguished Voltaire scholar, René Pomeau, who also wrote the first volume, *D'Arouet à Voltaire, 1694–1734*. The second, *Avec Mme. Du Châtelet, 1734–1749*, by René Vaillot, is scheduled for publication in 1988. This biography, like the new edition of the *Complete Works*, is published by the Voltaire Foundation at Oxford.

Ira O. Wade, *The Intellectual Development of Voltaire* (Princeton 1969) is a standard work on Voltaire's ideas in different fields. Section IV, which runs to nearly 200 pages, is devoted to Voltaire's work in philosophy. More concise in his treatment of Voltaire's philosophy is Mason I, op. cit. Both books contain valuable information on the genesis of the *Treatise on Metaphysics*. Section IV of Wade's earlier *Studies on Voltaire* (Princeton 1947) includes several papers on the *Treatise* which demonstrate that it went through three different versions and that the text which has been preserved is of the second version. Voltaire's strictly philosophical ideas are critically and sympathetically examined by R. Z. Lauer in *The Mind of Voltaire—A Study in His "Constructive Deism"* (Westminster 1961). A particularly interesting discussion of Voltaire's early philosophical views, as contained in the *Treatise* and in the first version of the "Letter on Locke," which Voltaire thought too radical to publish at the time, is found in the last chapter of J. S. Spink, *French Free-Thought from Gassendi to Voltaire* (London 1960). A new critical edition of the French text of the *Treatise*, edited by W. H. Barber, is due for publication in 1988 in Vol. 14 of the *Complete Works*.

The influence of Locke and Newton on Voltaire's thought is discussed in most of the biographical and critical works mentioned earlier. The influence of Bayle, the author of the *Historical and Critical Dictionary*, which was a model for Voltaire's *Philosophical Dictionary*, is traced in great detail in H. Mason, *Pierre Bayle and Voltaire* (Oxford 1963). Mandeville's influence on both Voltaire and Mme. du Châtelet is examined in Chapter 2 of Wade's *Studies on Voltaire*, op. cit. The influence of Hobbes is traced in L. Thielemann, "Voltaire and Hobbism," *Studies in Voltaire and the Eighteenth Century*, Vol. 10 (1959). This important series, about which more will be said later, is abbreviated from here on as *SVEC*. The impact of Samuel Clarke on Voltaire is described in W. H. Barber, "Voltaire and Samuel Clarke," SVEC, Vol. 179 (1979). The same author's *Leibniz in France* (Oxford 1955, Photoreprint, New York and London, 1985) discusses the influence, both positive and negative, of Leibniz and also includes an extended discussion of Voltaire's early optimism and his very gradual shift to the views expressed in

Candide and such articles as "Tout est bien" in *The Philosophical Dictionary*. The Cirey period during which much of this development took place is the subject of Barber's "Voltaire at Cirey: Art and Thought," in *Studies in Eighteenth-Century French Literature Presented to Robert Niklaus*, ed. J. H. Fox et al. (Exeter 1975). Voltaire's "Poem on the Lisbon Earthquake" and its impact on philosophical and religious controversies are discussed in W. H. Barber, *Leibniz in France*, op. cit., and in Chapter 27 of Besterman's biography. There is a version of the Poem with a much gloomier conclusion than the one that was published. We are indebted for this information to G. R. Havens whose research is summarized in his "Voltaire's Pessimistic Revision of the Conclusion of the 'Poème sur le désastre de Lisbonne,'" *Modern Language Notes*, December 1929. Many interesting details about the motives inspiring Rousseau to write the letter to Voltaire (printed as an Appendix to this volume) may be found in R. A. Leigh, "Rousseau's Letter to Voltaire on Optimism," SVEC, Vol. 30 (1964) and in C. W. Hendel, *Jean-Jacques Rousseau: Moralist*, Vol. 1, Chapter 10 (New York 1934). Rousseau's letter was a kind of dress rehearsal for the more elaborate defense of fideism in his "Confession of Faith of a Savoyard Vicar," published as part of *Emile* in 1762. Voltaire never directly responded to Rousseau's fideistic "solution" of the problem of evil. Bertrand Russell did it on his behalf in a stinging critique in the chapter on Rousseau in his *History of Western Philosophy* (London and New York 1946).

Voltaire's discovery and use of Meslier's Testament is the subject of A. Morehouse, *Voltaire and Jean Meslier* (New Haven 1936). Additional information about Meslier may be found in I. O. Wade, *The Clandestine Organization and Diffusion of Philosophical Ideas in France from 1700 to 1750* (Princeton 1938), in J. S. Spink, *French Free-Thought from Gassendi to Voltaire*, op. cit., in R. Niklaus, "Clandestine Philosophical Literature in France," *Encyclopedia of Philosophy*, Vol. 2, pp. 114–118, and in A. Vartanian's article on Meslier in the *Encyclopedia of Philosophy*, Vol. 5, pp. 283–284. M. Waterman's *Voltaire, Pascal and Human Destiny* (New York 1942) is a fascinating short study of Voltaire's critique of Pascal. Unfortunately all the numerous lengthy passages from Voltaire and Pascal are quoted in the original French.

Norman L. Torrey's *Voltaire and the English Deists* (New Haven 1930) is the standard book on the influence of the deists on Voltaire. E. Royston Pike, *Slayers of Superstition* (London 1931), an excellent short history of English deism with chapters devoted to Toland, Collins, and Woolston, the three deists whom Voltaire quotes most frequently. Selections from all the major deists are reprinted in E. Graham Waring (ed.), *Deism and Natural Religion* (New York 1967). P. Gay's (ed.) *Deism* (Princeton 1968) contains selections from the English deists, the German deist Reimarus, and the two outstanding American deists, Thomas Paine and Elihuh Palmer, as well as Voltaire. Much of Vol. 1 of Leslie Stephen's justly famous *History of English Thought in the Eighteenth Century*, which first appeared in 1876, is devoted to the controversies provoked by the English deists.

Voltaire's attack on the Cartesian soul and his view that thinking is an attribute of human and animal bodies played a highly significant part in the development of eighteenth-century materialism. It was pointed out in the Introduction to the present volume that although Voltaire was not a materialist in the sense of identifying thought with brain states, he *was* a materialist in the broader sense of holding that mental processes cannot exist without a physiological foundation; and he was of

course quite clear in his mind that such a position rules out survival after death
except in the form of bodily resurrection which he regarded as incredible. The story
of the rise of materialism in France and Voltaire's important role in it is told in
A. Vartanian's fascinating book, *Diderot and Descartes—A Study of Scientific Natural-
ism in the Enlightenment* (Princeton 1953). The same author also produced a critical
edition of *La Mettrie's L'Homme Machine* ("Man a Machine," Princeton 1960). In
his introductory monograph Vartanian describes Voltaire's influence on La Mettrie
in some detail. It may be of interest to note that on the title page of the early
editions of *L'Homme Machine* La Mettrie quoted a short poem by Voltaire which he
removed in later editions because of his desire not to embarrass Voltaire. Voltaire's
role in this history is also noted in F. A. Lange's famous *History of Materialism*, Book
I, Section 4. This book, originally published in 1865, whose English translation
appeared in 1877, was reissued with an introduction by Bertrand Russell in London
in 1925. The development of materialism in France is also described in several
chapters of Spink, *French Free-Thought from Gassendi to Voltaire, op. cit.* Voltaire's
defense of the view that matter *can* think was anticipated in the writings of Anthony
Collins in the course of his correspondence with Samuel Clarke. The question
continued to be discussed throughout the eighteenth century by numerous minor as
well as by major thinkers. It was one of the topics debated by Richard Price and
Joseph Priestley, Price defending the Cartesian position and Priestley a materialism
closely akin to that of Voltaire. It may be of some interest to note that very recently
Richard Swinburne revived the views of Clarke and Price (and also of course of
Descartes) in Chapter 9 of *The Existence of God* (Oxford 1979). Swinburne's
arguments are much more sophisticated than those of earlier writers, but the
conclusion is the same. Swinburne's arguments are criticized in Chapter 7 of J. L.
Mackie, *The Miracle of Theism* (Oxford, 1982). The story of materialism in eigh-
teenth-century Britain has recently been told in J. W. Yolton, *Thinking Matter*
(Oxford 1984). This book contains a superb bibliography. The exchanges between
Collins and Clarke and Price and Priestley are also discussed in Vol. 1 of Leslie
Stephen, *History of English Thought in the Eighteenth Century, op. cit.* Intimately
connected with the question of thinking matter is that of the "animal soul," a topic
that greatly exercised both materialists and anti-materialists, Cartesians and anti-
Cartesians in the seventeenth and eighteenth centuries. In addition to the books by
Vartanian, Spink and Yolton, mention should be made of L. C. Rosenfield's *From
Beast-Machine to Man-Machine* (New York 1941) and R. M. Young's article, "Animal
Soul" in the *Encyclopedia of Philosophy*, Vol. 1, pp. 122–127. Rosenfield and Young
contain extensive bibliographies.

Richard Swinburne's defense of the design argument discussed in the Introduction to this book may be found in Chapter 8 of *The Existence of God* (Oxford 1979),
Louis Dupré's discussion in "The Argument of Design Today," *Religious Studies*
(1974), and Diderot's nontheological explanation of the order of the universe in his
"Philosophical Thoughts" (1746), which is available in English translation both in
Margaret Jourdain (ed.), *Diderot's Early Philosophical Works* (New York 1916) and
in L. G. Crocker (ed.), *Diderot Selected Writing* (New York 1966). The anthropic
principle is explained and defended in Paul Davies, *God and the New Physics*
(London and New York 1983) and in very great detail in J. D. Barrow and F. J.
Tipler, *The Anthropic Cosmological Principle* (Oxford 1986). Chapter 2 of the last-
mentioned book contains a long and useful history of the different versions of the

design argument. An earlier statement of the same idea occurs in Chapter 23 of Freeman Dyson's autobiography, *Disturbing the Universe* (New York 1979). The argument is of course very much older and goes back not only to Voltaire but even to Newton, who stated it quite clearly in the first of his "Four Letters to Richard Bentley," which are reprinted in numerous collections, e.g., in H. S. Thayer (ed.), *Newton's Philosophy of Nature* (New York 1953). The argument is incisively criticized in Chapter 5 of W. T. Stace, *Religion and the Modern Mind* (New York 1952). Dyson is critized by Stephen J. Gould in "Mind and Supermind," *Natural History* (1983), reprinted in his *The Flamingo's Smile* (New York 1985). Gould refers to an essay by Mark Twain, "The Damned Human Race," which contains similar criticisms. In Chapter 8 of *Religion and Science* (London 1935), Bertrand Russell advances substantially the same objections to numerous "anthropic" biologists who wrote in defense of "cosmic purpose" in the decades between the two wars. The anthropic principle itself is criticized in H. R. Pagels, "A Cozy Cosmology," *The Sciences* (1985), and in a highly critical review of Barrow and Tripler's book by M. Gardner in *New York Review of Books* (1986). In *The Miracle of Theism* (Oxford 1982), J. L. Mackie criticizes Swinburne's argument on grounds different from those advanced in the Introduction to this volume. Swinburne has replied to Mackie in "Mackie, Induction and God" in *Religious Studies* (1983). In "God and Probability," *Religious Studies* (1969), D. H. Mellor questions whether the various probability assertions (and denials) of the existence of God have any clear sense. A. J. Ayer's "Chance," to which prominent reference is made in the Introduction, is reprinted in his *Metaphysics and Common Sense* (London 1969). The following is the full text of the passage quoted from Charles Peirce. "The relative probability of this or that arrangement of Nature is something which we should have a right to talk about if universes were as plenty as blackberries, if we could put a quantity of them in a bag, shake them well up, draw out a sample, and examine them to see what proportion of them had one arrangement and what proportion had another." This passage occurs in Peirce's "The Probability of Induction" (1878), which has been reprinted in numerous collections, e.g., M. R. Cohen's collection of Peirce's papers entitled *Chance, Love and Logic* (New York 1923).

The Molyneux problem, which Voltaire discusses in the chapter from *The Elements of the Newtonian Philosophy*, reprinted on pp. 98–103, was stated in Locke's *Essay Concerning Human Understanding*, II, ix, Section 8. Locke had no doubt that the congenitally blind man who had suddenly been given sight would not be able to distinguish a cube from a sphere. Berkeley, in his *New Theory of Vision* (1709), gave the same answer and so, of course, did Voltaire. However, unlike Locke and Berkeley, Voltaire's answer was not speculative but based on the cataract operation performed by Cheselden and the behavior of his patient after he had acquired the ability to see. Later in the eighteenth century, several of the Enlightenment philosophers discussed Cheselden's operation without endorsing the negative answer to the Molyneux problem. In his *Histoire naturelle de l'âme* ("The Natural History of the Soul" 1745), La Mettrie maintained that the formerly blind man would be able to discriminate a cube from a sphere by visual means alone. The fact that the patient on whom Cheselden had operated could not do this was due to temporary damage to his eyes after the operation. In fairness to La Mettrie it should be mentioned that his answer to the Molyneux problem was not a wild *a priori* speculation but based on empirically founded views concerning the "sensory compensation" that takes place in individuals who are deprived of one or more senses. The sense of touch of the blind man, for example, enables him to form spatial and geometrical notions that are produced in normal individuals primarily by the sense of sight. Condillac took up these questions both in his *Essai sur l'origine des connaissance humaines* (1746) and the more famous *Traité des sensations* (1754, English translation 1930). His answer to the Molyneux problem is substantially the same as La Mettrie's. In his *Letter on the Blind for the Use of Those Who See* (1749), Diderot develops a theory of "sensory compensation" very similar to La Mettrie's and gives the same answer to the Molyneux problem as La Mettrie and Condillac. It should be remarked in passing that Diderot's *Letter* is a fascinating work dealing with many other questions including the existence of God (see Voltaire's *Letter to Diderot* pp. 211–212). Readers interested in this topic should not fail to consult Aram Vartanian's "La Mettrie and Diderot Revisited," *Diderot Studies*, Vol. 21 (1983), which traces the influence of La Mettrie on Condillac and Diderot and explains why neither of these otherwise admirable writers mentioned their indebtedness to La Mettrie. La Mettrie's writings, openly defending atheism, materialism, and free love, had scandalized large sections of the public and it was the better part of wisdom not to associate oneself with such a notorious person. (La Mettrie managed to survive chiefly because Frederick the Great offered him protection in Potsdam where he was a member of the Royal Academy of Science as well as personal physician to the king.) Diderot's *Letter* as well as D'Alembert's article on blindness in the Diderot-D'Alembert *Encyclopedia* (which is little more than a summary of Diderot's *Letter*) are available in English translation in M. Jourdain (ed.), *Diderot's Early Philosophical Writings*, op. cit. The distinguished British neuropsychologist, R. L. Gregory, has discussed the problem in several places. In *Eye and Brain* (3rd ed., London and New York 1978), he notes that there are now nearly 100 cases on record with sufficient evidence of early lack of vision to be at least prima facie relevant. Some of these clearly support the Lockean answer, but apparently some do not. One of the latter is described by Gregory and J. G. Wallace in "Recovery from Early Blindness: A Case Study," *Exp. Psychol. Soc. Monograph No. 2* (Cambridge 1963), reprinted in R. L. Gregory, *Concepts and Mechanisms of Perception* (London 1974). J. L. Mackie discusses the topic in *Problems from Locke* (Oxford 1976), arguing that Molyneux's problem confusedly amalgamates two questions. Although the answer to one of them is probably in the negative, Mackie maintains that the Gregory-Wallace case appears to favor an affirmative answer to the other question. Gregory's *Eye and Brain* contains additional references to twentieth-century work on this subject.

No complete translation of Voltaire's *Commentary* on Beccaria's book is currently in print. However, as noted earlier, substantial portions are included in Block's *Candide and Other Writings*. Beccaria's own *On Crimes and Punishments*, which is a slim volume of less than 100 pages, is available in two paperback editions. The earlier, a Macmillan paperback, is translated by H. Paolucci; the other, translated by D. Young, was published by Hackett (Indianapolis 1986). Both have excellent introductions. The standard book in English on Beccaria's influence on Voltaire is M. T. Maestro, *Voltaire and Beccaria As Reformers of Criminal Law* (New York 1942). This book contains numerous lengthy extracts from Voltaire's minor writings on legal reform. The article "On Cato and Suicide," which originally appeared in the *Questions Concerning the Encyclopedia* in 1770, and is available in English in the Hunt and the Fleming editions of the *Philosophical Dictionary*, contains a much fuller discussion of suicide than the selection reprinted in this volume. Here Voltaire is not only concerned to show the absurdity of religious and legal prohibitions of suicide; he also discusses such still unsolved mysteries as why children occasionally kill themselves at the same age and in the same manner as one of their parents. There is a fascinating discussion of eighteenth-century attitudes to suicide, with special reference to Voltaire's views, in J. McManners, *Death and the Enlightenment* (Oxford 1985). The following books are entirely devoted to the case of Calas: F. H. Maugham, *The Case of Jean Calas* (New York 1928), D. D. Bien, *The Calas Affair* (Princeton 1960), and E. Nixon, *Voltaire and the Calas Case* (London 1961). Just as there are people who still deny the existence of the Nazi death camps, royalists and extremists in the Church continued to insist for several decades that Jean Calas was guilty and that Voltaire created the entire case in order to embarrass the magistrates of Toulouse and the Catholic Church. Joseph de Maistre, the royalist quoted in the Introduction, who, as a Toulousian, was doubly concerned to vindicate the magistrates, wrote in 1817 that "nothing has been less proved than the innocence of Calas. There are a thousand reasons to doubt it, even to believe the contrary."

The account of the gruesome case of Gabriel Malagrida (see p. 198, note 13) is based primarily on H. V. Livermore, *A New History of Portugal* (Cambridge 1966), R. Fülöp-Miller, *The Power and Secret of the Jesuits* (New York 1930), and the article on Malagrida by T. Beal in the *New Catholic Encyclopedia* (New York 1967, Vol. 9, p. 103). Livermore's coverage of this episode is comprehensive and does not betray any bias. He places some of the blame on the papacy for not doing more to save Malagrida and two other Jesuits who were also executed at Pombal's behest. The article in the *New Catholic Encyclopedia* is sober and well informed. Fülöp-Miller's volume is one of the most famous books about the Jesuits and the author does not seem to grind any axes. The book is extremely well written, but frequently inaccurate. J. H. Pappas, "Berthier's Journal de Trévoux and the Philosophes," *SVEC,* Vol. 3 (1957), contains some interesting but all-to-brief remarks on the case.

One of the best critical evaluations of Voltaire's philosophical and religious ideas is contained in David Friedrich Strauss' *Voltaire: Sechs Vorträge,* first published in Leipzig in 1870. Strauss (1808–1874) was one of the leading German freethinkers of the nineteenth century whose controversial and highly influential *The Life of Jesus Critically Examined* (1835–1836, translated by George Eliot in 1848) resulted in his dismissal from the University of Tübingen. By 1870 he had become a fervent nationalist and the book on Voltaire was intended to downgrade Voltaire's place in history, but Strauss was unable to suppress his admiration for Voltaire's criticisms of traditional religion and his extremely well-written book had the result of making many friends for Voltaire in the German language ambit. It was in effect the beginning of a revival of interest in Voltaire in Germany and Austria. During the first half of the nineteenth century, German academic and intellectual life was very largely dominated by nationalist reactionaries to whom Voltaire was the symbol of all that they hated most — skepticism, the appeal to reason, liberalism, pacifism, and the opposition to every variety of mysticism. The Hirschel affair was commonly used as a pretext for dismissing Voltaire as a greedy and corrupt man whose work could be safely ignored. The picture changed with the rise of liberalism and social democracy. In addition to Strauss, special credit for the rehabilitation of Voltaire's good name belongs to the above-mentioned F. A. Lange, who repeatedly refers to Voltaire with great respect in the *History of Materialism* and to the distinguished physiologist and philosopher of science, Emil Du Bois-Reymond (1815–1896), who was a descendant of a French family that settled in Potsdam during the reign of Frederick the Great. In 1868 Du Bois-Reymond gave a lecture to the Prussian Academy of Science, "Voltaire in seiner Beziehung zur Naturwissenschaft" ("Voltaire and His Relation to the Natural Sciences") in which he not only described Voltaire's work and ideas in science but also emphasized his unequaled contributions to freedom of inquiry. Du Bois-Reymond's lecture was reprinted several times and did a great deal to clear the air. In the long run, however, nobody contributed more to Voltaire's rehabilitation than Nietzsche, who spoke in glowing terms about Voltaire in *Human All-Too-Human* (1878) and again in his posthumously published *Ecce Homo* (1908). As early as 1832 Heinrich Heine had expressed his admiration of Voltaire in his "Französische Zustände" ("Conditions in France"). Heine's admiration is hardly surprising. He possessed similar satirical gifts and he was the only German writer to command a similarly graceful, sharp-edged, lucid, and freely flowing prose. However, as a Jew, a champion of radical ideas, and, worst of all, a "cosmopolitan," Heine's praise probably served only to confirm the nationalistic reactionaries in their violent dislike of Voltaire. One other book that deserves to be mentioned, especially since it contains a detailed analysis of many of Voltaire's philosophical theories, is Josef Popper's *Voltaire—Eine Charakteranalyse* (Dresden 1905). This book, by the Viennese positivist, pacifist, and militant opponent of all supernaturalism, defended Voltaire against the many accusations, mostly libelous, that had been leveled against him by German and also by some French writers during the preceding century. Popper (1838–1921), who came to be known as Popper-Lynkeus, was a friend and associate of Ernst Mach and was much admired by Einstein, Freud, and the members of the Vienna Circle. There is an article about him in the *Encyclopedia of Philosophy* (Vol. 6, pp. 401–407).

Voltaire was intensely interested in science and kept abreast with the best thought of his time in several fields. During the Cirey period, he and Mme. du Châtelet spent much of their time, conducting experiments in chemistry and biology. He himself took special pride in an essay on the nature of fire (1739), which he submitted to the Academy and which was published along with the prize-winning essays by Euler and two Cartesian scientists. A useful summary of Voltaire's scientific work is found in Part III, Chapter 7 of I. O. Wade, *The Intellectual Development of Voltaire*, op. cit. The standard book in English on Voltaire's place in the history of science — M. S. Libby, *The Attitude of Voltaire to Magic and the Sciences* (New York 1935) — admits his importance as a popularizer of Newton, but concludes that Voltaire's achievements are "hardly beyond the attainment of an intelligent amateur." Unlike Diderot whose speculations on the subject were admittedly on the wild side, Voltaire totally rejected all evolutionary ideas.

Voltaire repeatedly described basic moral principles as "natural laws," but he did not always mean the same thing by this expression. Occasionally the "natural laws" of morality are utilitarian principles grounded on our experience of what is and what is not conducive to human welfare. At other times he claims or at least suggests that they possess logical necessity like the truths of mathematics. Voltaire adopts the former position in the *Treatise on Metaphysics,* but he inclines to the latter in *The Ignorant Philosopher,* in several articles of the *Philosophical Dictionary,* especially the one entitled "On Laws" and also in the "Poem on the Natural Law" of 1755, which he had sent to Rousseau along with the "Poem on the Lisbon Earthquake." What he says on this topic is doubly confusing because he repeatedly castigates the "natural law" philosophy of Grotius, Pufendorf, and other legal theorists as nonsense or even "rubbish." The conflict between Voltaire's empiricism and the view that moral principles are logically necessary is discussed in Ernst Cassirer's *Philosophy of the Enlightenment* (1932, English translation, Princeton 1955). An illuminating account of Voltaire's contradictory pronouncements on natural law is found in Appendix I of P. Gay, *Voltaire's Politics* (2nd ed., New York 1965). This valuable book covers a much wider area than its title might suggest and its Appendix contains a useful list of the many places in which Voltaire wrote about natural law.

The following works that are likely to be of interest to students of Voltaire could not be easily fitted into any of the previous groups. René Pomeau, *La religion de Voltaire* (rev. ed., Paris 1969), is the standard work in French on Voltaire's views on religious topics, including, of course, the arguments for the existence of God. Nothing remotely as comprehensive exists in English. A. Bachman, *Censorship in France from 1715 to 1750: Voltaire's Opposition* (New York 1934), is a fascinating account of the obstacles that free-thinkers encountered in France during the first half of the eighteenth century. Several chapters of A. Cobban, *In Search of Humanity—The Role of the Enlightenment in Modern History* (New York 1960), deal with Voltaire's work, primarily as an opponent of Christianity and of optimism. Cobban suggests reasons why Voltaire's opposition to atheism may have been a charade, allowing him to be all the more effective in his war on Christianity. Reneé Haynes, *Philosopher King—The Humanist Pope Benedict XIV* (London 1970), traces the relations between Voltaire and Benedict XIV to whom the play "Mahomet" was dedicated. B. N. Schilling's *Conservative England and the Case against Voltaire* (New York 1950) is a study of how in the wake of the French Revolution public opinion in Great Britain, stirred up by religious and political conservatives, turned against Voltaire. Among other things, Schilling tells the story of the publication in several editions, French and English, expensive and cheap, in five volumes, in two volumes, and in an abridgement in one volume of the *Memoires Illustrating the History of Jacobinism* (1795) by the Abbé Augustin Barruel, a Jesuit refugee who had settled in England. Barruel was concerned to demonstrate that the French Revolution was a devilish conspiracy hatched by Voltaire and abetted by his fellow *philosophes* to destroy all religion and government. The *Memoires* also contained lurid descriptions of the alleged torments Voltaire experienced on his deathbed. The intellectual level of Barruel's book is about the same as that of the "Protocols of the Elders of Zion," but like the latter it was widely believed. Endorsed by Edmund Burke and several other famous men, it had an enormous circulation.

Something should be said about the valuable series bearing the title *Studies in Voltaire and the Eighteenth Century,* which was started by Besterman in 1955 and is currently edited by Haydn Mason. So far no less than 250 volumes have been published. Many, though by no means all, essays included in these volumes deal with Voltaire, and their level is generally very high. Vol. 9 of this series (1959) contains a list of all books in Voltaire's library, which is now housed in Leningrad. The list was compiled by G. R. Havens and N. Torrey on the basis of firsthand research in Leningrad. The quotation from Bertrand Russell on the title page of the present volume is taken from a little-known piece, "Voltaire's Influence on Me," *SVEC*, Vol. 6 (1958). Like many other people, Voltaire habitually wrote comments on the margin of the books he read. An editorial team in Leningrad has for some time been engagd in the project of publishing Voltaire's marginalia. Three volumes of this *Corpus des notes marginales de Voltaire* have appeared at the time the present book went to press. Unfortunately the letter "H" has not yet been reached. We know how greatly Voltaire admired Hume and it would be of special interest to see his detailed comments.

Voltaire knew he was an important man, but even he might be amazed at the interest that his life and work continue to arouse in scholars all over the world.